NOT APPOINTED TO WRATH

Recovering the True Promise of His Return

Joshua Dobbs

Foreword by Stan Eure, Composer of Second Coming: The Rock Musical

TRUTH IN CHRIST
JOSHUA DOBBS MINISTRIES

Not Appointed to Wrath: Recovering the Promise of His Return
By Joshua Dobbs

Cover Image: Not Appointed to Wrath Cover
© Joshua Dobbs, 2025
All rights reserved.
  Truth in Christ – Joshua Dobbs Ministries™ is a trademark of
  Joshua Dobbs.

Unless otherwise noted, all Scripture quotations are taken from the
King James Version of the Holy Bible, which is in the public
domain.

Printed in the United States of America.

ISBN: 979-8-9994851-0-6
First Edition

Dedication

To Jesus my Lord,
who challenged the traditions of men.
I thank God my Father, from whom comes every good gift, and who
will vindicate His saints at the return of our Lord Jesus Christ.

To my parents,
who instilled in me the value of doing what is right
and taught me to have the strength to walk away from the
crowd going the wrong way.

To those who have opened the Bible
and accepted the truth over the traditions of men.
May your eyes see, and your ears hear.

Joshua Dobbs delivers the 'Fiery Truth' that King Jesus promised in His Word through sound, biblical scholarship for such an End Time as this."
—Stan Eure, Composer
Second Coming: The Rock Musical

"Joshua Dobbs, with Truth in Christ, provides a most needed voice for the historic premillennial view of eschatology held by the early church fathers. Mr. Dobbs not only promotes biblical literacy, but he also defends the plain reading of the Biblical text. A rock-solid ministry with a rock-solid message."
—Matthew Miller, Maranatha Ministries

"Not Appointed to Wrath" is a much-needed systematic theology of the posttribulation rapture and the first to define God's wrath with true biblical precision. Joshua Dobbs lays out the scriptural case with clarity while directly confronting the key objections of dispensational pretribulationism. This book restores confidence in God's justice and equips the Church to endure with hope, not fear. A bold and timely resource for a prepared Church.

— Ken Kovach, B.Div., D.B.C., D.C.E., Th.M.
International Certified Christian Chaplain

"We are living in a time where even secular people sense that it simply cannot continue in the direction that it is going. Instead of Christians boldly declaring what is just ahead for the world, there is a deafening silence. This is a direct result of a spirit of apathy from our pulpits on sound eschatology and a complete failure on the part of Christians to simply read the Bible. As a result, most Christians cannot accurately relay what the end holds for the Church or the world. They have received their 'education' from fictional books and films sensationalized by Hollywood, rather than the only reliable source: the Bible. This book separates fact from fiction by exploring and expounding on what God has plainly stated in His Word. A proper and accurate understanding of the days just ahead is desperately needed in the Church. Joshua strives to put forth the knowledge you need in this book. He provides the Scriptures that show God's seamless narrative of how the rule of man comes to its conclusion and Jesus Christ begins His reign. Do yourself a favor and read this book. Become convinced of the truth not because someone told you what to believe, but because you can see it for yourself."

— Rev. Bill Craft, Jr.
Veteran pastor and Bible teacher with nearly four decades of ministry experience, including 28 years in pulpit leadership and 35 years of in-depth biblical instruction

Table of Contents

Foreword
Not Appointed To Wrath

God's Word is holy, true, and entirely accurate. Yet prophecy remains one of the most debated topics among believers on the job, in the church, online, and across the marketplace. Books, podcasts, pulpits, and movies alike declare a wide array of conflicting eschatological views, often sowing confusion just as the End Times unfold before our eyes.

We need answers. We need truth. And we need unity.
As the modern Church drifts from the narrow way and marches toward apostasy, we stand at a prophetic crossroads. It's here that clarity must prevail. In Not Appointed To Wrath, Joshua Dobbs restores biblical order to End Times events by harmonizing Scripture with Scripture going deep into the original biblical Greek texts to reveal the plain meaning often lost in tradition and fear-based teaching.

Come on this journey and discover the peace that comes from understanding prophetic truth.

—Stan Eure
Composer of The Second Coming: A Rock Musical

Preface: Why This Book was Written

This book was born out of a burden, stirred by a growing unease with how Scripture is misinterpreted and misapplied in today's end-times teaching. I did not arrive at the posttribulation view through books written by popular teachers or by instruction from the pulpit. I arrived at it the way every doctrine should be tested: through a natural, Spirit-led reading of the Word of God. It is through a natural reading of the Holy Scriptures that one learns to rightly divide the word of truth.

It was only after my conversion that I began to hear about the so-called "pretribulation rapture," a view that claimed God would secretly remove believers from the earth before the tribulation ever begins. Pretribulation adherents would cite isolated verses like, "one taken, one left," or "not appointed to wrath" as if a single line, stripped from its context, could overturn the entire prophetic timeline laid out in Scripture. But something never sat right with me about what I was hearing from people evangelizing this foreign and strange doctrine. I went back to revisit the very Scriptures people claimed supported a pretribulation rapture. But as I examined them more closely, their interpretation didn't align with the full counsel of Scripture on the topic. That forced a question: Does the Bible contradict itself or have these verses been misinterpreted? Once I looked at the surrounding context, the answer became clear. The contradiction wasn't in the text, but in how pretribulationists had skewed it. The natural reading supported a posttribulational return of Christ, while the pretribulation narrative stood exposed as a misinterpretation.

Much of this misinterpretation was inherited at the local church level, where sincere ministers, trained through isolated proof-texting and theological tradition, were persuaded it was apostolic truth. I realized the reason this doctrine seemed so foreign is because it wasn't present in the plain reading of the text.

That was the moment I discovered scriptural harmony, and it changed everything. That realization didn't just shift my theology; it stirred a burden within me. I saw the consistent thread running from the prophets to Christ, from Christ to the apostles, and from the apostles to the Revelation, with a consistent exhortation that the saints must endure tribulation with patience and faith, and then the Lord returns in glory to deliver and vindicate them and to judge the wicked.

One of my motivations for authoring this book is that this truth is rarely found in your average Christian bookstore. The pretribulation rapture narrative has overwhelmed the shelves, saturating the market with fiction and fantasy, with terrifying sensationalism, while suppressing the only true narrative preserved in Scripture: that Christ gathers His people after the tribulation. This book pushes back against that flood, not with speculation, but with the clarity of God's Word. My aim is not to force a system onto the text, but to recover what the early Church believed and what the Bible plainly reveals. Not through charts, not through tradition, but through a Spirit-led return to the Word of God.

Over time, it became evident to others, as it had already become clear in my own study, that the Lord had given me a deep desire and ability to rightly divide His Word intuitively. Not by carving it apart to suit modern trends, but by cutting a straight path through Scripture, preserving its harmony and truth. That conviction eventually grew into a teaching ministry, both in person and online. Today, I host the Truth in Christ YouTube channel, with a mission to restore sound doctrine to the center of Christian instruction, especially concerning biblical prophecy.

The need for clarity has never been greater. A time for a sound Christian apologetics concerning the rapture. We are living in an age of deception, where emotional appeals have replaced exegesis, where people are taught to be terrified of being "left behind" rather than prepared to endure persecution faithfully like the early Christian communities. The pretribulation rapture doctrine exploits this fear. It paints a distorted image of God, as though He will brutalize His own redeemed saints with plagues if they happen to repent after the so-called "secret coming," and in some cases many pretribulationists teach not believing in a pretrib rapture though its not taught in scripture is enough to be left behind. It teaches that "rightly dividing the word" means chopping Scripture into isolated segments, carving out inconvenient verses, and undermining the unity of the Bible in the process. In reality, many of its arguments rest on contextomy (the act of quoting out of context), circular reasoning, and doctrinal conjecture dressed up as certainty. The conclusion is always assumed, and Scripture is forced to conform. This book is my answer to that distortion.

The Bible is not only consistent; it is clear. The Scriptures speak plainly to those who will listen humbly. Eschatology is not meant to be reserved for scholars with charts and systems. It's for the body of Christ. It's for the faithful servant who wants to be found watching when the Master returns.

My purpose here is not to win a theological debate, but to restore confidence in the Word of God. We must stop building doctrines on fear and speculation and return to letting the text speak for itself. That's why the method throughout this book will be simple: let Scripture interpret Scripture. When needed, I will include historical and linguistic insights. But our foundation will be the Word of God in context, read naturally, without interjecting presuppositions.

In the discourse of doctrine when passions run high, people forget the humanity of each other. My argument is directed at the arguments of those who hold to a pretribulation or "pretrib" rapture and not the persons themselves.

We will begin with a verse often used as a theological "mic drop" by pretribulationists: "For God hath not appointed us to wrath" (1 Thessalonians 5:9). This verse is used to bypass the entire conversation, to claim the debate is settled before it even begins. But the truth is, the meaning of that verse, like every other, depends on how we define the terms, how we read the context, and whether we are willing to harmonize it with the rest of Scripture. In Chapter 1, I will show that Paul is not offering an escape from hardship, but a promise of vindication when the wrath of God is poured out; not before the tribulation, but at the end of it, when Christ returns in glory.

This book will confront the assumptions of pretribulationism, expose its theological inconsistencies, and present a better way and one rooted in Scripture, not sentiment. What makes this book unique is it will directly engage with the arguments of pretribulation rapture from a historic premillennial position, and I will show throughout this book that this is the original doctrine historically taught by the early church.

It's time to return to sound doctrine. It's time to wake the Church from its slumber.

Interpretive Framework: How This Book Approaches Scripture

1. Scripture Interprets Scripture (Scriptural Harmony)

The Bible is a unified revelation. We do not pit one verse against another or isolate passages to build doctrines. Difficult or disputed texts must be interpreted in light of clearer ones. All relevant passages should be harmonized during study. If your doctrine creates contradiction, your interpretation is wrong.

2. Contextual Consistency

No verse exists in a vacuum. Chapter and verse numbers were added centuries later and can often interrupt the flow of thought. We must read passages in full context, across chapters when necessary, and trace the author's argument without artificial breaks. For example, parts from 1 Thessalonians chapters 4 and 5 form a single continuous teaching that must be interpreted together.

3. Biblical Language Interpretation

Sound doctrine starts with sound definitions. Greek and Hebrew terms must be studied based on how they are used throughout

Scripture, not redefined to fit preconceived notions or systems. The Greek word "orgē " ("wrath") in the book of Revelation refers specifically to God's final judgment at the Second Coming, not to tribulation, persecution, or the general sufferings of man.

4. Literal Interpretation (With Literary Awareness)

Taking the text at face value unless the genre or context clearly indicates symbolic language. A literal approach is not the same as a literalistic one. We respect metaphors, apocalyptic imagery, or any literary device without turning every passage into an allegory or flattening every symbol into wooden literalism.

5. Theological and Narrative Unity

Truth does not contradict itself. The Bible, from Genesis to Revelation presents one divine Author and one redemptive storyline. Doctrines built on isolated proof texts and disconnected from the biblical whole are dangerous. God's consistent pattern is deliverance through judgment, not escape from it. This theme runs from Noah to Egypt to Revelation.

In addition to presenting a clear biblical case for the posttribulation or "posttrib" return of Christ, the chapters in this book will include a rebuttal and answer section that will address many common objections raised by pretribulation teachers and believers. These arguments are often repeated with such confidence and frequency that they create an illusion of certainty, yet most collapse under the weight of context and scriptural consistency.

Each rebuttal will be addressed clearly and directly, not as a distraction, but to equip the reader with the discernment to separate truth from tradition. I will not avoid tough questions. On the contrary, I welcome them, because truth has nothing to fear from scrutiny. My aim is not merely to expose error, but to restore clarity where confusion has taken root.

Because many of the topics in this book are deeply interconnected, some Scriptures and theological points will naturally appear more than once. This is not redundancy, it's reinforcement. Biblical eschatology is a tightly woven tapestry, not a linear chart. Certain verses intersect across multiple doctrines, and their repetition serves to reinforce the harmony of Scripture, not dilute it. When a passage reappears in another chapter, it will be approached with fresh emphasis or in a different light, demonstrating its relevance to the broader theological framework. Scripture's beauty is in its consistency, and this book is designed to reflect that.

I do not write this out of pride, nor from an argumentative spirit, but out of grief for what has been lost for many and zeal for what must be restored. Like Paul, I must speak plainly:

"I say the truth in Christ, I lie not, my conscience also bearing me witness in the Holy Ghost, That I have great heaviness and continual sorrow in my heart."
(Romans 9:1–2)

I carry that sorrow for the Body of Christ; for those who have been misled, for those who fear what God never meant them to fear, and for those who no longer know what His return is meant to inspire: not dread, but hope. May this book be a light in that confusion.

A Note on Why I Use the KJV

I grew up reading the King James Version, and it remains the most widely accepted translation among English-speaking believers. While some find its archaic English challenging, I found it sharpened me, forcing me into deeper study, stronger discipline, and even the lost art of using a dictionary. I still supplement my reading with lexical tools and examine the syntax closely, but I've come to believe the issue isn't the difficulty of the language… it's the lack of desire to rise to the challenge. Truth isn't found by dumbing things down; it's revealed to those zealous enough to dig deeper. That's the zeal of the Lord.

Chapter 1:
Not Appointed to Wrath? An Introduction to 1 Thessalonians 5:9

"For God hath not appointed us to wrath, but to obtain salvation by our Lord Jesus Christ."
(1 Thessalonians 5:9, KJV)

As I said in the preface, pretribulationists often treat this verse like a theological mic drop, as though its mere quotation is sufficient to prove the church will be absent during the tribulation. But this misuse of 1 Thessalonians 5:9 exposes one of the most common interpretive errors in modern prophecy circles: the tendency to isolate a verse from its surrounding context, inject it with doctrinal conjecture and assumptions, and then build an entire eschatology around it. This is not exegesis. This is presuppositionalism in disguise.

Restoring the Flow of Paul's Thought

To understand what Paul truly meant when he wrote that "God hath not appointed us to wrath," we must start by restoring the continuity of the passage. It's important to remember that the chapter and verse divisions we see in our modern Bibles were not part of the original biblical text. Chapter divisions were introduced by Stephen Langton, Archbishop of Canterbury, in the early 13th century, while verse numbers were later added by Robert Estienne, a 16th-century printer. These editorial additions are helpful for reference, but they often fracture the flow of thought and create the illusion of subject breaks where none exist. As noted in the Encyclopedia Britannica, Langton's chapter system became standard in the Latin Vulgate and was eventually adopted across Bible translations. What Paul wrote, however, was a continuous letter. One unfolding message that connected resurrection, return, and judgment in a single prophetic event. The pretrib system of theology capitalizes on these artificial chapter breaks, which interrupt the natural flow of thought. In fact, the entire system thrives on contextomy, taking advantage of readers' assumptions about chapter divisions and leading them to believe a new chapter signals a new subject. But in reality, many of these breaks are poorly placed and serve only as reference markers.

The Artificial Break Between Chapters 4 and 5

Many pretribulationists, though sincere in their convictions, interpret 1 Thessalonians chapters 4 and 5 as describing two entirely different prophetic events. In their view, chapter 4 refers to a secret, signless rapture of the Church that occurs before the tribulation begins, while chapter 5 introduces the Day of the Lord as a separate, subsequent time of judgment that comes upon the world after the Church has been snatched up in the rapture. This interpretive break is not drawn from the flow of Paul's letter but rather from a doctrinal framework imposed upon it.

Classical dispensationalism is especially rigid in this division, often going so far as to equate the "thief in the night" language with the rapture itself arguing that it represents Christ's secret, imminent coming for the Church. More moderate pretribulationists may allow some overlap in tone or theme between chapters 4 and 5 but still maintain a chronological gap between the rapture and the Day of the Lord. Yet in both cases, a textual separation is assumed rather than demonstrated.

In order to sustain this model, the natural continuity between resurrection, rapture, and judgment must be interrupted. The phrase "caught up… to meet the Lord in the air" (1 Thessalonians 4:17) is isolated from the "sudden destruction" (5:3) and "wrath" (5:9) that follow just a few verses later. Yet Paul makes no such distinction. He gives no indication that these events are divided by years or separated by dispensations. In fact, his repeated use of transition words like "but," "for," and "therefore" reinforces the uninterrupted flow of thought from one event to the next.

Immediately after describing the catching away of the saints in 4:17, Paul continues in 4:18 with, "Wherefore comfort one another with these words." Then, in the very next sentence, he writes, "But of the times and the seasons, brethren, ye have no need that I write unto you" (5:1), indicating he is not beginning a new subject but continuing the same prophetic framework. In 5:2–3, he warns of coming judgment, saying, "For yourselves know perfectly that the day of the Lord so cometh as a thief in the night… For when they shall say, Peace and safety; then sudden destruction cometh upon them." Again, Paul uses "for" to explain the continuity and immediacy of the danger tied to Christ's coming. Later in verse 6, he exhorts believers to remain watchful: "Therefore let us not sleep, as do others; but let us watch and be sober." These transitions link the resurrection hope with the call to readiness in the face of coming judgment.

Far from supporting a hidden, pretribulational rapture followed by a delayed Day of the Lord, Paul's seamless argument moves from the resurrection of the dead in Christ to the sudden judgment upon the unprepared; without any textual signal that these are separate events divided by time. All of it unfolds as one prophetic sequence tied to the return of Christ.

One Continuous Eschatological Vision

Chapters and verses may help us flip through our Bibles, but they were added centuries after Paul laid down his pen. In the original letter, there was no "Chapter 4" break, no neat "Chapter 5" heading. There was only one unstoppable surge of thought about Jesus' coming in glory, an unbroken stream of exhortation, hope, and warning written to be read aloud as a single message to the Church. These modern divisions, while useful for navigation, can mislead readers into thinking Paul shifted topics where he did not. What we now call the end of chapter 4, and the beginning of chapter 5 were never meant to be read as distinct subjects. Paul drives straight into the vision of resurrection and rapture, saying, "Wherefore comfort one another with these words," and then, without missing a beat, he leans in again with, "But of the times and the seasons, brethren, ye have no need that I write unto you." He isn't changing gears; he is plunging deeper into the same single, radiant event of the Lord's return.

Even the "thief in the night" motif, often isolated by pretrib interpreters, is part of this same continuous message. It is sandwiched between two calls for comfort: first, the comfort of the resurrection in 4:18, and later, the comfort of identity and salvation in 5:11, where Paul writes, "Wherefore comfort yourselves together, and edify one another." This structure reinforces the unity of the section. From resurrection to return, from warning to watchfulness, from sudden destruction to sober encouragement, Paul presents one seamless prophetic vision meant to prepare the Church, not remove it, for the Day of the Lord.

The language of both chapters clearly points to a single event. Paul describes the Lord descending from heaven with a shout (4:16), the dead in Christ rising, the living being caught up, and all believers meeting the Lord in the air (4:17). Without shifting focus, he immediately continues by warning that the Day of the Lord will come as a thief in the night (5:2), bringing sudden destruction upon the wicked. In the same breath, he urges the faithful to remain sober and watchful. There is no break in subject or theme, only a seamless unfolding of resurrection, return, and judgment as one continuous message

Defining "Wrath" (ὀργή)

This raises the question: What, then, is the "wrath" we are not appointed to?

The Greek word used here is orgē (ὀργή), a term that consistently refers to God's final, eschatological judgment throughout the New Testament, especially in the Book of Revelation. It is never used to describe tribulation, persecution, or the ordinary trials of life. It does not refer to suffering inflicted by men, but to retribution poured out by God. This wrath is not random or indiscriminate. It is measured vengeance, aimed with precision at the ungodly who rejected the truth and afflicted the righteous. And it is always tied to the return of Christ in power and glory, when justice will no longer wait and every wrong will be brought into judgment. This is not the fire we endure. It is the fire that falls on those who oppressed us. (More on the Greek word orgē and its purpose in Chapter Three.)

Paul affirms this in the very next verse: "Who died for us, that, whether we wake or sleep, we should live together with him" (5:10). This is resurrection language, a direct continuation of the promise outlined in chapter 4. Our hope is not escape from tribulation, but eternal life at Christ's appearing. Once again, Paul concludes with a call to encouragement: "Wherefore comfort yourselves together, and edify one another" (5:11). The repetition of this phrase, first in 4:18 and now in 5:11, functions like a set of bookends. It reinforces the continuity we have already traced, showing that Paul never changed subjects. From resurrection to return, from warning to comfort, the message remains the same: Christ is coming, and we will live with Him.

The Thief-in-the-Night Motif

And the nail in the coffin for the pretrib interpretation is Paul's use of the phrase "as a thief in the night" (1 Thessalonians 5:2). Since we have already established that chapters 4 and 5 form a continuous narrative, one seamless vision of Christ's return, resurrection, and reckoning, it becomes even more significant that Paul introduces the thief motif at this very point. Pretribulationists often claim that this imagery suggests a secret or stealthy coming, as though Christ will slip in quietly to remove the Church before the world takes notice. But the biblical usage of the thief motif, especially when cross-referenced with the rest of Scripture, reveals a very different picture. The thief comes to bring sudden, devastating judgment upon the unprepared, not to whisk the faithful away in secrecy.
Paul writes:

"For yourselves know perfectly that the day of the Lord so cometh as a thief in the night. For when they shall say, Peace and safety; then sudden destruction cometh upon them, as travail upon a woman with child; and they shall not escape."
(1 Thessalonians 5:2–3)

Notice carefully: the thief imagery is for the wicked, not the righteous. It is tied to inescapable destruction, not deliverance. This warning belongs to the same flow of thought we have traced from resurrection to wrath, with no indication of a hidden phase or separate event. And Paul is not alone in this. As we will soon see, when the thief returns in Revelation, it is never in silence or secrecy, but always in the context of final judgment and visible glory.

Revelation 16:15–16: The Ultimate Thief Imagery

Perhaps the most definitive confirmation that the thief imagery refers to the Second Coming is found in Revelation 16. There, in the very chapter where the kings of the earth are gathering for the battle of Armageddon, Jesus Himself interrupts the narrative with a warning—not to the world, but to His people—invoking the thief language one final time:

"Behold, I come as a thief. Blessed is he that watcheth, and keepeth his garments, lest he walk naked, and they see his shame."
(Revelation 16:15)

And what follows? The climactic confrontation of Armageddon:

"And he gathered them together into a place called in the Hebrew tongue Armageddon."
(Revelation 16:16)

This is staggering. The only time in Revelation that Jesus speaks of coming "as a thief" is not before a secret event or hidden removal, but immediately before the final battle, when the beast and the kings of the earth are mustered for open war. This is not seven years before His return. This is the final hour. The moment of judgment. The true Second Coming in glory.

In 2 Thessalonians 1:7–8, Paul makes this even more explicit:

"And to you who are troubled rest with us, when the Lord Jesus shall be revealed from heaven with his mighty angels,
In flaming fire taking vengeance on them that know not God, and that obey not the gospel of our Lord Jesus Christ."

Here again, the revealing of Christ is not divided into multiple phases. It is the moment of wrath, vengeance, and fire. It is also the time when the Church is given rest from tribulation. The Lord is revealed "from heaven," echoing 1 Thessalonians 4:16, but now we are shown another dimension of that same event: He appears with His angels to bring justice upon the wicked and to vindicate His saints. There is no mention of a separate, earlier coming to secretly extract the Church. There is no hidden phase tucked seven years behind this visible return. What we see is what we get the glorious, public, retributive return of Christ.

And that raises the irony. In the pretribulational system, the so-called "Second Coming" is actually the third. The rapture is made into a secret first return, followed later by a visible one. But Scripture does not make that distinction. In natural reading, the instinct of most believers is to harmonize all these descriptions of Christ's return into one unified event. I have spoken with pretrib believers who have candidly admitted that it is easy to "conflate" the rapture and the Second Coming. And why is that? It is because the plain reading of the text draws them together. The reason so many people intuitively read the return of the Lord as taking place after the tribulation is because that is the natural flow of the biblical narrative. And if we simply let the Word speak, that is where it leads.

The True Comfort of 1 Thessalonians 5:9

So, when Paul says in 1 Thessalonians 5:9 that "God hath not appointed us to wrath," he does not mean we will escape tribulation. He means that when Christ returns in fire and fury to destroy the armies of the beast and judge the wicked, we will be rescued. Not removed seven years beforehand but delivered in that very moment. We will be raised. We will be gathered. And we will be glorified at His appearing.

Paul's message does not shift from suffering to escape; it moves from suffering to vindication. This is the consistent gospel pattern. We are not promised exemption from affliction, but rest at the return of the Lord. And that is exactly what Paul teaches in 2 Thessalonians 1. He asks us to consider: When do we rest? The answer is given plainly: "When the Lord Jesus shall be revealed from heaven with his mighty angels." And who is punished at that revelation? Again, Paul tells us: "In flaming fire taking vengeance on them that know not God, and that obey not the gospel of our Lord Jesus Christ." These are not future hypotheticals; they are the defining moments of the Second Coming. That is when the wicked are judged. That is when the righteous are relieved.

This passage does not describe two separate events. There is no invisible return in view. There is one moment when the Lord is revealed, when vengeance is rendered, and when the saints are comforted at last. The justice of God is not about removing His people from tribulation but about reversing their affliction at Christ's appearing. Paul's theology is not escape theology. It is resurrection theology. Pretribulationalism undermines this by reframing the comfort Paul offers. Rather than teaching believers to endure tribulation with patience and faith, knowing they will be vindicated at Christ's return, it offers an escape hatch that bypasses the very suffering Scripture tells us to overcome. Yet in Revelation 14:12–13, we are told:

"Here is the patience of the saints: here are they that keep the commandments of God, and the faith of Jesus. And I heard a voice from heaven saying... Blessed are the dead which die in the Lord... that they may rest from their labours."

This is the consistent message. Saints endure. Saints overcome. Saints are saved not through rapture, but through resurrection and eternal life. Our hope is not in vanishing, but in victory.

Rebuttal & Answer:
"But Pretrib is the Majority View!"

One of the more common defenses of the pretribulation rapture is that it is "the majority view." You will hear this fallacy tucked into sermons, books, online videos, and podcasts, as if somehow the popularity of the position settles the matter before the Bible is ever opened. But let's be honest. That is not a biblical argument. It is a numbers game. And numbers do not determine the truth.

If they did, the early Church would have bowed to Rome, accepted pagan compromise, and silenced the gospel to avoid persecution. But it did not. The gospel advanced because a faithful minority refused to be swept away by the crowd. The appeal to majority—or argumentum ad populum—is a fallacy dressed in religious clothing. It argues that something must be true simply because most people believe it. But Scripture never says, "Check the polling data." It says, "What saith the scripture?"

Pretribulationists lean heavily on rhetorical appeal rather than scriptural foundation. The suggestion is often made that to reject their view is to step outside the bounds of historic Christian faith, as if disagreeing with pretribulationalism is akin to rejecting the Bible itself. But that is not intellectual rigor. That is intimidation by peer pressure. It is the same mindset Jesus confronted in the religious elite of His day. They loved consensus, tradition, and the approval of men. But Jesus pulled back the veil:

"Ye do err, not knowing the scriptures, nor the power of God."
(Matthew 22:29)

And Paul's warning feels timelier than ever. He said the time would come when believers "will not endure sound doctrine," but would gather teachers to scratch their itching ears (2 Timothy 4:3). We are living in that time. And in this kind of environment, biblical loyalty will look like dissent. The irony, of course, is that pretribulationism is not even the historic majority view. But that truth is often kept quiet, tucked behind assumption and tradition. Let us examine the real historical record and the results may surprise you.

Historical Majority? A Narrow Minority, Actually

The truth is, the pretrib movement has functioned as a loud minority, not a theological majority. It floods the marketplace with books, conferences, media productions, and internet personalities who repeat the same talking points. But repetition does not equal inspiration, and volume does not equal truth. The reach of pretribulationalism has always outpaced its foundation. It spread by system-building, not Scripture-following. And now that more believers are waking up and testing the claims, its grip is weakening.

Statistically, the pretrib doctrine does not hold majority ground, not globally and not even nationally within the full range of theological diversity. When we examine the broader spectrum of eschatological views including amillennialism, postmillennialism, premillennialism, and its older, more rooted counterpart, historic premillennialism, it becomes clear that pretribulationalism is not the prevailing voice. It is a subcategory within dispensational premillennialism, which is itself a relatively recent and niche expression within the larger premillennial tradition. In plain terms, pretrib is not the foundation. It is a refinement layered on top of a system that itself diverged from the historic framework of the early Church.

A 2016 LifeWay Research study reported that only 36 percent of U.S. Protestant pastors affirmed a pretribulational rapture. Twenty-five percent interpreted the rapture non-literally, while 18 percent held to a posttrib view. The remainder were divided among midtrib, prewrath, or expressed uncertainty. And that is in the United States, the nation most responsible for broadcasting pretribulationalism to the rest of the world. While the doctrine was born in the British Isles through the teachings of John Nelson Darby in the nineteenth century, it was in the United States that it found a platform, an audience, and a distribution machine.

The turning point was the publication of the Scofield Reference Bible in 1909. For the first time, Darby's dispensational framework, and with it, the pretrib rapture, was inserted directly into the margins and footnotes of Scripture. That one volume became a theological pipeline, shaping generations of pastors, churches, and seminaries. It was not just a study Bible. It was a study system. Scofield's notes gave dispensationalism the appearance of biblical inevitability, and for many, the notes came to hold as much weight as the text itself.

If you believe in the pretribulational rapture, there is a strong chance that influence traces back to Scofield. Whether you encountered it through your church, your pastor, your parents, or a popular prophecy teacher, the pathway almost always leads to the same source. And you have done nothing wrong in receiving it. Many of us inherit our theology before we ever examine it. But it is important to acknowledge where these ideas come from and whether they align with what Scripture actually says. The pretrib doctrine did not arise naturally from centuries of Christian consensus or continuous exegesis. It was introduced, published, and promoted until it became familiar. Familiarity, however, is not the same as faithfulness.

On the global stage, the pretrib position remains a minority view. It is not a theological default. It is a theological export, heavily marketed to English-speaking evangelicals, often assumed to be the norm simply because it is the loudest voice in certain Western circles. But volume does not establish truth, and majority perception does not make a doctrine apostolic.

Early Church Witness vs. Modern Invention

This raises a crucial question: if pretribulationism is supposedly the biblical and historic view, why is it missing from the first eighteen centuries of Church history? The answer is simple—it wasn't there. Historic premillennialism, not pretribulationism, was the position of the early Church. The Church fathers didn't speculate about multiple comings of Christ or hidden phases of return. They expected one glorious appearing after the tribulation. Irenaeus, Justin Martyr, Tertullian, Papias, and Lactantius all affirmed a visible Second Coming that would follow the rise of the Antichrist and a time of great tribulation. More on early church testimony later in this book.

Tregelles on Modern Revelation

Samuel P. Tregelles, a 19th-century biblical scholar, Greek expert, and translator of the New Testament, was no outsider to theology or church scholarship. He stood firmly within the world of serious exegesis and classical Christian study. Yet when he first encountered the idea of a secret pretribulational rapture, his reaction was telling. He wrote:

"I am not aware that there was any definite teaching that there would be a secret rapture of the Church at a secret coming until this was given forth as an 'utterance' in Edward Irving's church, and it was from that supposed revelation that the modern doctrine and the modern phraseology arose."
—The Hope of Christ's Second Coming, p. 26

Tregelles called it out for what it was. A modern doctrine, born not from Scripture, but from speculative revelation and emotional fervor. He soundly refuted it, and not because he doubted the return of Christ, but because he believed the Bible had already spoken plainly. For him, faith in the Second Coming did not require a split timeline or a secret schedule.

And let us be honest. If the secret rapture is real, it may be the best-kept secret in biblical history. It was so secret, in fact, that the apostles never mentioned it, the Church Fathers never taught it, and the vast majority of clergy in Darby's own century had never even heard of it. A doctrine this recent, introduced through a supposed utterance in the 1800s, should not be accepted as gospel simply because it found a microphone in the 20th century.

Tregelles' critique reminds us that popularity does not confer pedigree. The test of truth is not novelty, but faithfulness to what has already been revealed. If the early Church could cling to the hope of Christ's return without splitting it into stages, so can we.

Dispensationalism's Load-Bearing Wall

Pretribulationism did not emerge from the plain reading of the Bible. It emerged from Darby's system. It is often described as a subcategory within dispensational premillennialism, and that is true, but it is more than a footnote in the system. It is one of the load-bearing walls. Without a secret rapture to separate the Church from Israel, the entire dispensational timeline collapses. In that sense, pretrib is not simply part of dispensationalism. It is the glue that holds it together.

And that is the problem. If your doctrine only exists to preserve your chart, then you have not begun with the Word of God. You have built on a blueprint, not on the solid rock of Scripture. And when the storm of serious Bible study comes, that structure begins to shift. The foundation cracks. The dispensational framework, built on the sand of speculation and separation, is now sinking. The load-bearing wall of pretribulationism is buckling, and with it, the whole system is faltering.

According to data published by Christianity Today and LifeWay Research, support for pretribulationalism is shrinking, especially among younger pastors and those trained in deeper theological study. In 2016, LifeWay found that only 36 percent of U.S. Protestant pastors affirmed a pretribulational rapture. Among pastors under the age of 45, that number dropped to 28 percent. Meanwhile, support for posttribulationalism rose to 23 percent in that same younger group, suggesting a quiet but steady return to a simpler reading of Scripture. Twenty-five percent of pastors interpreted the rapture non-literally, while the remainder were divided among midtrib, prewrath, or uncertain.

This is not just a generational trend. It is a return to biblical clarity. The more grounded a teacher becomes in the whole counsel of Scripture, the more likely they are to abandon the system. The conferences, films, and novels may have kept it afloat for a time, but the foundation has never been solid. The doctrine is not gaining ground. It is bleeding credibility.

The Only Vote That Counts

So, the question isn't, "What do most people believe?" The question is, "What did Jesus say?" And in the end, that's the only vote that counts.

As we close this chapter, remember that the promise of verse 9 isn't an escape hatch but a lifeline thrown to every believer in the face of divine judgment. We're not sidestepping the storm. We're anchored in the hope that when Christ appears, all wrath will be turned away from us and poured out on our foes. Cling to that comfort. Let it steady your heart.

Next Revelation:
The Timing of Wrath and the Day of the Lord

As we turn the page into Chapter 2, we will follow the thread of divine judgment from the prophets into Revelation itself, tracing the Greek orgē ("wrath") through trumpet blasts, seal judgments, and the climactic Day of the Lord. You will see that what Scripture calls "wrath" is never poured out at the first seal or the midpoint of Daniel's week but held in reserve for that one appointed hour when Christ returns in glory. We will unpack the difference between orgē and thumos, compare Paul's sudden destruction language with John's Armageddon vision, and let the text's own timeline reveal that the Church's rescue occurs in that very moment of reckoning, not before. By the end, the supposed gap between rapture and return will vanish, and the sequence of trumpet, wrath, and vindication will stand in clear, unbroken relief.

Chapter 2:
The Timing of Wrath and the Day of the Lord

As we shift from the foundation laid in Chapter 1, it becomes clear that the question is not simply whether the Church will face hardship, but what kind of judgment God has truly promised to spare His people from. The issue at stake is not suffering in general, but the specific kind of "wrath" Paul had in view. While many pretribulationists continue to quote 1 Thessalonians 5:9 as a quick retort to posttribulational teaching, the verse cannot carry their argument alone. Quoting Scripture is not the same as interpreting it, and citing a promise without context often leads to presumption rather than clarity. A single verse, when removed from the thread that holds it to the rest of Paul's message, becomes a loose stone. And a doctrine built on a loose stone will not stand.

As we saw in Chapter 1, Paul's flow of thought in 1 Thessalonians 4 and 5 is seamless. His exhortation to comfort one another with the hope of resurrection does not end with chapter breaks or subject changes. It flows directly into the warning that the Day of the Lord will arrive with sudden destruction. That entire arc from resurrection to reckoning is one continuous message of encouragement to the faithful and a sober warning to the unprepared. Paul does not pivot from comfort to catastrophe for dramatic effect. He does it to frame the full picture of what the return of Christ will mean. For the saints, it is hope fulfilled. For the wicked, it is judgment unleashed.

In this chapter, we will revisit that continuity, not just to affirm the structure of Paul's epistle, but to drill deeper into what Paul actually meant by "wrath." We will test the claim that this wrath refers to the entire seven-year tribulation and examine what the Greek text and surrounding context truly reveal. We will see that Paul's warning is not about escaping the afflictions brought by Antichrist or man, but about being preserved through them until the wrath of God falls in full force upon the enemies of Christ. That wrath, as we will trace through Scripture, is not arbitrary, and it is not scattered. It is appointed. And it arrives at the very moment Jesus returns in power and glory.

The Technical Meaning of Apantēsis

This brings us to a crucial detail that reinforces the continuity we traced in Chapter 1 and affirmed again at the beginning of this chapter. The unity of 1 Thessalonians chapters 4 and 5 is not just a literary observation. It is theological bedrock. The return of Christ, the resurrection of the saints, the sudden destruction of the wicked, and the comforting promise of deliverance from wrath are not isolated events scattered across unrelated timelines. They are part of one prophetic sequence, tied together by Paul's unbroken thought and vocabulary.

This continuity is critical. The seamless narrative from chapter 4 into chapter 5 directly contradicts the idea that the rapture is a separate event from the Second Coming. In fact, the Greek word used in 1 Thessalonians 4:17 for "meet" (ἀπάντησις, apantēsis) carries a very technical meaning: it refers to a formal greeting of a dignitary, where a delegation goes out to welcome and meet a person of honor and then accompanies them to their destination. This term is used the same way in Matthew 25:6 (the parable of the ten virgins) and Acts 28:15 (when believers go out to meet Paul). There are no U-turns back to where the dignitary departed from in these examples. There is no suggestion that believers go up to heaven and remain there for seven years while tribulation unfolds on the earth. Jesus departs from heaven, and we meet Him in the clouds, and since there is no U-turn for the King in apantēsis, we must return with Him to earth.

To further illustrate that this was not a rare circumstance or poetic speech on Paul's part, we must understand the conventional usage. The Greek noun apantēsis, translated "to meet" in 1 Thessalonians 4:17, carries a specific cultural and linguistic connotation, especially in Greco-Roman contexts where a delegation would go out to meet a dignitary, then return with him—Acts 28:15; 1 Thess 4:17; Matt 25:6."

- Josephus uses the word in precisely this manner when describing the public reception of Vespasian: "The whole multitude waited for Vespasian's approach... [and] poured forth to meet (apantēsis)

- Likewise, W. E. Vine notes that the term denotes "a formal meeting of a dignitary" No where in this meeting is a hint of a king turning back from his point of departure and this consistent meaning underlies the use of apantēsis in all New Testament passages where it occurs.
- Also, it say in BDAG, the 3rd edition (2000), p. 97:ἀπάντησις—meeting, encounter— in our lit., as a technical term for the civic custom of meeting a visiting dignitary, to accord him honor by going out to meet him and escorting him partway back: Mt 25:6; Ac 28:15; 1 Th 4:17.
- NT Wright states: Greek word for 'meeting' was used ... when a king or emperor was visiting a city. The citizens would go out to meet him, and then escort him back into the city."
—Abridged from N. T. Wright, Surprised by Hope: Rethinking Heaven, the Resurrection, and the Mission of the Church (New York: HarperOne, 2008), 133.

The implications are unavoidable. The Church does not meet Christ in the air to detour back to heaven for a heavenly honeymoon while the world burns. We meet Him because He is returning, and we accompany Him because He is coming to reign. The linguistic scholars are not debating this. They are in full agreement. Paul was not describing a departure. He was describing a procession. The saints are not caught up to leave the world behind, but to welcome the King back to the world He is about to judge and restore. That is what apantēsis means. That is what the Church is appointed to. And that is what every eye shall see.

Reception, Not Departure

Considering this, the picture painted of the meeting is one of reception. The saints meet the Lord in the air as He is descending, and they accompany Him to the earth, specifically to the Mount of Olives, as foretold in Zechariah 14:4. As it is written in Acts 1:11, the angel said at the Mount of Olives, from where Jesus departed, that He would return "in like manner." This means physically and visibly to the Mount of Olives.

The idea of a secret, invisible coming seven years earlier is not only absent from this passage but also contradicted by the plain language of the text. The angel does not give the disciples two comings to watch for. He gives them one. There is no mention of a hidden phase, no delay before the Second Coming, and no hint that the Church should expect a private rapture before Christ's public descent. If such a paradigm were essential to the hope of the Church, here would have been the perfect moment to introduce it. But the record is silent. The only return Jesus is said to make is the one that brings Him back to the very place He left.

This is where the meaning of apantēsis becomes critical. The saints are not being called upward for an extended heavenly honeymoon. They are going out to meet the returning King, just as loyal subjects would go out to welcome a royal procession and escort him back into the city. That is the imagery Paul chose, and that is the expectation the early Church understood. There is no theological room for a round trip to heaven followed by a seven-year layover. The meeting in the air is not the end of the journey. It is the moment we join our returning Lord in His descent to establish justice on the earth.

The pretribulational attempt to separate the rapture of 1 Thessalonians 4 from the Second Coming of Zechariah 14 introduces a division that Scripture never makes. It creates an artificial gap between the meeting and the destination, as though the saints will greet the Lord in the clouds only to take a detour to heaven while He waits to fulfill the rest of His mission. But the angel was not ambiguous. The Lord who ascended from the Mount of Olives will come again in like manner to that same mountain. He is not stopping midway. He is not veering off course. He is returning, just as He left. And we are told to expect nothing less.

This sets the stage for the next crucial link in Paul's timeline. What follows the meeting is not a retreat. It is confrontation. Not a secret return, but a thief-in-the-night arrival that catches the world off guard and brings wrath upon the wicked. And that moment is not years before Armageddon. It is Armageddon.

The Thief in the Night and Armageddon

Now, turning again to 1 Thessalonians 5:1–3, as I've stated before, we see that the "Day of the Lord" comes suddenly, like a thief in the night, while people are saying "peace and safety." This warning comes directly on the heels of Paul's description of the Lord descending from heaven in chapter 4. It is not a new subject, but a continuation of the same sequence—the return of Christ, the resurrection of the saints, and the reckoning that follows.

This thief imagery is not isolated to Paul. It is mirrored almost word-for-word in Revelation 16:14–16, where demonic spirits go out to gather the kings of the earth to battle against God. This is the scene of Armageddon. And right in the middle of this climactic confrontation, Jesus interjects with a statement that echoes Paul's words:

"Behold, I come as a thief. Blessed is he that watcheth, and keepeth his garments, lest he walk naked, and they see his shame."
(Revelation 16:15)

Then immediately, the narrative continues:

"And he gathered them together into a place called in the Hebrew tongue Armageddon."
(Revelation 16:16)

This is not a secret rapture. This is a declaration of open war. The thief comes, not for a quiet rescue mission, but to break into the strong man's house and take back what belongs to Him. This is the same Jesus whom the angel said would return "in like manner" to the Mount of Olives. And now, in Revelation 16, He is doing just that—coming with vengeance, interrupting the world's false peace with unstoppable judgment.

Ironically, the language so often used by pretribulationists to suggest imminence ends up working against their own model. The thief is not lurking in the shadows before the seals are opened. He is not creeping in before the first trumpet sounds. He does not appear until the kings of the earth have already been gathered. The thief is only imminent when the armies are assembled in Megiddo. That is the context. That is the timing. The moment of crisis is the moment of coming.

The real issue here is not about getting the dispensation right. It is about rightly dividing the word of truth by cutting a straight line from 1 Thessalonians to Revelation without inserting artificial gaps or manmade timelines. Paul's warning is not about some hidden phase of escape but about the collision between Christ's arrival and the rebellion of the nations.
The implications are clear:

- The Day of the Lord comes like a thief (1 Thessalonians 5:2)
- Jesus says, "I come as a thief" (Revelation 16:15)
- And what follows is Armageddon (Revelation 16:16)

This is the moment Paul spoke of when he said, "sudden destruction cometh upon them, and they shall not escape" (1 Thessalonians 5:3). The thief does not come to steal away the Church in secrecy. He comes to confront the rebellious, to judge the nations, and to vindicate the saints. This is not a rapture moment. It is a wrath moment.

This is the wrath we are not appointed to. And to understand exactly what Paul meant by that, we need to look closely at the word he used, orgē. What is this destruction that overtakes the world while the faithful are watching? What is this firestorm that follows the shout, the trumpet, and the appearing of Christ? That word, orgē, appears again in the Book of Revelation, written by the apostle John under the inspiration of the Holy Spirit. Though Paul and John were addressing different churches in different contexts, the Spirit of God uses the same term with purpose and precision. To truly define what this wrath is and not just repeat the phrase, we will follow its usage through Revelation in the next chapter. Many posttribulationists rightly say we are spared from wrath, but few take the time to show what that wrath actually is, when it arrives, or who it targets. We are going to take that step. But before we turn the page, we need to finish what Paul started. Because the comfort he offers in 1 Thessalonians is not about evading suffering but about standing firm in the promise that when Christ returns, justice will be done.

Comfort Through Resurrection and Vengeance

As I have said in the earlier chapter, this continuous flow is reinforced by Paul's closing statement in 1 Thessalonians 4:18,

"Wherefore comfort one another with these words."

He echoes the same phrase again in 5:11,

"Wherefore comfort yourselves together, and edify one another."

These bookends are not just pleasantries. They serve as markers, tying everything together. Paul has not changed the subject. He has not veered into a new timeline. He is still speaking of one event—the return of Christ, the resurrection of the saints, and the final reckoning with the wicked.

The comfort Paul offers is not rooted in escaping hardship. It is grounded in the unshakable hope of bodily resurrection at Christ's glorious return, and in the promise that every wrong will be made right. This is exactly what Paul affirms in his second letter to the Thessalonians. Those who suffer for Christ do so with purpose and expectation, because their vindication is bound to the moment Christ is revealed:

"And to you who are troubled rest with us, when the Lord Jesus shall be revealed from heaven with his mighty angels,
In flaming fire taking vengeance on them that know not God, and that obey not the gospel of our Lord Jesus Christ."
(2 Thessalonians 1:7–8)

Here, the relief does not come from being taken out of the world, but from Christ coming into it to bring justice. That is the rest Paul promises.

This ties directly into the cry of the saints in Revelation. They are not hiding from tribulation, but they are enduring it with holy expectation. Twice, John emphasizes their defining trait:

"Here is the patience and the faith of the saints."
(Revelation 13:10)

"Here is the patience of the saints: here are they that keep the commandments of God, and the faith of Jesus."
(Revelation 14:12)

In both cases, the patience and faith of the saints are not disconnected from the judgment that follows. Their endurance is not blind waiting, but it is a cry for justice, a hope rooted in the coming retribution upon those who persecuted them. The very next scenes in Revelation describe the fall of Babylon, the reaping of the earth, and the winepress of God's wrath being trodden. Patience and vengeance are not at odds. They are intertwined. God delays not because He has forgotten, but because He has appointed a day.

Patience. Endurance. Faith. That is what defines the Church in the tribulation—not escape, but perseverance unto vindication. When Christ returns, He will raise the righteous and repay the wicked. And that dual action, that collision of resurrection and retribution, is the comfort Paul offers to the Church. Not because the saints will be removed before it happens, but because they will be vindicated when it does.

This theme of God repaying the wicked and avenging His saints who have suffered persecution with patience and faith is a common thread tying together the eschatological teachings of Paul and John, a thread that is unusually left unexplored by pretribulationists.

Wrath and Final Judgment

Then we have another thread that ties the true eschatological narrative together, which is the alignment between 1 Thessalonians 5 and Revelation 16. This makes it undeniably clear: Paul's reference to "wrath" is connected to the final judgment, not to general tribulation or persecution that believers may endure. The wrath is poured out when Christ returns, when Babylon falls, when the beast and the false prophet are destroyed, and when those who received the mark are cast into the lake of fire, as you will later see in this book.

The fall of Babylon is not merely symbolic, it is described as a moment of finality, soaked in the language of divine fury. Consider the words of Revelation 16:19:

"And the great city was divided into three parts, and the cities of the nations fell:
and great Babylon came in remembrance before God,
to give unto her the cup of the wine of the fierceness of his wrath."
(Revelation 16:19)

This is not ordinary suffering. It is the culmination of God's settled indignation. Babylon receives the cup of wrath precisely because her sins have reached heaven, and the time for mercy has closed. Paul's use of "wrath" in 1 Thessalonians finds its full counterpart in scenes like this, where judgment does not come in stages, but in an unstoppable flood.

Dispensational teachers have insisted that the Church will escape all persecution and suffering during this time, but this idea is nowhere supported in the biblical text. It is a comforting lie, a false peace, that has rocked countless believers to sleep. The truth is that saints will face tribulation, but they are not appointed to God's wrath at the Second Coming. The Antichrist and all his followers are appointed to this wrath.

The text itself makes it clear that both chapters 4 and 5 of 1 Thessalonians speak of the same event: the visible, victorious return of Christ. Once we eliminate the artificial chapter break and allow the text to flow as Paul originally intended, the illusion of a pretribulation rapture collapses. The rapture and resurrection of the saints occur at the end of the tribulation, when Jesus comes not in secret, but as a conquering King.

When we let Paul speak without interruption and stop slicing his words into disconnected segments, we discover a seamless narrative. The resurrection of the saints, the sudden destruction of the wicked, and the promise of comfort all belong to one unified return—not two. And what is especially powerful is that when we align Paul's unbroken flow in 1 Thessalonians with John's vivid scenes in Revelation, we find perfect harmony. Paul describes the Lord descending from heaven with a shout, with the voice of the archangel, and with the trumpet of God. John shows us that same trumpet echoing through judgment, climaxing in the wrath poured out on the kingdom of the Beast.

Together, these two apostles paint a complete picture: the return of Christ is not a drawn-out process with hidden phases. It is a singular, cataclysmic event. It is the day when the dead are raised, the saints are gathered, Babylon falls, and the wrath of God is poured out. When we let Scripture speak on its own terms and resist the temptation to impose artificial divisions, the pattern becomes unmistakable. One return. One resurrection. One reckoning. And that is the hope the Church is meant to hold fast to—not escape from tribulation, but vindication at the coming of our Lord.

Harmony with the Words of Jesus

This harmonizes precisely with the words of Jesus Himself in Matthew 24:29–31:

"Immediately after the tribulation of those days shall the sun be darkened, and the moon shall not give her light, and the stars shall fall from heaven, and the powers of the heavens shall be shaken: And then shall appear the sign of the Son of man in heaven: and then shall all the tribes of the earth mourn, and they shall see the Son of man coming in the clouds of heaven with power and great glory. And he shall send his angels with a great sound of a trumpet, and they shall gather together his elect from the four winds, from one end of heaven to the other."

There is no gap. No hidden interval. The coming of the Son of Man takes place immediately after the tribulation, and it is at that very moment that the elect are gathered. This aligns precisely with Paul's account in 1 Thessalonians 4, where the Lord descends with a shout, with the voice of the archangel, and with the trumpet of God.

As in the Days of Noah

Many pretribulationists try to turn the days of Noah into a depiction of a pretrib rapture. But the irony is hard to miss. Jesus places the coming of the Son of Man immediately after the tribulation and then compares that very coming to the days of Noah. If we are going to force this into a rapture argument, then the pretrib position still collapses, because in the Noah story, the judgment is what comes first. The rains are poured out. The wicked are swept away. And only then is Noah's ark lifted above the flood.

Jesus also likens His coming to the days of Noah in Matthew 24:37–39:

"But as the days of Noe were, so shall also the coming of the Son of man be. For as in the days that were before the flood they were eating and drinking, marrying and giving in marriage, until the day that Noe entered into the ark, And knew not until the flood came, and took them all away; so shall also the coming of the Son of man be."

This is not an arbitrary comparison. It is a direct warning. The days of Noah are not about escape. They are about sudden judgment. In Genesis 7:11–13, we are told that "the same day were all the fountains of the great deep broken up," and it was on that very day that "Noah entered into the ark." The rain, God's judgment, began as Noah was sealed inside. He was not raptured away. He was preserved through it.

And what did the rain do? It took the wicked, all of them, away. The plagues that pretribulationists say we will escape do not take away the Antichrist and his followers in their entirety. They are part of a larger series of judgments that unfold over time. But the Second Coming of Christ does bring a final, decisive reckoning. That is when the wrath of God is poured out. That is when the fire falls. That is when the beast and the false prophet are thrown alive into the lake of fire, and the armies of rebellion are crushed. And yet we, my friend, are not appointed to that wrath, but have obtained salvation through our Lord Jesus Christ.

That is exactly what Jesus is saying. The coming of the Son of Man follows the same pattern. It happens after the tribulation, not before. And when it does, it will not be a secret departure for the Church. It will be a cataclysmic return that takes away the ungodly in one final, unmissable act of judgment. Just like the flood.

And just like Noah was lifted up in the ark, not to escape the world, but to rise above the judgment that swept it clean, so shall we be lifted up when Christ appears. Not because we earned it. Not because we avoided suffering. But because we are not appointed to wrath of the Lamb. Whether we are awake or asleep, alive or dead, watching or resting, we will rise. We have obtained salvation through our Lord Jesus Christ. The floodwaters will fall, but we will be sealed. The fire will come, but we will be gathered. Not in fear, but in triumph. Not in secret, but in glory.

Just as the ark was sealed by the hand of God, so too are we sealed by the promise of the Spirit. The same God who remembered Noah in the midst of the storm will remember His saints in the hour of shaking. When the earth gives way and the heavens split open, our hope will not tremble. We are not drifting aimlessly in the dark. We are held fast by the One who commands the storm.

So, take heart. The judgments that will break the pride of nations will not break the promise made to you. The fire that devours the wicked will not touch the righteous who are hidden in Christ. The wrath that falls will pass over those who are marked by the blood of the Lamb. When that day comes, it will not be a rescue in panic. It will be a victory long foretold. And we will rise, not as fugitives, but as heirs.

Rebuttal & Answer:
"Revelation 3:10 says, I also will keep thee from the hour of temptation."

Pretribulationists often appeal to Revelation 3:10 as though it were an airtight guarantee of a pretrib rapture. The verse reads:

"Because thou hast kept the word of my patience, I also will keep thee from the hour of temptation, which shall come upon all the world, to try them that dwell upon the earth."

On the surface, this may sound like a promise of removal. But once again, the interpretation hinges not on what the text says, but on what the interpreter assumes it must mean. The key lies in the word "keep."

The Greek word here is τηρέω (tēreō), which does not mean to evacuate, snatch away, or remove. According to Thayer's Greek Lexicon, it means "to attend to carefully," "to guard," "to watch over," and "to keep one in the state in which he is." The idea is preservation, not extraction. It is about being kept safe within a trial, not being lifted out of it. This same word is used in John 17:15, where Jesus prays to the Father:

"I pray not that thou shouldest take them out of the world, but that thou shouldest keep them from the evil."

The phrase "keep them from" is tēreō ek, just like Revelation 3:10. And here, Jesus explicitly rejects the idea of removal. He does not ask the Father to take His disciples out of the world, but to preserve them spiritually while they remain in it. The grammar and the meaning are consistent. God's promise is not that the Church will raptured out, but that the faithful will be guarded through what is coming.

And frankly, if Revelation 3:10 were promising a rapture, it would be a strange way to say it. Keeping someone "in the state they are in" is hardly the transformation Paul describes when he says that we will be changed "in a moment, in the twinkling of an eye" and "caught up together… to meet the Lord in the air" (1 Corinthians 15:52, 1 Thessalonians 4:17). There is nothing sudden or glorified about being kept as you are. That is preservation, not glorification. And it certainly does not describe resurrection power.

In fact, this interpretation fits perfectly with the broader context of Revelation. The Church is seen enduring trials, bearing witness, and overcoming the beast not vanishing from the narrative. The saints are sealed, not removed. They are victorious, not absent.

To claim that Revelation 3:10 teaches a secret rapture is to isolate the verse, import foreign assumptions, and ignore the plain meaning of the Greek. The promise is not to airlift believers out of testing, but to preserve them through it, just as God has always done with His people.

Rebuttal and Answer:
"But the Bible Says One Taken, One Left"

Then, some pretribulationists point to Jesus' words in Matthew 24:40–41— "Then shall two be in the field; the one shall be taken, and the other left"—as though it were a hidden breadcrumb trail leading to a secret pretribulation rapture. But once again, the claim relies not on what the text says, but on what they read into it.

This is another example of shifting goalposts. When Revelation 3:10 does not hold up under scrutiny, then their argument may slide over to Matthew 24:40 as a backup proof. But the context is no friend to their position.

In the verses prior to this, Jesus lays down the framework:

"But as the days of Noe were, so shall also the coming of the Son of man be."
(Matthew 24:37)

This reference to Noah is not abstract. It is Jesus' own interpretive lens for understanding what follows. He continues:

"For as in the days that were before the flood they were eating and drinking, marrying and giving in marriage, until the day that Noe entered into the ark, And knew not until the flood came, and took them all away; so shall also the coming of the Son of man be."
(Matthew 24:38–39)

It is no coincidence that Jesus connects the "taking" to the judgment of the flood. Those who were taken were not the faithful, they were the unrepentant. They were swept away in destruction. As we already explored earlier in this chapter, the Noah comparison is not about removal from danger, but about preservation through it. Noah was lifted in the ark while judgment fell. He was not taken away. The ones "taken" were those overtaken by wrath. And Jesus says His coming will follow the same pattern.

That context continues into verses 40 and 41. The "one taken" is not raptured to glory. He is seized in judgment. This is not a depiction of a quiet disappearance. It is a warning about sudden destruction.

Jesus seals the meaning with a vivid image that many skip over:

"For wheresoever the carcase is, there will the eagles be gathered together."
(Matthew 24:28)

This is apocalyptic language. It points to death, aftermath, and judgment. In Luke's account, the disciples ask Jesus directly, "Where, Lord?" meaning, where will the individuals in question be taken to? His answer is just as jarring:

"Wheresoever the body is, thither will the eagles be gathered together."
(Luke 17:37)

Jesus is not being vague. He is giving a prophetic snapshot of divine retribution. The ones "taken" are the ones whose bodies lie on the battlefield, while the birds of prey descend. Some translations even render "eagles" as "vultures," because the imagery is unmistakable: death, not deliverance. This is not a heavenly reunion. It is a scene of judgment.

And friend, you do not want to be "taken" in that context. You do not want to be the carcass. You do not want to be the one left in the field while the birds circle above. The pretribulational narrative flips the imagery completely, suggesting comfort where Jesus clearly declares condemnation.

But Jesus does not leave us in the dark. This is a battlefield, not a banquet. Or rather, it is both. Because in Revelation 19, John shows us the full picture:

"And I saw an angel standing in the sun; and he cried with a loud voice, saying to all the fowls that fly in the midst of heaven, Come and gather yourselves together unto the supper of the great God; That ye may eat the flesh of kings, and the flesh of captains, and the flesh of mighty men..."
(Revelation 19:17–18)

That is not the rapture. That is the final military confrontation between the Lord Jesus and the armies of the beast. The enemies of Christ are first gathered to a staging ground called Armageddon, as Revelation 16:16 states plainly:

"And he gathered them together into a place called in the Hebrew tongue Armageddon."

But the actual battle unfolds in and around Jerusalem, just as Zechariah 14:2 foretells:

"For I will gather all nations against Jerusalem to battle; and the city shall be taken..."

This climactic showdown happens at the same time as the marriage supper of the Lamb (Revelation 19:6–9). These two great events are not distant from each other. They unfold in tandem. One is a celebration of union between Christ and His redeemed. The other is a public display of covenantal vengeance, where the vultures feast upon the flesh of kings. The marriage supper is a table of joy. The battlefield is a table of judgment. And both take place when the King returns. Because when Christ reunites with His beloved Bride everyone eats at the marriage supper, even the fowl that circle overhead.

So, let's trace the trail:
- Matthew 24 describes the coming of the Son of Man after the tribulation.
- The "taken" are swept away like those in the flood.
- The "eagles" (or vultures) gather over the battlefield.
- Revelation 19 paints the fulfillment: Christ returns, the Beast and his army are defeated, and the birds of heaven feast on the bodies of the slain.

In short, the so-called "rapture" in Matthew 24:40–41 is not a rescue mission. It is a reckoning. It is the wrath Paul described in 1 Thessalonians 5:3:

"For when they shall say, Peace and safety; then sudden destruction cometh upon them... and they shall not escape."

This is the Day of the Lord. It is not the beginning of a secret departure. It is the climax of an open confrontation.

So, when pretribulational teachers leap from verse to verse, moving the goalpost from Revelation 3:10 to Matthew 24:40, hoping to find a foothold for a secret rapture, they miss the bigger picture. The ones "taken" are not the Church. They are the targets of judgment. Just like in the days of Noah.

We've now seen that 1 Thessalonians 5 does not promise an escape from tribulation, but from a specific kind of wrath—which is the final outpouring of judgment when Christ returns to the Mount of Olives. We've also exposed how pretribulational interpretations distort Jesus' warnings, turning scenes of judgment into imagined rapture events. That confusion depends on interrupting the flow between chapters 4 and 5, because when we read them together, the illusion falls apart. But this leads us to a bigger question. What does Paul actually mean by wrath?

Next Revelation:
Not Appointed to Wrath: But When Is Wrath Poured Out?

Pretribulationists often assume it begins at the start of the tribulation, but Scripture speaks differently. In the next chapter, we will trace the word orgē through the Book of Revelation. We will see exactly when it falls, who it falls on, and why that matters for understanding what believers are truly spared from in 1 Thessalonians 5:9.

Chapter 3
Not Appointed to Wrath: But When Is Wrath Poured Out?

At this stage in our study, we must go beyond merely identifying the misuse of 1 Thessalonians 5:9. I will now endeavor to define the nature and timing of divine wrath more precisely through lexical and scriptural analysis. Pretribs have long relied on fear as a theological weapon, conflating the wrath of God at the Second Coming with the tribulation plagues that fall upon the earth before Christ returns. In doing so, they have distorted the character of God and the meaning of Scripture, telling believers that if they are not raptured before the tribulation, they will be "left behind" to suffer the wrath of God. This is not only unbiblical, but also logically incoherent and theologically reckless.

The Greek term used in 1 Thessalonians 5:9, ὀργή (orgē), is not some vague reference to hardship, general suffering, or persecution. It is a technical word with a very specific meaning in the New Testament, especially in the Book of Revelation, where it is consistently used without deviation to describe God's final and decisive judgment poured out at the return of Jesus Christ. The term never describes the tribulation plagues themselves, nor is it applied to the trials the saints endure at the hands of the Beast. I must reiterate that orgē in every single instance for the wrath that is unleashed at the second coming of Christ. This is not a prolonged season of hardship. It is a climactic, world-shattering event. It is the floodwaters of divine judgment that will sweep away the wicked, just as the flood came and took them all away in the days of Noah.

"For God hath not appointed us to wrath (ὀργή), but to obtain salvation by our Lord Jesus Christ."
(1 Thessalonians 5:9)

But this raises a critical question that is rarely examined with biblical precision: When is the wrath of God actually poured out? To answer this, we must define our terms carefully and allow Scripture to speak for itself. As I've already noted, the Greek word in question, a word that appears repeatedly throughout the Book of

Revelation, has nothing whatsoever to do with the experience of being "left behind" and enduring the chaos of the tribulation. That narrative is a fictional invention propped up by sensationalist theology, not a faithful rendering of the biblical text. Orgē is a specific term that consistently refers to the final, climactic outpouring of God's righteous fury, poured out not on His Church, but on the unrepentant world at the return of Jesus Christ.

In other words, wrath in the sense that 1 Thessalonians 5:9 uses it is not what happens throughout the tribulation; it is what happens at its end. The more we trace the language of judgment and redemption through the epistles and Revelation, the more obvious it becomes that the resurrection of the dead saints, the rapture of the living, and the outpouring of wrath all occur in a single sequence, at the return of Christ, after the tribulation. What becomes increasingly clear is that pretribs confuse the categories entirely. They conflate the wrath of God with the wrath of the Beast. They confuse satanic persecution with divine judgment. And in doing so, they terrify the Church with threats of abandonment when God has promised vindication.

This distinction between the two is crucial for proper exegesis. The tribulation, biblically speaking, is marked by persecution of the saints at the hands of the wicked, empowered by the Beast. Scripture is unambiguous on this point. Daniel prophesied that the Antichrist would "make war with the saints, and prevail against them" (Daniel 7:21), and Revelation echoes the same, saying the Beast "was given unto him to make war with the saints, and to overcome them" (Revelation 13:7). Since John's Revelation reiterates Daniel's vision, and since both plainly describe the saints as targets of the Beast's fury, there is no room for confusion. There is no removal before the persecution. The tribulation is the time of refining, not escape. It is the battlefield where faith is tested and proven.

This is the tribulation, the time of testing and endurance for God's people under satanic assault. But the wrath that we are not appointed to is something entirely different. It is not what the Church suffers; it is what the wicked receive as recompense for tribulating the saints. This wrath is unleashed when Christ returns in power and glory. As Paul declares:

"Then shall that Wicked be revealed, whom the Lord shall consume with the spirit of his mouth, and shall destroy with the brightness of his coming" (2 Thessalonians 2:8).

Tribulation is what the saints endure at the hands of Antichrist and his followers, though God will recompense tribulation on those who trouble the Church. Wrath is what Antichrist, and his followers receive at the hands of Christ.

Let's begin by tracing this term through the Book of Revelation to see how Scripture itself defines and places the wrath of God.

The Wrath of the Lamb: Every Use of Orgē Points to the Second Coming

Let's look at where this Greek word appears in key moments in the Book of Revelation, and in each case, it is tied to end-of-age judgment. Revelation 6:16–17 is the first mention:

"And said to the mountains and rocks, Fall on us, and hide us from the face of him that sitteth on the throne, and from the wrath [orgē] of the Lamb: For the great day of his wrath is come; and who shall be able to stand?"
(Revelation 6:16–17)

This passage does not describe the beginning of the tribulation, but its crescendo. It declares "the great day of his wrath," the Day of the Lord, when the sky is opened and heaven is revealed, and Christ in His glory is made manifest. This terrifying unveiling of the Lamb and the declaration that "the great day of his wrath is come" prompts the unrepentant to flee and hide. They do not tremble before vague divine displeasure or symbolic metaphors, but from the face of the Lamb Himself. And they are not hiding from a season of plagues spread out over years, but from one singular, overwhelming day—the day of His wrath. This is the Second Coming in view, not a preliminary phase or extended process.

It mirrors other Day of the Lord imagery throughout Scripture, such as Isaiah 2:19, which states, "And they shall go into the holes of the rocks, and into the caves of the earth, for fear of the LORD, and for the glory of his majesty, when he ariseth to shake terribly the earth." Similarly, Joel 2:11 declares, "For the day of the LORD is great and very terrible; and who can abide it?" These verses, like Revelation 6, portray the breaking in of divine glory upon a sinful world. It is not subtle. It is not spread over seven years. It is a sudden, cataclysmic unveiling that causes the wicked to beg for the mountains to cover them.

What follows in Revelation 7 is not a thematic detour, but a direct continuation of the sixth seal, a pattern consistent with the interpretive principle that chapter divisions are artificial and often interrupt the inspired continuity of the text. The question raised at the end of chapter 6, "Who shall be able to stand?" is immediately answered in chapter 7 by the sealing of the 144,000 and the vision of the great multitude. This is not a flashback, but a heavenly zoom-out that answers the question with two categories of people who will "stand" in the day of wrath: the sealed servants of God (Revelation 7:3–8), and the redeemed from every nation who have "come out of great tribulation" and now stand before the Lamb in victory (Revelation 7:9–17).

"After this I beheld, and, lo, a great multitude, which no man could number, of all nations, and kindreds, and people, and tongues, stood before the throne, and before the Lamb, clothed with white robes, and palms in their hands... These are they which came out of great tribulation, and have washed their robes, and made them white in the blood of the Lamb."
(Revelation 7:9, 14)

This scene is undeniably eschatological. The great multitude is seen in the presence of God, waving palm branches, a symbol of triumph, and clothed in white robes, signifying purity and resurrection. Their location— "before the throne"—is not symbolic of an intermediate state. It is the consummation of redemption. They are no longer on earth suffering tribulation at the hands of God's enemies. They have emerged from it victorious, and are now recipients of divine comfort after the orgē was poured out on their tormentors:

"They shall hunger no more, neither thirst any more; neither shall the sun light on them, nor any heat. For the Lamb which is in the

midst of the throne shall feed them, and shall lead them unto living fountains of waters: and God shall wipe away all tears from their eyes."
(Revelation 7:16–17)

This moment parallels Revelation 21:4, which clearly places these blessings after the return of Christ and the renewal of all things. The convergence of these images—the fear of the wicked at Christ's appearing in Revelation 6 and the vindication of the saints in Revelation 7—makes it unmistakably clear: the wrath of the Lamb, first introduced in chapter 6, finds its full context in the visible return of Jesus. Far from being separated by a seven-year gap, the wrath and the resurrection are inseparably linked. Judgment falls upon the wicked, while deliverance and glorification are granted to the faithful. This is the Day of the Lord.

The next key usage of orgē is found in Revelation 11:18, and once again, it is unmistakably placed at the climactic end of the age:

"And the nations were angry, and thy wrath [orgē] is come, and the time of the dead, that they should be judged, and that thou shouldest give reward unto thy servants the prophets, and to the saints, and them that fear thy name, small and great; and shouldest destroy them which destroy the earth."
(Revelation 11:18)

Here, we find the perfect convergence of final judgment, resurrection, reward, and wrath. The phrase "thy wrath is come" is paired with "the time of the dead, that they should be judged." This is not a random act of judgment disconnected from the resurrection. It is the precise moment when God rewards His servants and judges the rebellious. Once again, orgē is not describing a general atmosphere of hardship or divine disapproval but it is pinpointed at the moment of Christ's visible return, the vindication of His saints, and the destruction of His enemies. It is the thunderclap of divine justice, not a murmur of warning.

And if we are honest with the biblical text, this placement dismantles the fear-based structure that pretribs so often lean on. When every instance of orgē in Revelation is traced carefully, it becomes overwhelmingly clear that the wrath we are not appointed to is not the plagues of the tribulation, but the final act of divine retribution when Christ is revealed from heaven. It is the same day Paul described in 2 Thessalonians 1, when Christ comes "in flaming fire taking vengeance on them that know not God." There is no fear in this day for the saints. There is vindication. There is glory. There is comfort. The terror belongs only to the enemies of the cross.

Another appearance of orgē occurs in Revelation 14:10, within one of the most sobering warnings in Scripture. Here, the angel declares the fate of those who worship the Beast and receive his mark:

"The same shall drink of the wine of the wrath [orgē] of God, which is poured out without mixture into the cup of his indignation; and he shall be tormented with fire and brimstone in the presence of the holy angels, and in the presence of the Lamb."
(Revelation 14:10)

This is direct retributive justice. The imagery is severe, but so is the offense: worshiping the Beast in defiance of the living God. The orgē mentioned here is not diluted or deferred. It is "poured out without mixture," meaning full strength, undiluted justice. This cup is not sipped slowly over the course of seven years. It is dumped out with fury at the appointed hour of judgment. And it is not poured out during the tribulation to test the saints. It is the final consequence for those who aligned themselves with the Antichrist after defying every opportunity to repent. The wrath is punitive, not purifying.

Then in Revelation 14:19, orgē is again used in vivid harvest imagery:

"And the angel thrust in his sickle into the earth, and gathered the vine of the earth, and cast it into the great winepress of the wrath [orgē] of God."
(Revelation 14:19)

This is apocalyptic judgment language rooted in the prophetic tradition. The winepress motif echoes Isaiah 63:3, where the Lord declares, "I have trodden the winepress alone... their blood shall be sprinkled upon my garments." The winepress is the instrument of wrath. It is where grapes are crushed underfoot, and here, it is the wicked who are crushed beneath the fury of God's judgment. Notice again: this takes place after the angelic warnings, after the calls to repentance, after the Beast has risen. This is not an early or intermediate act of wrath. It is the harvest final, total, and executed by divine hand. The righteous are not trampled here. The righteous are gathered elsewhere. This is wrath upon the enemies of God.

Next, we encounter orgē in Revelation 16:19, a scene situated within the outpouring of the seventh bowl judgment. It reads:

"And the great city was divided into three parts, and the cities of the nations fell: and great Babylon came in remembrance before God, to give unto her the cup of the wine of the fierceness of his wrath [orgē]."
(Revelation 16:19)

This is the culmination of Babylon's rebellion. The harlot city, representing spiritual corruption and worldly power, is finally remembered by God—not in forgetfulness but in long-delayed vengeance. The "cup of the wine of the fierceness of his wrath" is the execution of divine justice. Babylon is not simply judged; she is destroyed. The timing, again, is unmistakable. This is the final stage of history before Christ's return in Revelation 19. It is not a wrath that hovers in the background of the tribulation. It is decisive, visible, and terminal.

And finally, we see orgē one last time in Revelation 19:15, in the climactic return of Jesus Christ:

"And out of his mouth goeth a sharp sword, that with it he should smite the nations: and he shall rule them with a rod of iron: and he treadeth the winepress of the fierceness and wrath [orgē] of Almighty God."
(Revelation 19:15)

This is the moment of vindication, vengeance, and visible glory. Christ Himself treads the winepress. He does not commission angels to do it. He does it personally. And He does it at His return. The same winepress we saw in chapter 14 is now pressed beneath the feet of the King of kings. This is the wrath that all previous uses of orgē have pointed toward. It is not passive. It is not abstract. It is the Messiah crushing the systems and armies of rebellion at the zenith of human history. The Beast is cast down. The false prophet is destroyed. The armies of the earth are slain. And the saints are vindicated before the watching heavens.

Let the reader understand: in every case where the word orgē appears in the Book of Revelation—chapter 6, chapter 11, chapter 14, chapter 16, and chapter 19—it refers without exception to the final wrath of God at the visible Second Coming of Jesus Christ. Not once is orgē used to describe the tribulation period as a whole. Not once is it applied to the early stages of judgment. Not once is it directed at the Church. It is always final. Always climactic. Always poured out upon the wicked.

This dismantles the fear-based narrative of pretrib teaching, which equates tribulation with wrath and uses it to threaten believers into clinging to a secret escape. The biblical text does not support that interpretation. Instead, it offers something far greater: the assurance that the Church will endure tribulation with faith, and will be rescued not from trouble, but from the final wrath that falls on the ungodly at Christ's return. This is the consistent witness of Revelation. And it is the true hope of the saints.

The Wrath of the Lamb: Distinguishing Thumós and Orgē

It is crucial to recognize the lexical distinction between the Greek words orgē (ὀργή) and thumós (θυμός), as both are often translated into English as "wrath," yet carry distinct connotations in the original Greek texts. These differences are not semantic trivia; they carry significant implications for understanding the timing and nature of divine judgment in the end times.

According to lexical studies, thumós denotes a passionate, momentary outburst of anger or indignation. It conveys the idea of God's immediate and intense response to wickedness or rebellion. In contrast, orgē refers to a more deliberate and settled anger, an enduring disposition of divine justice that accumulates over time and is executed in a single, climactic act.

Vine's Complete Expository Dictionary defines thumós as indicating rage or passionate anger, often vivid and explosive. Orgē, by contrast, is consistently understood as controlled and judicial—righteous wrath that builds and is ultimately expressed in deliberate judgment. The BDAG lexicon (Bauer-Danker-Arndt-Gingrich) echoes this contrast, defining thumós as a sudden, emotional reaction and orgē as a settled state of anger grounded in moral and judicial principles.

Biblically, this distinction is not merely theoretical. It plays out in vivid detail within the Book of Revelation. Thumós is especially associated with the escalating judgments poured out during the tribulation period, particularly in the trumpet and bowl judgments. These show the progressive outpouring of divine displeasure in response to increasing human rebellion. Revelation 15:1 and 15:7 both refer to the "seven plagues, which are the last, for in them is filled up the wrath [thumós] of God." This culminates in the command to release the final judgments:

"And I heard a great voice out of the temple saying to the seven angels, Go your ways, and pour out the vials of the wrath [θυμός, thumós] of God upon the earth."
(Revelation 16:1)

This passage demonstrates that thumós is tied to the bowls of wrath the sequential, temporal judgments poured out during the tribulation. These are fierce and terrifying, but they are not final. They are momentary and intensifying responses, not the ultimate verdict. They do not represent God's eternal decree of retribution. Rather, they are God's passionate protests against sin as the world races toward its conclusion.

In contrast, orgē refers to the climactic, final judgment that comes at the return of Christ. This is the wrath from which the Church is promised deliverance. It is not part of an ongoing tribulation period but is instead the culmination of divine justice, executed when Jesus is revealed in glory. As shown in the previous section, every instance of orgē in Revelation appears in direct connection with the Second Coming. The most vivid of these is Revelation 6:16–17:

"And said to the mountains and rocks, Fall on us, and hide us from the face of him that sitteth on the throne, and from the wrath [ὀργή] of the Lamb: For the great day of his wrath [ὀργή] is come; and who shall be able to stand?"
(Revelation 6:16–17)

Here, orgē does not describe an ongoing process. It announces a singular event the "great day" of His wrath. The heavens are opened, Christ is revealed, and the unrepentant cry out in terror. Not because of a plague, but because they now face the unveiled justice of the Lamb. This is not one bowl in a series. It is the final reckoning. The decisive judgment. The end of the age.

This distinction between thumós and orgē helps clarify what sensationalist theology has confused. The bowls of wrath, filled with thumós, belong to the tribulation sequence and build in intensity until Christ returns. But the orgē—the wrath that believers are not appointed to—is what happens when He returns, when judgment is no longer restrained and the enemies of God are consumed by His appearing.

In this light, the message of Revelation becomes not a tale of fear, but one of hope and precision. The Church may endure persecution, but it is not appointed to orgē, the final outpouring of wrath that falls upon the wicked when Christ comes in power and glory.

Understanding these lexical nuances reinforces the hope of the saints and dismantles the fear-driven teaching that blurs God's temporary judgments with His ultimate verdict. The wrath we are not appointed to is not a plague, not a trumpet, not even a bowl. It is the winepress of divine justice at the Second Coming. And that, Scripture assures us, is reserved for the enemies of the cross and not for the redeemed who overcome by the blood of the Lamb.

The Wrath of the Son in Psalm 2 and Revelation

It would be a mistake to think the vocabulary of wrath in Revelation is a sudden innovation. The language of divine indignation both settled and burning was already embedded in the Psalms long before John ever recorded his vision. One passage does stand-out with striking clarity: Psalm 2. Not only does this coronation psalm feature both orgē and thumós in the Greek Septuagint,[1] but it also identifies the Anointed One (Christos), the Son of God, as the very agent of that wrath. The themes of rebellion, enthronement, judgment, and mercy all converge in this brief but loaded chapter. When read in light of Revelation, Psalm 2 is not merely typology—it is a prophetic frame, foretelling the final outpouring of wrath at the return of the Christ. What follows is a closer look at this psalm and its decisive role in confirming that the orge of God is not a general force, but a personal, Messianic judgment delivered by the returning King.

Psalm 2 may be only twelve verses long, but it delivers a complete eschatological blueprint. This ancient coronation psalm does not simply anticipate a local king in Zion—it prophetically unveils the final return of the Lord's Anointed. The very same elements that appear in the book of Revelation—divine wrath (orge), royal judgment, global rebellion, and the identity of the Christ—are all here. Early Christians did not have to force typology into the Psalms. They recognized what the Spirit had written plainly. Psalm 2 is filled with terms and themes that reappear at the Second Coming, including explicit references to orge and Christos in the Greek Septuagint.

The rebellion begins with the nations raging against "the Lord and against His Anointed." The Greek word used here is Χριστός (Christos)— "His Christ." The psalm then pivots toward the response of heaven. God laughs, not because He is amused, but because their rebellion is futile. What follows is divine wrath. In verse 5, the Lord speaks to them "in His wrath," and in verse 12, the language intensifies with a dual warning: orgē and thumós—the same pairing found in Revelation's vision of final judgment.

"Lay hold of instruction, lest the Lord be wrathful, and ye perish from the righteous way, when His anger is suddenly kindled. Blessed are all they that trust in Him."[2]
(Psalm 2:12, LXX)

The phrase "lest the Lord be angry" uses the Greek ὀργισθῇ—a verbal form of ὀργή (orgē), meaning judicial wrath. It

---

[1] A Greek translation of the Old Testament often cited by the New Testament.
[2] Adapted from Brenton—emphasis mine.

signifies not mere irritation but the settled, righteous anger of a King rendering judgment. The second phrase, "His wrath is kindled," uses θυμός (thumós), a word that conveys burning indignation. These are not redundant terms. When orgē and thumós appear together, they describe a full outpouring: the verdict and the execution, the judicial decree and the flaming sword.

This precise pairing occurs three climactic times in Revelation, each tied to the Second Coming:

"The same shall drink of the wine of the wrath (thumós) of God, which is poured out without mixture into the cup of His indignation (orgē)..."
(Revelation 14:10)

"...to give unto her the cup of the wine of the fierceness (thumós) of His wrath (orgē)."
(Revelation 16:19)

"...He treadeth the winepress of the fierceness (thumós) and wrath (orgē) of Almighty God."
(Revelation 19:15)

All three refer not to preliminary warnings or partial judgments, but to the full expression of God's wrath at the visible return of Jesus Christ. Psalm 2 foretells this very event. The nations rage, the Son is installed on Zion's hill, and then the wrath of God is revealed from heaven. There is no gap between the exaltation of the Son and the execution of judgment. The orge of God is what happens when the Christ returns.

This is why the psalm ends with an urgent plea to the kings of the earth:

"Be wise now therefore, O ye kings: be instructed, ye judges of the earth.
Serve the Lord with fear, and rejoice with trembling.
Kiss the Son, lest he be angry, and ye perish from the way, when his wrath is kindled but a little.
Blessed are all they that put their trust in him."

(Psalm 2:10–12)

The phrase "Kiss the Son" is a powerful command of submission. It is not merely poetic affection. It is covenantal loyalty and surrender to the King. The warning that follows ties directly to orge: "lest he be angry." This shows that the Son—not just the Father—is the executor of divine wrath. This again matches Revelation, where it is Jesus, the Lamb, who pours out wrath and treads the winepress. The same "Christ" the world rejected is the One who returns in judgment. And He is also the refuge for all who submit to Him.

Psalm 2 therefore functions as a prophetic seed. It contains:
- The rebellion of the nations against the Lord and His Christ
- The declaration of the Son's divine identity
- The promise of inheritance over all nations
- The judicial wrath (orgē) and burning indignation (thumós) that accompany His return
- The call to repent, submit, and take refuge in the Son

What is planted in Psalm 2 blossoms fully in Revelation 19. The wrath of the Lamb is not a contradiction—it is the fulfillment of God's covenant promise to give all nations to His Son, and to destroy those who refuse to bow. But the mercy remains: "Blessed are all they that put their trust in Him."

The Wrath That Destroys Babylon

The fall of Babylon is one of the most vivid demonstrations of God's wrath and His final and unrelenting judgment. Revelation 16:19 places this moment at the climax of the seventh vial, when God's wrath reaches its full and irrevocable intensity. Babylon, the spiritual and economic stronghold of the Beast's empire, is not merely weakened; it is violently overthrown as part of the divine retribution poured out at Christ's return. This is not incremental chastisement. It is the irreversible collapse of a system that has defied God to the very end.

"And the great city was divided into three parts, and the cities of the nations fell: and great Babylon came in remembrance before God, to give unto her the cup of the wine of the fierceness of his wrath." (Revelation 16:19)

The phrase "the fierceness of his wrath" combines thumós (fierceness) and orgē, signaling the culmination of both God's burning indignation and His settled, judicial sentence. Babylon does not experience partial judgment or incremental discipline. She is made to drink the full concentration of God's anger and ire. This is not like the escalating judgments of the tribulation. This is orgē, the stored wrath of God, released in its undiluted final form. Just as Belshazzar was judged for drinking from the holy vessels in defiance of heaven, Babylon, having drunk from the cup of spiritual fornication, now receives the cup of divine fury. Her destruction is not a separate prelude to Christ's return. It is an integrated part of the wrath that is poured out at His appearing.

As we now broaden our field of view through the lens of Scripture, we see that thumós reaches its climax in the tribulation judgments, but it gives way to orgē—the wrath of the Lamb—which falls in full at the return of Jesus. This is the wrath Paul referenced in 1 Thessalonians 5:9. The bowls of wrath conclude, and the final stroke is delivered not in symbolism, but in the literal and visible return of Christ. Having clarified the difference between the passionate outbursts of thumós and the deliberate final judgment of orgē, we now turn to the details of how that final wrath falls upon Babylon in Revelation 18 and 19.

The fall of Babylon in Revelation 18 is not a separate, symbolic event, nor is it merely a prelude to the return of Jesus. It is an essential part of the final, climactic outpouring of God's orgē. The phrase "Babylon is fallen, is fallen" (Revelation 18:2) deliberately echoes the prophetic cry of Jeremiah 51:8, where ancient Babylon was judged and destroyed: "Babylon is suddenly fallen and destroyed: howl for her; take balm for her pain, if so be she may be healed." This is not poetic coincidence. It is a prophetic parallel that draws a straight line between the fall of ancient Babylon and the eschatological destruction of the final world system that exalts itself against the Most High.

This collapse is not a political or economic. It is divine justice in motion. In Revelation 16:19, Babylon is split by a great earthquake, and God gives her "the cup of the wine of the fierceness of his wrath." This directly alludes to the cup of wrath spoken of in Jeremiah 25:15–17, where God commands the nations to drink of His fury. Babylon, representing the spiritual, economic, and political center of rebellion, is forced to drink it down to the bitter dregs. This is not warning. This is final execution.

But the wrath does not stop with the city. It culminates in the destruction of its king and false prophet. In Revelation 19, Jesus returns from heaven as King of kings and Lord of lords, riding a white horse, eyes as a flame of fire, and many crowns upon His head. His return is not symbolic or secret. It is an open conquest of righteousness and fury.

"And I saw the beast, and the kings of the earth, and their armies, gathered together to make war against him that sat on the horse, and against his army. And the beast was taken, and with him the false prophet... These both were cast alive into a lake of fire burning with brimstone."
(Revelation 19:19–20)

This is the moment of divine vengeance. The Antichrist and the False Prophet are not simply removed from power. They are the first to suffer the final judgment of eternal damnation. They are cast alive into the lake of fire, bypassing even the Great White Throne judgment. Those who worshiped the Beast, took his mark, bowed to his image, and pledged allegiance to his system are not far behind.

Revelation 14:10 declares that they "shall drink of the wine of the wrath [orgē] of God, which is poured out without mixture into the cup of his indignation," and that they "shall be tormented with fire and brimstone... and the smoke of their torment ascendeth up for ever and ever." Without mixture is a terrifying expression. In the ancient world, wine was normally diluted with water to temper its potency. But Jesus, in His return, pours out the undiluted wrath of Almighty God upon the Beast and all who follow him. This is not for correction. This is for condemnation. They did not obey the gospel. They persecuted His people. They defiled the earth and blasphemed His name. Now they drink the pure cup of divine judgment.

This is the fulfillment of wrath in its final and complete form of God's unrestrained, righteous judgment poured out at the Second Coming. It is not allegory. It is not speculative prophecy. It is the climactic, irreversible sentence upon the enemies of God. The Beast, the False Prophet, and all who follow them suffer the wrath of damnation.

But here is the great dividing line of hope. We who are in Christ Jesus are not appointed to this wrath. God will not spare any part of the Beast's empire: not the Beast, not the False Prophet, not their followers, and not the city that sat atop it all—Babylon.

The same event that brings ruin to Babylon brings rescue to the saints. While the wicked drink the cup of wrath, we rejoice in the cup of salvation. While the earth quakes under judgment, we stand firm in resurrection hope. The Church is not removed to escape hardship but is preserved through tribulation and vindicated when Christ appears.

The wrath that falls at the Second Coming is not distributed across seven years. It is not scattered over bowls and trumpets. It is final and concentrated. It is not aimed at the saints. It is poured out upon the Beast, his kingdom, and all who rebel against God. It is the fire of vengeance that comes when Christ is revealed from heaven to judge the world in righteousness.
As Paul declared with confidence:

"God hath not appointed us to wrath, but to obtain salvation by our Lord Jesus Christ."
(1 Thessalonians 5:9)

This is gospel hope. When Jesus comes again, we will not suffer the wrath of damnation. We will see the triumph of our King. This is the wrath we are not appointed to—the wrath that destroys Babylon, condemns the Beast, and brings the age of rebellion to an end.

The Wrath of God = The Second Coming of Christ

All of this leads to one inescapable conclusion: the wrath that believers are not appointed to is not the general tribulation, nor the escalating judgments that unfold during it though we are protected from those, as we will see later in this book. It is the final wrath, the orgē of God, unleashed in full force at the return of Christ.

This aligns with Romans 2:5–6, where orgē is described as something stored up for the day of wrath. It aligns with the testimony of Revelation. It aligns with the justice and precision of God. The saints may face persecution and trial, but they will never suffer the vengeance of divine wrath. That vengeance is not chaotic or misdirected. It falls with purpose upon the unrepentant, the Beast, the False Prophet, and the final world system of apostasy.

To claim that the Church must be removed before tribulation to escape wrath is to misidentify what wrath is, when it comes, and whom it targets. The wrath we are not appointed to is the wrath that ends the age and inaugurates the kingdom of Christ. That wrath is not now but it is coming soon.

Rebuttal & Answer: "The Church Isn't Mentioned After Revelation 3"

A well-worn argument among dispensationalists is the claim that the Church must be absent from the tribulation because the word church isn't used after Revelation 3. At first glance, this may sound persuasive to the uninitiated, but upon closer inspection, the entire argument collapses under the weight of its own logic.

Let's start with the basics. The claim is technically false. Revelation 22:16 explicitly uses the word churches when Jesus says, "I Jesus have sent mine angel to testify unto you these things in the churches." So, the word itself isn't absent from the book after the third chapter. It appears in both the opening and the closing of the Revelation. But let us assume, for the sake of argument, that we grant their premise. Even if the word church were absent after Revelation 3, is that really a valid proof of absence?

If we are going to argue from silence, then we must be consistent. The term Jew also doesn't appear after Revelation 3. Are we to believe, by that same logic, that the Jewish people have also vanished from the end-time scenario? Dispensationalists would never accept such a conclusion, nor should they. Their eschatology requires the presence of Jews at the center of prophetic fulfillment. Yet they make no mention of this silence when arguing for the Church's supposed disappearance. The moment consistency is applied; their argument unravels. Selective silence is not exegesis. It's reaching.

Exposing a Double Standard

At this point, their fallback response is predictable: "The 144,000 sealed from the twelve tribes of Israel—that's the Jews!" And just like that, they've proven our point. They are willing to identify the Jewish people without requiring the word Jew to appear. They accept that a group can be called something else and still be the same group. But if they can make that allowance for Israel, then they must allow it for the Church as well. The saints in Revelation—those who resist the Beast, suffer persecution, keep the commandments of God, and are ultimately resurrected and rewarded are not a different class of believers. They are the Church by another name.

This creates a theological dilemma. If they insist the Church is gone because the word is not used, then they must also concede that the Jews are gone too. That would require dismantling the very framework dispensationalism depends on. But if they argue that the Jews are still present, just under a different designation, then they are forced by their own logic to admit the Church is also still present referred to not as church, but as saints, elect, or servants of God. They cannot have it both ways.

The Church and The Saints, One and The Same

To make matters worse, many Bible translations of Revelation 22:21 refer to the recipients of the book as saints. Why? Because ancient manuscripts like Codex Sinaiticus use the word saints[3]in that verse to describe the audience of the message. In other words, the Church is addressed as saints at the conclusion of the Revelation. The attempt to draw a hard line between church and saints is a modern invention. The text itself does not draw that line— dispensationalism does.

---

[4] Greek Interlinear (Codex Sinaiticus):
Ἡ (The) χάρις (grace) τοῦ (of the) Κυρίου (Lord) Ἰησοῦ (Jesus) Χριστοῦ (Christ) μετὰ (with) πάντων (all) τῶν (the) ἁγίων (saints). Ἀμήν (Amen).

Let us also remember how the word church (Greek: ekklēsia) is used throughout the New Testament. It simply means assembly. It appears in three primary ways: as a local congregation (such as the church of Ephesus), as a collective reference to multiple assemblies in different locations, and as the singular, universal body of Christ. But here's the irony: even before Revelation 3, the phrase the Church as a reference to the universal body does not appear. Every use of the word is local or regional. Not once in chapters 1 to 3 does John refer to the universal Church as a singular entity. So, when pretribulationists insist the Church disappears after Revelation 3, they are asking us to believe that something not mentioned explicitly before chapter 3 has somehow gone missing afterward. Their argument presumes what the text never affirms. It is built on presupposition, not inspiration.

Patterns of Denial

And then the trained response from the pretribulationist's position always arrives on cue: "It's not the same." The saints in Revelation? Not the same as the Church. The last trumpet in Revelation? Not the same as the last trumpet in 1 Corinthians 15. The elect gathered after the tribulation in Matthew 24? Not the same as the Church. This is not biblical exegesis. It is theological gymnastics. It is a reflex, not a reason. When every inconvenient passage is waved away with "not the same," the interpreter is no longer following Scripture. He is forcing it to follow him.

What we see is a pattern, an interpretive strategy driven not by careful study, but by predetermined conclusions. It reveals the underlying engine of dispensational theology: doctrinal fear, double standards, and a relentless attempt to avoid what the text plainly says. When you have been indoctrinated to live in fear of the plagues that God will use to avenge us, and you have built your hope on escaping the tribulation He has called the Church to endure, then you will cling to silence as if it were a verse and use absence as if it were evidence. But absence is not evidence. It is desperation.

Ultimately, the absence of the word church after Revelation 3 proves nothing—except the frailty of a theological system that must rely on gaps and word games to avoid contradiction. The saints of Revelation are the Church. The elect gathered at Christ's return are the Church. The ones who overcome the Beast by the blood of the Lamb are the Church. Call them saints, servants, witnesses, or overcomers—it makes no difference. They are the body of Christ. They are the Bride. They are present when Jesus returns in glory. And they are not the ones who vanished, they are the ones who overcame.

The testimony of Scripture is clear. The wrath believers are not appointed to is not the tribulation, nor the judgments unfolding within it. It is the orgē of God—His final, unrestrained fury—poured out at the visible return of Jesus Christ. To confuse tribulation with wrath is to blur God's justice, misread His promises, and rob the Church of its prophetic endurance. The saints are not raptured to escape trouble; they are preserved through it and vindicated in the fire of Christ's coming.

Next Revelation:
The Resurrection Happens at the End

If wrath falls at the return of Christ, then the resurrection must occur at the same time not seven years before. In Chapter 4, we will dismantle the myth of a pretribulation resurrection by following Jesus' own words, Paul's inspired teaching, and John's apocalyptic vision. There is no secret rapture. There is no multi-staged first resurrection. The dead in Christ rise at the last day and the trumpet that sounds is the final one.

Chapter 4:
The Resurrection Happens at the End

The biblical testimony is unequivocal: the resurrection happens at the end. It does not occur secretly at the beginning of a fabricated pretribulational rapture scenario, but openly and visibly at the end of this present age, coinciding with Christ's glorious return. The concept of a secret resurrection or rapture occurring seven years before Christ's visible coming is not found anywhere in Scripture. Instead, Jesus Himself repeatedly emphasized that He would raise His people "at the last day" (John 6:39–40, 44, 54), explicitly placing the resurrection at the final moment of history not in stages, not secretly, and certainly not before a supposed seven-year period of tribulation.

The phrase "last day" used by Jesus is critically important. It is definitive and final, signifying the ultimate culmination of time when human history intersects with eternity. It is not indicative of a series of events spread across multiple stages or separated by years. If there were multiple days or events leading to the resurrection, Jesus would have said so plainly. But He did not. Instead, He unequivocally spoke of a singular, decisive event occurring precisely "at the last day."

"And this is the Father's will which hath sent me, that of all which he hath given me I should lose nothing, but should raise it up again at the last day."
(John 6:39)

"And this is the will of him that sent me, that every one which seeth the Son, and believeth on him, may have everlasting life: and I will raise him up at the last day."
(John 6:40)

By repeating this phrase, Jesus leaves no ambiguity about the timing. He firmly anchors the resurrection to the conclusion of this age, making it impossible to insert an earlier, secret resurrection event without contradicting His explicit words. This is critical because pretribulationism requires believers to accept an event that

Jesus Himself never mentions a separate, invisible coming prior to the visible return at the end.

The doctrine of a pretribulational rapture, though popularized in modern evangelical circles, finds no basis in Christ's teachings. Jesus consistently teaches one resurrection at one clearly defined time: at the end of the age. To claim otherwise is to construct a doctrine unsupported by the biblical text, forcing Scripture to bend around a preconceived theological narrative.

In contrast, the scriptural record is consistent and clear. The resurrection occurs openly, universally visible, and unquestionably glorious, coinciding with Christ's return at the culmination of history. The "last day" is exactly what it implies: the ultimate and concluding day when Christ appears, time ceases, and eternity begins.

Revelation Confirms the Resurrection Happens After Tribulation

This is further confirmed in Revelation 20, where we read of the "first resurrection" coinciding with the Second Coming of Christ. This event is not pretribulational; it is unmistakably posttribulational. The text plainly states that those who participate in this resurrection are specifically those who "were beheaded for the witness of Jesus, and for the word of God," and who "had not worshipped the Beast, neither his image, neither had received his mark." These individuals clearly lived through the tribulation. They experienced firsthand the Beast's reign, endured intense persecution, and many sacrificed their lives due to their unwavering faithfulness to Christ. It is precisely these saints whom Revelation explicitly identifies as participating in the first resurrection.

Yet, pretribulation teachers, faced with this undeniable biblical contradiction to their doctrine, have conveniently invented an entirely fictitious class of believers. They propose a separate category of "tribulation saints." These invented saints are necessary only because their system demands someone to fulfill the role that clearly contradicts their timeline. They say necessity is the mother of invention, and indeed, pretribulation theology demonstrates that vividly. The doctrine creates imaginary saints to bridge gaps and reconcile inconsistencies rather than accepting the straightforward testimony of Scripture.

Nowhere in the New Testament do we find the Church being replaced or succeeded by another group of believers during the tribulation. The very idea undermines the unity of the body of Christ. Scripture says plainly, "There is one body, and one Spirit... one hope of your calling" (Ephesians 4:4). To create a new class of saints is to divide what God has made one.

If there were truly a resurrection of the Church prior to the tribulation, surely the Book of Revelation, which lays out the tribulation in detail, would mention it. But it does not. There is no scene where the Church is resurrected or raptured before the seals are opened or the judgments begin. Instead, we are introduced to saints on the earth, persecuted, praying, and waiting for vindication. Revelation's silence on a pretrib resurrection is not accidental. It is theological testimony.

By inventing a fictitious class of tribulation saints, pretribulationism not only violates the integrity of Scripture but leaves the true Church unprepared for the trials to come. Rather than equipping the saints to endure, it teaches them to expect escape. But Jesus said, "In the world ye shall have tribulation" (John 16:33). He did not promise deliverance from it, but victory through it. Neglecting the spiritual welfare of the Church by failing to equip believers to endure tribulation is dangerously irresponsible. Moreover, teaching believers to fill in the gaps left by Scripture with imagination instead of accepting its plain testimony can have devastating effects. Such an approach, once subconsciously inherited from the pulpit, opens the door for a variety of heresies. When believers are conditioned to reconcile doctrinal presuppositions through imagination rather than through careful exegesis of clear biblical statements, the Church's doctrinal purity and spiritual resilience suffer greatly.

"Blessed and holy is he that hath part in the first resurrection: on such the second death hath no power, but they shall be priests of God and of Christ, and shall reign with him a thousand years."
(Revelation 20:6)

This verse is unambiguous. It leaves no room for a separate earlier resurrection of a distinct class of believers. Revelation clearly portrays a singular resurrection event involving believers who directly confront and overcome the tribulation, further confirming that the pretribulational narrative is a constructed system lacking scriptural foundation.

Pretribulationists often stumble here and default to a worn-out default claim: "That's not the same resurrection." But Scripture does not make such a distinction. This is the first resurrection. If there were another resurrection before this, it would not be the first. To call a resurrection prior to this one "first" would require the apostle John to be wrong in his numbering. That is not a minor oversight. It is a direct contradiction. But John, writing under the inspiration of the Holy Ghost, makes no mistake.

We really do not need to expand much further here; the absurdity of the claim speaks for itself. But even so, we will revisit this evasive tactic in greater detail in the rebuttal and answer section later in this chapter. There, we will expose the full extent of the multistage resurrection theory, dissect its theological inconsistencies, and demonstrate how it stands in open defiance of the biblical narrative.

For now, it is enough to say: Scripture says what it means, and it means what it says. This is the first resurrection. There is no prequel. There is no fragmented rollout. Just the plain and powerful truth of God's word.

This harmonizes perfectly with what both Daniel and Revelation affirm: the Beast makes war with the saints and prevails for a time (Daniel 7:21; Revelation 13:7). These saints are not a separate class or a new group they are the Church, God's people, faithful to the end. And when Christ returns, it is these very overcomers who are part of the first resurrection and reign with Him for a thousand years.

The Harmony of the Gospels and Epistles

Yet dispensational teachers insist on removing Matthew 24 from the discussion, claiming it only applies to Israel, not the Church. This insistence arises from a misunderstanding of the biblical command to "rightly divide the word of truth" (2 Timothy

2:15). Rather than interpreting "rightly dividing" as maintaining the coherence and unity of the biblical narrative, they mistakenly view it as an instruction to isolate certain passages or events, particularly when those passages disrupt their preferred eschatological framework.

Three passages: Matthew 24, 1 Thessalonians 4, and 1 Corinthians 15 describe the same unmistakable event: the resurrection of the dead, the transformation of the living, and the gathering of the elect at the visible return of Christ. The clouds, the trumpet, and the appearing of the Son of Man are not scattered fragments. They are harmonized expressions of one glorious event, spoken from three inspired angles. Yet pretribulationists insist on severing Matthew 24 from this harmony to preserve a theological system that cannot withstand the unified testimony of Scripture. This is not rightly dividing the word of truth. It is dividing what God has joined together.

Furthermore, the final trumpet mentioned by Paul is exactly what he calls it the last trumpet. It is not part of a fragmented sequence or a coded signal in a secret heavenly event. It is the decisive and earth-shaking blast of the trumpet of God, marking the culmination of His redemptive plan. Paul declares plainly:

"At the last trump... the dead shall be raised."
(1 Corinthians 15:52)

This final trumpet signals nothing less than the visible return of Jesus Christ, the resurrection of the righteous dead, the transformation of living believers, and the inauguration of the Kingdom of God. Revelation 10:7 confirms this truth explicitly:

"But in the days of the voice of the seventh angel, when he shall begin to sound, the mystery of God should be finished, as he hath declared to his servants the prophets."
(Revelation 10:7)

We also see this trumpet theme tied inseparably to the Greek word parousia,[4] the visible return of Christ in several other key passages:

"For this we say unto you by the word of the Lord, that we which are alive and remain unto the coming (parousia) of the Lord shall not prevent them which are asleep."
(1 Thessalonians 4:15)

"For the Lord himself shall descend from heaven with a shout, with the voice of the archangel, and with the trump of God: and the dead in Christ shall rise first. Then we which are alive and remain shall be caught up together with them in the clouds, to meet the Lord in the air: and so shall we ever be with the Lord."
(1 Thessalonians 4:16–17)

"For as the lightning cometh out of the east, and shineth even unto the west; so shall also the coming (parousia) of the Son of man be."
(Matthew 24:27)

"They shall see the Son of man coming in the clouds of heaven with power and great glory. And he shall send his angels with a great sound of a trumpet, and they shall gather together his elect from the four winds."
(Matthew 24:30–31)

"Now we beseech you, brethren, by the coming (parousia) of our Lord Jesus Christ, and by our gathering together unto him."
(2 Thessalonians 2:1)

---

[4] The Greek word παρουσία (parousia) is commonly translated as "coming" or "presence." In the New Testament, it refers specifically to the visible return of Christ in glory (e.g., Matthew 24:27; 1 Thessalonians 4:15; 2 Thessalonians 2:1, 8). The term was also used in secular Greek to describe the arrival or official visit of a king or dignitary, reinforcing the royal and public nature of Christ's return—not a secret event.
See: BDAG, παρουσία, 1; Thayer's Greek Lexicon, παρουσία, "the advent, i.e. the future visible return from heaven of Jesus"; Louw & Nida, Semantic Domain 13.69, "the arrival of a person to be present."

These verses tie together the themes of trumpet, clouds, resurrection, and gathering with the visible return of Christ. They do not point in different directions. They do not divide into phases. They declare one singular return.

Nevertheless, pretribulationist teachers argue that the "last trumpet" is not truly last, and that the "first resurrection" is not genuinely first. This is more than simply incorrect theology. It unintentionally pushes them into intellectual dishonesty by forcing them to redefine clear biblical terms in ways that Scripture itself does not support. If the "first resurrection" is not truly the first, and if the "last trumpet" is not truly last, biblical prophecy devolves into semantic gymnastics rather than clear divine revelation.

This pattern of shifting meanings to preserve an eschatological system creates unnecessary confusion within the Church. But God is not the author of confusion. He has spoken clearly, plainly, and consistently. He meant exactly what He said, and He said exactly what He meant. Rightly dividing the word of truth means cutting a straight, consistent line through Scripture, preserving the unity and coherence of its message—not isolating verses or chapters to protect doctrines that Scripture itself plainly contradicts.

In the rebuttal and answer section of this chapter, we will examine this multistage resurrection theory further. We will demonstrate how Scripture decisively refutes the claim that the resurrection of believers occurs in multiple, disconnected stages. The truth will be evident: God's Word presents one unified, glorious event, the visible and triumphant return of our Lord Jesus Christ.

There is no secret resurrection. There is no invisible coming. The parousia, the Greek word used in 1 Thessalonians 4:15, Matthew 24:27, and 2 Thessalonians 2:1 refers to a visible presence, not a hidden removal. It means a public arrival, a royal unveiling, a glorious appearance witnessed by all. According to Thayer's Greek-English Lexicon, parousia (Strong's G3952) is defined as, "The future visible return from heaven of Jesus, to raise the dead, hold the last judgment, and set up gloriously the kingdom of God." This definition is not obscure or disputed. It is plain, authoritative, and devastating to the claims of a secret rapture. Every time parousia is used in the context of Christ's return, it refers to this visible, cosmic event—the singular and climactic moment when the King of Glory appears and all the world beholds Him. There is no secret version, no two-stage rollout. There is only one return.

This truth dismantles the myth of a hidden rapture occurring before the tribulation. When the parousia happens, the dead in Christ rise, the living are caught up, the trumpet of God shakes creation, and Jesus appears in radiant glory.

"Behold, he cometh with clouds; and every eye shall see him, and they also which pierced him: and all kindreds of the earth shall wail because of him."
(Revelation 1:7)

This is the visible, undeniable, world-shaking return of Jesus Christ. It is the climactic moment of redemptive history. The trumpet, the clouds, and the resurrection are not markers of different prophetic programs. They are the unified elements of one glorious event: the parousia of our Lord, the visible return of the King, and the blessed hope of His Church at the end of the age.

Rebuttal & Answer: "The First Resurrection Happens in Stages. It's Not Just One Event"

One of the more desperate evasions in pretribulational theology is the claim that the first resurrection described in Revelation 20 is not truly "first" in any chronological sense. Instead, they argue that it is merely the final stage of a multi-part resurrection process. Depending on the teacher, you may encounter either a two-part or a three-part first resurrection theory. This rebuttal focuses primarily on the three-part version, since that model has gained significant traction in many dispensational circles. That said, the arguments presented here also dismantle the two-part model, particularly by demonstrating that the return of Christ, the resurrection of the dead, and the rapture of the living are not separated across time. They occur together in a singular, climactic event.

Part of the multi-stage resurrection argument has already been dismantled earlier in this chapter, where we showed that the resurrection in Revelation 20 explicitly includes those who endured the tribulation and were killed by the Beast. Scripture calls that moment the first resurrection plainly, publicly, and without ambiguity. But since that inconvenient truth does not fit the pretribulationist narrative, some resort to redefining "first" to mean "final installment in a series." That is not biblical exegesis. It is narrative control. What they are doing is not interpretation. It is theological redirection designed to protect a fragile system from collapsing under the weight of Revelation 20.

Breaking Down the Three-Part Model

Let us summarize what the three-part first resurrection theory claims:

1. Phase One: Old Testament saints were allegedly resurrected and ascended with Christ at His resurrection (citing Matthew 27:52–53).
2. Phase Two: At the so-called secret rapture, Christ will invisibly return to resurrect and rapture the New Testament Church before the tribulation.
3. Phase Three: After the tribulation, Christ will come again to resurrect the "tribulation saints" who were left behind.

The purpose of this model is transparent. It is an attempt to neutralize Revelation 20:4–6, which plainly places the first resurrection after the tribulation. By labeling it "phase three," they hope to strip it of its force and context pretending it does not contradict their timeline. But that tactic does not succeed.

Scripture nowhere describes a multi-phase resurrection. The idea that the first resurrection can be subdivided into installments the Old Testament saints in one wave, Church saints in another, tribulation saints in a third is never taught in the Bible. It is not a product of exegesis. It is a clever narrative maneuver, crafted to preserve a doctrinal structure that collapses under honest examination.

This maneuver is theological sleight of hand. And much like a rigged card game, the rules are being rewritten on the fly to guarantee the right outcome for the one holding the theological deck. If you try to quote Revelation 20 and point out that the first resurrection includes saints who were killed during the tribulation, dispensational teachers will respond, "You can't play that verse because it doesn't count. That's not really the first resurrection." If you point out that the saints mentioned there are clearly part of the Church, they reply, "You can't say that because they're a different group called tribulation saints."

It is like playing a game with someone who constantly changes the rules to protect their position. "You can't move there," they say. "You can't play that hand." Ask them to prove it in the rule book—the Bible—and you will find that they appeal to speculation. The entire scheme is a construct of theological imagination. Conjecture passed off as biblical doctrine.

But the Bible speaks plainly. The resurrection of the righteous is not divided across dispensational categories. It is not broken into parts. It is consistently presented as a single event that takes place at the visible return of Jesus Christ. The trumpet sounds. The dead are raised. The living are transformed. The Lord appears in glory. That is the first resurrection and there is no other.

Addressing Their Favorite Proof Text: 1 Corinthians 15:20–23

Some of the most popular pretribulationist teachers who promote the three-part resurrection theory frequently appeal to 1 Corinthians 15:20–23, where Paul refers to Christ as the "firstfruits of them that slept." Because the term firstfruits appears in plural form in English, they argue that Christ was not alone in this category. They claim it must also include those saints who rose from the dead in Matthew 27. But this is a distortion of both the language and the logic of Paul's argument.

The Greek word used here is ἀπαρχὴ (aparchē), which is singular and collective in meaning. It refers to the first portion of a greater harvest, much like a sheaf offered to God that represents the full crop to follow. It is a singular offering that signifies more to come. Thayer's Greek-English Lexicon defines aparchē as "the beginning of a sacrifice," or "the first portion, as the pledge and guarantee of the rest." It does not imply that others participated with Christ in a glorified resurrection or ascension. Rather, it affirms that Christ alone was the first to rise in immortality, first in both chronology and preeminence.

This is exactly Paul's point. Christ is not merely the first among others who rose with Him. He is the firstfruits. He is the prototype. He is the firstborn from the dead (Colossians 1:18), and as Romans 8:29 affirms, He is the firstborn among many brethren. He rose first to secure the harvest, and the rest of His brethren will follow—not sporadically, not in disconnected waves, but together at the appointed time.

His resurrection guarantees the harvest to come, which will not be reaped until His return. If other saints had ascended into heaven in glorified bodies with Him, Paul would surely have mentioned them in a passage where he is explicitly discussing the order and timing of resurrection. But he does not. The burden of proof lies on those who insist that others share Christ's identity as firstfruits. Scripture gives them no such support.

Paul's message is simple and clear. Christ is the singular firstfruits of those who have died. Then, and only then, those who belong to Him will be raised at His coming:

"But every man in his own order: Christ the firstfruits; afterward they that are Christ's at His coming."
(1 Corinthians 15:23)

This verse is devastating to both the two-part and three-part resurrection theories. It presents a divinely ordered sequence. First, Christ rose. Then afterward and not in between, not across phases but afterward, those who belong to Him rise at His coming. The Greek word for "coming" in this verse is parousia, the same term used earlier in this chapter and throughout the New Testament to describe the visible, bodily return of Christ from heaven.

As we saw earlier, parousia does not refer to a secret or partial event. According to Thayer's Lexicon, it means "the future visible return from heaven of Jesus, to raise the dead, hold the last judgment, and set up gloriously the kingdom of God." This is exactly what Paul is describing. Not multiple returns. Not fragmented phases. One return. One harvest. One parousia, the singular moment when the dead in Christ will rise and the Kingdom of God will be revealed in glory.

So let the record stand. Christ alone is the firstfruits. The rest of the harvest is gathered at His coming. There is no resurrection of saints occurring quietly behind the scenes. There is no earlier wave to anticipate before the Lord appears in power and great glory. The firstfruits has already risen, and the field will not be harvested until the King returns.

What About the Saints in Matthew 27?

Some may object and say, "What about the saints who rose from the dead in Matthew 27:52–53?" The answer is simple. That text says nothing about glorified bodies, nothing about ascension, and nothing about them entering heaven permanently. Their resurrection was a local sign to the people of Jerusalem and an affirmation of Christ's authority over death. These saints were a testimony, not a firstfruits harvest.

It is telling that pretribulationist teachers dwell on passages like this, not because they are clear, but precisely because they are vague enough for conjecture to sneak in. Where the Bible is specific, they remain evasive. Where the Bible leaves room for speculation, they construct elaborate systems. But theology cannot be built on silence and speculation. The simple facts are these: Matthew says the saints appeared in the city after Christ's resurrection. He does not say they ascended. He does not say they were glorified. And he certainly does not say they entered heaven with the risen Lord.

More importantly, Scripture consistently reserves all firstborn and firstfruits titles of the resurrection for Jesus Christ alone. He is "the firstborn from the dead" (Colossians 1:18). He is "the first begotten of the dead" (Revelation 1:5). And He is "the firstfruits" (1 Corinthians 15:23). These are not poetic generalities. They are theological declarations. If others had been raised in glorified form and entered heaven alongside Him, then these titles would not apply exclusively to Christ. But they do. Because they are accurate. Jesus alone has risen in glory. The others still await that day.

They'll say, "But these people were resurrected." My response is simple: so was Lazarus. But neither he nor they ascended with Jesus because Scripture is clear. Christ ascended alone.

Peter's Pentecost Sermon Refutes Phase One

Now at this point, a pretribulationist might object, "Just because Scripture doesn't say they ascended doesn't mean they didn't." They might accuse this argument of being an argument from silence. But that claim falls flat, because this is not an argument from silence—it is an argument from what the Bible explicitly states. Scripture clearly affirms that David, one of the central Old Testament saints, was still dead and had not ascended into heaven at the time Peter preached on the Day of Pentecost. It is not silence we are appealing to. It is the direct, Spirit-filled testimony of Scripture. What is speculative is building an entire resurrection phase on a passage that says nothing of glorification or ascension.

Perhaps the most devastating refutation of phase one in the multi-stage theory comes from Peter himself, preaching on the Day of Pentecost. Under the unction of the Holy Ghost, Peter declares that David is both dead and buried, and did not ascend into the heavens:

"Men and brethren, let me freely speak unto you of the patriarch David, that he is both dead and buried, and his sepulchre is with us unto this day."
(Acts 2:29)

"For David is not ascended into the heavens..."
(Acts 2:34)

This demolishes the idea that Old Testament saints, including David, rose and ascended with Christ. If they had, Peter would not be standing in Jerusalem, pointing to David's tomb. The psalm he quotes— "Thou wilt not leave my soul in hell"—applies to Christ alone. The resurrection and ascension were His and His alone.

Peter is not vague. He says plainly and publicly, while filled with the Holy Ghost, that David did not ascend into heaven. And if David didn't, neither did the rest. If Peter, standing post-resurrection and post-ascension, filled with the Spirit, declares David's tomb to be sealed and his body still with us, then no honest reader can claim otherwise. The burden is not on us to prove that they did not ascend. The burden is on pretribulationists to show that they did—and Scripture gives them no such evidence.

To further bury the multi-stage idea, consider the Ascension itself. In Acts 1, Jesus ascends bodily into heaven while the apostles watch. The text makes no mention of any group of saints following Him. No glorified procession. No cloud of ancient patriarchs trailing behind Him. Just one man rising:

"While they beheld, he was taken up; and a cloud received him out of their sight."
(Acts 1:9)

And the angel says:

"This same Jesus, which is taken up from you into heaven, shall so come in like manner."
(Acts 1:11)

It is one Christ. One ascent. One return. No fragmented process. No hidden phases.

One Lord. One Resurrection. One People.

So let us put the pieces together. Christ rose first. Christ ascended alone. David did not rise. The tomb is sealed. The bones remain. The psalm pointed to Jesus, and Jesus alone is the firstfruits. Any doctrine that attempts to insert others into that category is crushed under the testimony of Peter and the explicit witness of Scripture. It is not silence that defeats the three-part resurrection theory, but it is the loud, Spirit-filled declaration of the apostles themselves.

Let the pretrib teacher wrestle with this. Peter says David is dead. The tomb is closed. The bones are still with us. There is no glorified procession. There is no secret ascension of Old Testament saints. The resurrection is not split across dispensational charts or imagined theological phases. It is a unified, glorious moment at the end of the age. And it will include all who belong to Christ whether they lived before the cross, after Pentecost, or through the tribulation.

No amount of theological acrobatics, driven by fear of suffering or discomfort, will change what Scripture declares. The resurrection happens at the end. Not before the tribulation. Not in phases. Not in shadows. At the end.

Faith must triumph over fear. God has not abandoned His people to wrath. He will avenge His saints. He will exonerate His Church. And He will raise us in glory together at the return of our King.

Next Revelation:
The Saints in Tribulation: God's Justice, Not His Wrath

So do not fear the tribulation, my friend. When we rightly divide the word of truth, we see it for what it truly is—not God's wrath against His people but His justice for them. The saints are not abandoned in the fire; they are vindicated through it. God's vengeance is not aimed at the Church but at her enemies. In Chapter 5, we will see the tribulation through the lens of Revelation and discover that it is not a curse to escape, but a stage for His glory.

Chapter 5:
The Saints in Tribulation: God's Justice, Not His Wrath

Throughout Scripture, God draws a sharp line between the righteous and the wicked. He does not pour out His wrath indiscriminately, nor does He punish the just alongside the unjust. Divine judgment is never arbitrary. It is always righteous, always targeted, and always in harmony with His covenant justice. As Paul wrote to the persecuted believers in Thessalonica, "It is a righteous thing with God to recompense tribulation to them that trouble you" (2 Thessalonians 1:6).

This principle of God avenging His people by turning the tables on their oppressors is not just a theological concept. It is a recurring pattern in redemptive history. We see it in the deliverance from Egypt, where God afflicted Pharaoh and his nation with plagues tailored to their defiance and cruelty. And we see it again in the final judgments of Revelation, where Babylon the great city that rides the beast is repaid for her crimes against God's people.

Revelation 18 paints a vivid picture of Babylon's judgment. This city, the capital of the beast's kingdom, is not just a symbol of immorality and idolatry. It is the hub of persecution, commerce, sorcery, and slavery. Revelation 17:6 describes her as "drunken with the blood of the saints, and with the blood of the martyrs of Jesus." This imagery is sobering. Babylon is not just indifferent to the suffering of God's people; she is intoxicated by it. She revels in the shedding of innocent blood. She rides the beast, but she is not merely a passive passenger. She is his consort in evil, profiting from his power while compounding his crimes.

The Beast is given authority to make war with the saints and to overcome them (Revelation 13:7), but Babylon drinks in the results. She is the face of the system that traffics not only in merchandise but in lives. Revelation 18:13 explicitly lists "slaves and souls of men" among her merchandise. This means she deals in human lives, reducing people to property including the saints. This is not metaphorical. It is economic, political, and spiritual enslavement.

The saints are not only martyred by the Beast. Many are taken as captives, enslaved, imprisoned, and abused by Babylon's empire of commerce and corruption. Revelation 13:10 confirms this captivity:

"He that leadeth into captivity shall go into captivity: he that killeth with the sword must be killed with the sword. Here is the patience and the faith of the saints."

This passage signals that unjust imprisonment is not only expected, but divinely foreseen. The faithful will endure captivity and death, and their endurance is a testimony that will be vindicated by God's retribution.

This is the context for the judgment that falls upon her. God is not acting capriciously. He is responding to rebellion, persecution, and cruelty. Revelation 18:6 declares:

"Reward her even as she rewarded you, and double unto her double according to her works: in the cup which she hath filled fill to her double."

This is targeted justice. This is the reversal of fortunes. Babylon falls because she made the saints fall. She is tormented because she delighted in their torment. The merchants who grew rich by her corruption weep, not for her crimes, but for their loss. But heaven rejoices, for the Lord has judged her with equity.

What we are seeing here is the consistency of God's justice. Just as He judged Egypt for enslaving Israel, He will judge Babylon for trafficking in the lives and blood of His saints. Many of the plagues are surgical in nature and aimed at the Beast, the false prophet, and the systems under their control. All of the plagues target the ungodly, but never the repentant. The wrath of God is not scattershot. It is exacting. Babylon falls because she filled her cup with the blood of the saints, and God fills it back with His fury.

Paul's Tribulation Paradigm

Paul lays the foundation for this principle in his second letter to the Thessalonians, a letter written to a church enduring tribulation at the hands of its persecutors. In chapter 1, Paul outlines what I call his tribulation paradigm: the righteous endure suffering now with patience and faith, but their persecutors will be recompensed with tribulation, and the saints will be vindicated at Christ's return. This is not mere theory. It is the divine pattern of redemptive justice. Those who afflict the Church will themselves be afflicted, and those who patiently endure will be granted rest. This reversal of fortunes is not postponed to some distant eternity; it begins with the visible return of Jesus Christ.

Paul's wording is deliberate. The Greek word he uses for the Church's affliction is thlipsis (θλῖψις), which means pressure, oppression, or tribulation. According to Thayer's Greek-English Lexicon, thlipsis refers to "a pressing, pressing together, pressure; metaphorically, oppression, affliction, tribulation, distress." It is used throughout the New Testament to describe both the general afflictions of the righteous and the specific period of end-time tribulation. Jesus Himself used this word in Matthew 24:21: "For then shall be great tribulation (thlipsis), such as was not since the beginning of the world..." The word defines the Church's present suffering, and it also defines the era to come.

This underscores the continuity between the Church's current afflictions and the great end-time tribulation. Both are described using the same Greek word. Jesus and Paul are not describing two separate peoples or prophetic programs, but one suffering, one body, and one glorious hope.

What makes Paul's declaration so profound is the parallel word he uses to describe what God will do to the persecutors. In 2 Thessalonians 1:6, he writes, "It is a righteous thing with God to recompense tribulation to them that trouble you." The word translated "trouble" is thlibō (θλίβω), the verb form of thlipsis. According to Thayer, thlibō means "to press, press hard upon; a compressed way; metaphorically, to oppress, afflict, distress." BDAG adds, "to cause trouble, afflict, oppress, to experience distress." In other words, Paul is using the same root term to describe both the suffering of the Church and the judgment that God will pour out upon its oppressors. The saints are thlibō-ed by the world, and God will thlibō the world in return.

This is not coincidental wordplay. It is a deliberate expression of divine retribution. God is not merely reacting to injustice. He is returning the favor. He is repaying pressure with pressure, affliction with affliction, tribulation with tribulation. That is the meaning of recompense—to reward in kind, to match the nature of what was done. The oppressors will receive back what they gave, measure for measure, and weight for weight. This is not cruelty. It is justice. It is the righteous and calculated vengeance of a God who promises to repay those who have crushed His people.

And here is where the contrast becomes unavoidable. Paul's tribulation paradigm is a far cry from the pretribulational model, where God's wrath is imagined as being poured out indiscriminately falling upon the just and the unjust, the repentant and the unrepentant alike, recklessly and without distinction. According to that framework, there is no clear justice. There is no retributive symmetry. The righteous suffer side by side with the wicked, and divine vengeance seems more like blind rage than righteous recompense.

Even more astounding is the fact that classical dispensationalism never meaningfully addresses Paul's doctrine of recompense. It sidesteps it. It ignores it. It treats Paul's inspired declaration—that "it is a righteous thing with God to recompense tribulation to them that trouble you"—as if it were irrelevant to the discussion of end-time judgment. The silence is deafening. The dismissal is doctrinally irresponsible. To build an entire theology of the tribulation without this foundational truth is not merely an oversight. It is a distortion.

God does not forget His people. He does not ignore their cries. He will not allow the suffering of His saints to go unanswered. The tribulation is not His rage turned against the Church. It is His righteous answer to those who have dared to touch the apple of His eye.

Let every believer take comfort in this: God will exonerate the saints in the sight of their enemies. He will not only vindicate them in eternity. He will reverse the pressure. He will tribulate those who tribulated His Church. That is the promise of 2 Thessalonians 1. That is the pattern of divine justice. And that is the heartbeat of the tribulation—not chaos, but covenant. Not fear, but faith. Not abandonment, but the righteous recompense of our God.

God Repays with Precision

While we wait for the blessed hope of Christ's return, God is not silent. He avenges His saints by recompensing tribulation upon those who trouble the Church. The saints endure with patience and faith, but God brings wrath upon their persecutors. Mystery Babylon is said to be drunk with the blood of the saints (Revelation 17:6), and God responds in kind—giving blood to drink in return. This is no isolated image. Revelation 14:8 declares that "all nations have drunk of the wine of the wrath of her fornication." The whole world has shared in Babylon's defilement, so the scope of some plagues is appropriately wide, not because God lacks precision, but because global guilt demands global justice.

One of the clearest examples of this divine distinction is found in the plague of blood in Revelation 16. The second and third vials are poured out upon the sea and rivers, turning them into blood. But these are not random acts of wrath. They are deliberate judgments targeted at those who have shed the blood of the saints.

"And I heard the angel of the waters say, Thou art righteous, O Lord, which art, and wast, and shalt be, because thou hast judged thus. For they have shed the blood of saints and prophets, and thou hast given them blood to drink; for they are worthy."
(Revelation 16:5–6)

This is not judgment against the Church. It is judgment for the Church. It is the vindication of the martyrs. It is the Lord declaring that vengeance belongs to Him. It is divine recompense, echoing Paul's declaration: "It is a righteous thing with God to recompense tribulation to them that trouble you" (2 Thessalonians 1:6). Do you see it, my friend? It is a righteous thing with God to repay tribulation with tribulation!

This plague is a theological sledgehammer. It obliterates the notion that God's wrath is poured out indiscriminately upon all the earth, including the faithful. God does not judge His people with the wicked. He does not pour out His fury upon those sealed by His Spirit and purchased by His Son. He avenges them. He defends them. He remembers their tears and repays their oppressors. This is scriptural harmony at work. This is the unwavering consistency of God's covenant justice.

A Consistent Pattern of Preservation

This is not a message of fear, but of faith. Even in the darkest hour, the Lord knows how to preserve His own. The blood judgment of Revelation 16 is heaven's answer to the blood of the saints. Far from beating His bride, God is avenging her honor with divine precision. It is God defending His bride and avenging the blood of His witnesses. Just as Pharaoh's Egypt suffered the plagues for persecuting Israel, so the Beast's kingdom will suffer fierce anger for persecuting the Church.

And this turns the tables on the common rhetoric aimed against the posttrib view. Pretrib teaching often claims it would be unjust for God to let His people suffer through tribulation. But the greater injustice, the far more blasphemous claim, is the pretrib rapture model itself: that God will unleash wrath, death, demonic torment, and famine upon those who turn to Him during the final hour of history. According to that system, those who repent after the rapture will be left unprotected, undefended, and slaughtered by God Himself.

But the judgments described in Revelation are not poured out on a mixed crowd of believers and unbelievers. They are precise. They are surgical strikes against the kingdom of the Beast, his worshipers, and his system of deception and blasphemy. God knows exactly who is marked and who is sealed. And not one hair on the head of a sealed saint will be harmed without His permission.

In Revelation 16:2, the first vial judgment is poured out, and its target is explicit:

"And the first went, and poured out his vial upon the earth; and there fell a noisome and grievous sore upon the men which had the mark of the beast, and upon them which worshipped his image."

Only those who take the mark are afflicted. Not one saint is touched. This pattern continues with surgical precision. The fourth angel pours out his vial upon the sun in verse 8, and power is given to it to scorch men with fire. And again, we are told who is affected:

"And men were scorched with great heat, and blasphemed the name of God..." (Revelation 16:9)

These are not the sealed servants of God. They are the rebellious who curse Him even under judgment. Then in verse 10, the fifth vial falls directly upon the political system of the Antichrist:

"And the fifth angel poured out his vial upon the seat of the beast; and his kingdom was full of darkness; and they gnawed their tongues for pain..." (Revelation 16:10)

The very throne of the Antichrist is assaulted. God is not attacking His Church. He is dismantling the infrastructure of rebellion.

This is the same covenant of grace that protected Noah in the flood, Israel in Goshen, and the three Hebrews in the fire. It is the same Spirit that shut the mouths of lions for Daniel, and it is the same blood of Christ that seals every believer until the day of redemption. The saints who live during the tribulation are sealed by that same covenant. They are not forgotten. They are not collateral damage.

Pretrib teachers must ask themselves honestly: if the Beast is already persecuting the saints, what sense does it make for God to pour out His wrath on them as well? Is that not doubling their punishment? The logic crumbles under Scripture. It is not God who afflicts His saints with wrath. It is the Beast who makes war against them, and it is God who judges the Beast for it.

The wrath of God is not reckless. It is not indiscriminate. It is justice. It is vengeance. It is deliverance. And it falls only upon those who bear the mark of rebellion, never upon those who bear the seal of redemption.

God Has Always Preserved His People in Judgment

This is why not a single plague in Revelation is said to touch the saints. God knows those who are His. He marks them, seals them, and guards them, just as He did in Exodus when the plagues of Egypt left Goshen untouched. While Egypt suffered frogs, flies, and boils, Goshen remained a sanctuary:

"Only in the land of Goshen, where the children of Israel were, was there no hail." (Exodus 9:26)

And while the death angel moved through the land, it passed over every door covered by the blood of the lamb. God distinguished between His people and their oppressors then, and He will do so again.

Noah too was not removed from the earth during judgment. He was protected in it. The flood came, and Noah was preserved inside an ark of divine design. He endured the flood from a place of safety, just as the sealed saints endure the Great Tribulation with God's protection upon them. If we are to compare the ark to the rapture, one must conclude that since, as we have already explored in this book, the rains represent the coming of the Son of Man immediately after the tribulation, and the rain represents the ὀργή-wrath, then the ark rising on the floodwaters represents a posttribulation rapture scenario. If we are looking for archetypes, it is more logical to conclude a posttrib motif, especially when we are seeking consistency and congruency across Scripture.

But often, in the absence of exegetical support, pretribulation teachers appeal to emotion. One of their most frequent tactics is to ask, "So you think God is going to let babies starve during the tribulation?" It is a cheap shot, a manipulative attempt to provoke fear and bypass reason. But we can ask the same question of their model. If tribulation saints are saved during that time, what about their children? Are they exempt from this supposed divine wrath, or are they just collateral damage in a world abandoned by grace?

The real answer is this: you do not know the Scriptures nor the power of God if you ask such a question. Did God not feed Elijah with a raven during a drought? Did not an angel deliver food to him, and he journeyed forty days on the strength of that meal? (1 Kings 17:6; 19:5–8). The same God who opened the heavens for manna in the wilderness is not suddenly limited in the end times. The same Shepherd who provides for His flock today will not abandon His sheep in the hour of trial.

Psalm 33:18–19 says:

"Behold, the eye of the Lord is upon them that fear him… to deliver their soul from death, and to keep them alive in famine."

The tribulation does not cancel God's covenant. It activates His protection with even greater clarity. While the Beast wages war on the saints, God sustains them. While Babylon drinks their blood, God prepares their vindication.

Fear-based theology says, "God must remove us to spare us." But faith says, "God can keep me wherever I am." And Scripture confirms that He does.

Typology Supports a Posttribulational Hope

The point is not merely typology. It is consistency. When we interpret Noah's Ark, the blood in Egypt, and the sealing of God's servants in Revelation, a pattern emerges: the righteous are protected through judgment, not removed before it.

This consistent pattern across Scripture refutes the pretribulation panic that assumes God's indignation cannot coexist with God's people. The truth is, God never judges the righteous with the wicked. He preserves the faithful even when judgment falls all around them.

Tribulation is not abandonment. It is the backdrop against which the glory of God's faithfulness shines brightest. Just as the ark rested on the waves, so the Church rests in the promises of a God who never fails.

We see this pattern again in the fiery furnace. The three Hebrews were not spared from the fire, but they were preserved in it. The flames raged, but they were not consumed. And in the fire, they met the One "like unto the Son of God." He did not deliver them from afar, but He walked with them in the midst of the fire.

And what about Daniel? He was not rescued from the sentence of the lions' den. He was thrown in. He spent the night surrounded by predators. But God shut the mouths of the lions and preserved His servant through the tribulation. And when morning came, Daniel was lifted out unharmed, while his accusers—the ones who had plotted his downfall—were thrown in and devoured. That is divine justice. That is tribulation turned back on the heads of the wicked.

It is the same pattern we find in the end. The saints may be thrown into the furnace of affliction, or lowered into dens of danger, but they will not be consumed. They are sealed. They are watched over. And when the time of vengeance arrives, God will turn the judgment upon their persecutors. This is not a promise of escape from all danger, but a promise of divine protection in the midst of danger. As Psalm 91 declares:

"A thousand shall fall at thy side, and ten thousand at thy right hand; but it shall not come nigh thee."
(Psalm 91:7)

Let the wicked fear. Let the Church endure. God's faithfulness has never failed, and He will not begin to fail now. The fire may come, the lions may roar, but the Lord is with those who trust in His name.

Correcting the Misrepresentation: God Is Not Beating His Bride

Persecution is something many pretribulationists hope to escape. And on a human level, I understand. Even Christ, in His humanity, asked if the cup could pass from Him. Yet He submitted to the will of the Father. He made it clear: "The spirit indeed is willing, but the flesh is weak." This not only reveals the dual nature of Jesus Christ as fully God and fully man, but it teaches us something vital about our own flesh. It is weak. It resists suffering. It recoils at tribulation.

But Jesus did not call us to follow our feelings. He called us to pick up our cross, deny ourselves, and follow Him. Peter wrote:

"Hereunto were ye called: because Christ also suffered for us, leaving us an example, that ye should follow his steps"
(1 Peter 2:21).

Jesus said, "Whosoever will lose his life for my sake shall find it." This exhortation to remain faithful under pressure is not a fringe idea. It is woven into the entire fabric of Scripture.

Yes, the flesh resists persecution. But doctrine must never be built on preferences or fear. We are called to be overcomers:

"To him that overcometh will I give a crown of life"
(Revelation 2:10).

God has not promised us exemption from tribulation. He has promised us victory through it.

Far from beating His bride, God will avenge her. Think of it this way: if a husband were away on a long journey and returned to find his wife battered and bruised by enemies, what would he do? Would he join in the assault, or would he unleash wrath on those who had harmed her? His fury would burn against the offenders. He would demand justice. He would see them punished.

This is exactly what the Bible says God will do. He will recompense tribulation to those who trouble the Church. He will not brutalize His bride. He will avenge her. The plagues of Revelation are not for the saints. They are the just sentence against their oppressors. The Lamb will return, not to beat His bride, but to make her enemies drink the cup they filled with her blood.

One of the most common fear tactics used by the pretribulation rapture camp is to accuse posttrib believers of portraying a cruel and abusive God, as if we teach that God will beat His own bride through the tribulation. This accusation is not merely unfair. It is an outright lie.

We do not believe God pours out His wrath on His Church. We believe exactly what Scripture says: "It is a righteous thing with God to recompense tribulation to them that trouble you" (2 Thessalonians 1:6). We believe God protects His people, just as He always has. His plagues are not random. They are vengeance upon those who persecuted His saints. And this is not creative interpretation. This is the clear teaching of the Word of God.

Pretribulationist rhetoric consistently misrepresents the posttrib position. They construct straw men and knock them down to scare people into adopting their system. "If you believe in a posttrib rapture," they say, "you believe God will brutalize His bride with wrath." That is emotional manipulation. It avoids honest exegesis by trading the Word of God for fear-based slogans.

But what does the pretrib model teach about God? According to their system, if you are left behind—if you do not make the rapture—you will suffer the horrors of the tribulation, and no amount of repentance will stay God's hand. He will harm, torment, and destroy you alongside the followers of the Beast, even if you repent,[5] even if you seek Him with all your heart.

That is not the God of Scripture. That is not the just Judge. My God does not persecute the repentant. My God does not ignore the blood of the Lamb and the sealing of His Spirit. My God draws near to those who call upon Him, even in the darkest hour. And my God remembers every tear, every testimony, every martyr, and He declares, "Vengeance is mine; I will repay."

He is not the God of escape. He is the God who walks in the fire. He is the God who shut the lions' mouths for Daniel and turned their hunger upon his accusers. He is the God who stood with Shadrach, Meshach, and Abednego in the furnace, preserving them without even the smell of smoke on their garments. He is the God who strengthens weary hearts and says, "Lo, I am with you always, even unto the end of the world."

The truth is simple. Pretribulationism not only slanders the posttrib view, but it also slanders the character of God. It claims to protect grace but denies mercy to those who will cry out to Jesus in the final hour.

May God indeed recompense tribulation upon those who trouble His Church. And may He exonerate every saint who endures to the end, not with wrath, but with rest. May every overcomer be crowned with righteousness. And may the Bridegroom return to avenge His bride and welcome her into glory.

Rebuttal & Answer: "The falling away is the departure in 2 Thessalonians 2:3. That's the rapture."

Not so fast, my friend. There are multiple inaccuracies and misrepresentations in that argument. It is a feeble attempt to explain away a clear contradiction to pretribulational doctrine.

In recent years, some pretribulationists have attempted to redefine the Greek word ἀποστασία (apostasía) in 2 Thessalonians 2:3 to mean a physical departure—specifically, a reference to the rapture. But this interpretation is not only lexically unsound, it is

---

[5] Grant R. Jeffrey, The Next World War: What Prophecy Reveals About Extreme Islam and the West (New York: WaterBrook Press, 2006), 186. **"Those who are on earth during the Great Tribulation will not be delivered from wrath but will be overcome."**

historically absent, theologically forced, and strategically inserted to preserve a doctrinal system that is collapsing under the weight of the text.

The verse reads:

"Let no man deceive you by any means: for that day shall not come, except there come a falling away first, and that man of sin be revealed..." (2 Thessalonians 2:3)

Some claim that "falling away" (apostasía) refers not to rebellion or apostasy, but to a literal, bodily departure from the earth. But this claim does not survive careful examination.

The standard Greek lexicons are unanimous. Apostasía means rebellion, defection, or a falling away from the faith—not physical relocation.

- Thayer defines it as "a falling away, defection."
- BDAG defines it as "defiance of established system or authority, rebellion, abandonment, breach of faith."

There is no mention of the rapture. There is no linguistic hint of a spatial departure. The word refers to spiritual revolt and always has.

The word apostasía appears only twice in the New Testament. The second instance is in Acts 21:21, where Paul is accused of teaching apostasía from Moses and not bodily disappearance, but doctrinal defection. It is a rejection of truth, not a relocation to heaven.

Despite this, some modern pretribulation teachers—most notably Andy Woods[6]—have promoted the idea that apostasía means a physical departure. This view is a recent innovation. It has no foundation in early church theology, and no serious Greek scholar

---

[6]Andy Woods, The Falling Away: Spiritual Departure or Physical Rapture? (Sugar Land, TX: Dispensational Publishing House, 2018). Woods is a leading advocate of the minority view that apostasía in 2 Thessalonians 2:3 refers not to a spiritual rebellion, but to the rapture of the Church. This reinterpretation has gained traction in some pretribulational circles but lacks support from early church usage, standard lexicons, or mainstream Greek scholarship.

outside of pretribulation circles affirms it. It is a manufactured definition, motivated by the need to protect the doctrine of imminence.

And that is the real reason this redefinition has gained traction. Redefining apostasía as the rapture salvages the pretrib model's collapsing timeline. Because if 2 Thessalonians 2:3 means what it plainly says, that the coming of Christ and our gathering to Him will not happen until there is a great falling away and the man of sin is revealed—then the doctrine of imminence is dead on arrival.

I have come across many testimonies from former pretribulationists who say 2 Thessalonians 2:1–3 was the turning point. The wording was too clear to ignore. They could not reconcile the plain reading with what they had been taught. And so, rather than redefining the word, they realigned with the truth.

If we take the pretrib redefinition at face value, the passage will effectively read: "We beseech you… by our gathering together unto Him… that day shall not come except there come a rapture first…" This is theological nonsense. It would mean that our gathering together unto Christ— the rapture—must occur before the rapture can occur.

Even worse, it would imply that the Antichrist is revealed after the Church is already gone in multiple phases. Not only is that incoherent, but it also completely undermines Paul's entire purpose. He was writing to reassure the Church that they had not missed the Day of Christ. He clearly says that day cannot come until two things happen first: a great falling away and the revealing of the man of sin. Not afterward. First.

This error is not harmless. It distorts Paul's timeline. It confuses the Church. And it perpetuates a myth of imminence that Paul directly dismantles in the opening verses of this very chapter. Tragically, many believers may find themselves unprepared for persecution because they placed their hope in a system built on theological slight-of-hand.

But there is hope. God will avenge His elect. He will recompense tribulation to those who persecute the saints. And when Christ returns, He will exonerate the faithful and silence every false prophecy that said the Church would be gone.

Let the Scriptures speak plainly. The apostasía is not a rapture. It is a rebellion. It is the great spiritual defection that will engulf the world in deception and prepare it for the man of sin. To claim otherwise is not exegesis. It is manipulation. It is forcing Scripture to serve a system, instead of submitting the system to Scripture.

What Paul describes is not a silent vanishing of believers, but a society-wide revolt against truth that sets the stage for Antichrist. And that moment will not come without warning. The Church will see it. The Church will endure it. And the Church will be delivered through it when the Lord Jesus Christ returns in glory.

I want to be clear that I'm not accusing Dr. Andy Woods or others who teach the "departure" view of apostasía of malicious intent. In fact, I believe many who hold this view are sincere. But sincerity does not exempt us from the influence of presuppositions, and I believe in this case Dr. Woods is operating from a framework that is coloring his interpretation. Whether consciously or not, he has approached the text with a conclusion already in mind and has read the meaning of apostasía through the lens of that desired outcome.

Lexical Roots and Early Translations of Apostasía

The Greek word ἀποστασία (apostasía) carries a rich etymology rooted in the idea of departure but not a spatial one. It derives from apostasis, meaning a political or religious revolt, and from apostasion, a term used for divorce or a departure from covenant, such as in marriage. These are not movements through space, but departures from relationship, loyalty, or established order.

This explains why many translations, including the ESV and NET Bible, render apostasía in 2 Thessalonians 2:3 as "rebellion." It captures the true force of the word as it is used throughout Scripture. Paul was not predicting a physical disappearance. He was warning of a massive falling away from the faith—a betrayal of truth that would leave the world spiritually desolate and prepared to receive the man of sin.

To go even deeper into the lexical roots of apostasía, we can examine its compound structure. The prefix apo means "away from" or "departure," and stasis means "a standing, place, or position." Thus, the word literally means "a departure from a position." But this is where some pretribulationists distort the term. They isolate the word "position" and treat it as if it must refer to a physical location—as in departing from the earth. However, in both classical and biblical usage, stasis does not refer to geography. It refers to standing in a political, moral, or covenantal sense.

In fact, apostasía does not signify a change in physical location at all. Its etymological ties to apostasis (rebellion) and apostasion (divorce) point consistently to defection, betrayal, and covenant breaking. Divorce is a departure from marriage. Apostasy is a departure from the faith. These are relational ruptures, not spatial relocations.

Even in modern language, when we say someone has "left their position," —whether it be political, religious, or any ideological position—we do not mean they vanished into thin air. We mean they defected. They betrayed trust or forsook duty. The emphasis is on disloyalty, not geography. A political defector is not someone who changes locations, but someone who changes allegiance. That is exactly what apostasía means—rebellion, defection, and abandonment of divine truth.

This is where we must exercise caution. The danger is not in disagreeing over a word. The danger is in bending the discipline of exegesis to fit a theological system. Dr. Woods is committing what scholars call the "root fallacy," the assumption that a word's etymology determines its present meaning. But language does not function that way. Words evolve, and context shapes their use far more than their roots.

To illustrate the error, imagine I told you that the English word understand does not mean to comprehend but literally means "to stand under." After all, under means beneath, and stand refers to a physical position. If we followed that line of thinking, we could redefine understand as the act of physically standing underneath something. But we know that's not how language works. Context, usage, and common sense tell us otherwise.

So too with Paul's use of apostasía in 2 Thessalonians 2:3. The departure he refers to is not a vanishing act. It is a societal revolt. A rejection of the faith. A mass defection from truth that prepares the world to embrace the man of sin. The context, the grammar, and the historical usage all support this. To read spatial departure into stasis is to force a modern framework onto an ancient word. Paul was not talking about air travel. He was talking about apostasy. And the Church must stop allowing theologians to twist Greek roots into doctrinal fantasies.

And make no mistake, there is a motive behind the pretribulational redefinition of this word. The reason some are so eager to ignore millennia of Greek usage and theological consistency to redefine apostasía as the rapture is simple: it places the doctrine of imminence in jeopardy. It flat out destroys it.

To be apostate means you have departed from the faith. And you cannot depart from something you were never part of. Just like you cannot divorce someone you never married, you cannot fall away from a truth you never embraced. This proves that Paul was warning about a spiritual rebellion among those who once stood in the truth—likely even among the visible Church.

Many readers can likely think of other doctrines, outside the rapture debate, that could be "rescued" if we allowed ourselves to redefine apostasía. That is the danger of this approach. The moment we redefine words to protect our golden calves, we repeat the sin of Israel at Sinai. The idol may stand a little longer, but we will drink the bitter water of its ruin, just as they did in Exodus 32.

We must not do violence to Scripture in order to protect our systems. Pretribulation teachers are ignoring generations of lexical evidence, historical theology, and the consistent usage of the word in the LXX—the Septuagint, the Greek translation of the Hebrew Bible often cited by New Testament writers. And in every instance where apostasía is used in the Septuagint, it always means rebellion against God. It never refers to a spatial departure.

For example:

- *Joshua 22:22 (LXX): "God forbid that we should (rebel) (ἀποστασίαν ποιησώμεθα) against the Lord."*
- *2 Chronicles 29:19 (LXX): "All the vessels which King Ahaz had cast aside in his reign, in his ἀποστασία (apostasy), we have prepared and sanctified."*
- *Jeremiah 2:19 (LXX): "Thine own ἀποστασία (apostasy) shall correct thee."*

In each of these passages, the word apostasía or its form refers to rebellion, defection, or unfaithfulness. Never once is it used to describe a rapture, relocation, or departure from one place to another. To redefine apostasía now, in light of this overwhelming evidence, is to abandon both linguistic integrity and the authority of Scripture.

Classic Translations Say Departure

To bolster this claim, they often appeal to a handful of early English translations that rendered apostasía as "departure" or "departing." This includes the Geneva Bible, and other classic translations. The argument typically goes like this, "The early translators knew that apostasia meant 'departure' a simple, neutral word. It doesn't have to mean rebellion or apostasy. Therefore, it refers to the Church departing from earth in the rapture."

At first glance, it sounds compelling—until you do what apparently many pretribulationists haven't done: read the margin notes those very translators provided.

Had they bothered to check, they would have seen that these same translators clarified what kind of departure they meant. It wasn't a spatial departure into the clouds. It was a departure from the faith. In other words, an apostasy—exactly how nearly every Greek lexicon and every major translation renders it today.

Let's look at the evidence directly.

"Let no man deceive you by any means: for that day shall not come, except there come a departing first, and that man of sin be disclosed, even the son of perdition."
The Geneva Bible (1599)

Margin note:

"many shall fall away from God to him."[7]

This is unambiguous. The Geneva translators understood the word to mean a spiritual defection, not a physical disappearance.

---

[7] "The Apostle foretelleth that before the coming of the Lord, there shall be a throne set up clean contrary to Christ's glory, wherein that wicked man shall sit, and transfer all things that appertain to God, to himself, and many shall fall away from God to him." 1599 Edition GB

The word apostasía was understood then exactly as it is now—a rebellion, a forsaking, a falling away from God. Friend, do you see how pretrib teachers and scholars lead with the conclusion? They never stopped and asked if the translator's idea of departing aligned with their assumptions. Unfortunately, the internet is flooded with misinformation declaring that the departure is from earth and not faith. There is a departure happening now; a departure from truth by trying to redefine words. Let me be clear the departure was never understood to be a rapture.

Let the Word of God speak plainly. Let our doctrines submit to its authority. Paul warned of a great rebellion. We must take him at his word. And we must be among those who stand when the world falls away.

Posttribulationism does not teach that God will beat His Bride it teaches that God will avenge her. It is pretribulationism that misrepresents His character, projecting the flaws of its own doctrine onto historic premillennialism. By accusing others of cruelty, it conceals the injustice of a system that leaves repentant souls exposed to wrath. We must let Scripture speak plainly and stop redefining words to protect theological traditions. Truth needs no manipulation. It only needs submission.

Next Revelation:
The Church Is Present in the Tribulation

The plagues of Revelation are not poured out randomly; they are triggered by the cries of the saints. Before a single trumpet sounds, God hears His people, and His judgments follow. Chapter 6 will show that the Church is not missing during the tribulation but is at the very center of its conflict. Persecuted, sealed, and sustained, the saints endure as living witnesses against the Beast. As we'll see, the book of Revelation does not exclude the Church it reveals her vindication.

Chapter 6:
The Church Is Present in the Tribulation

"And it was given unto him to make war with the saints, and to overcome them..."
(Revelation 13:7)

Many in the modern Church have been sold a fantasy by pretribulationist teachers and scholars. A generation of believers has been trained to expect escape, told they will be raptured away before the rise of the Antichrist, the great tribulation, and the judgments of God. But when we turn from sensationalism to Scripture, this entire narrative collapses. God's Word paints a very different picture, one in which the saints are not absent during tribulation, but central to its unfolding.

Let's demolish a myth frequently proclaimed by modern prophecy teachers: the Church is not missing from the book of Revelation. This claim must be destroyed at the outset. The saints are seen throughout the book suffering, crying out, praying, witnessing, and reigning. These are not a separate group called "tribulation saints" created to protect a system. They are the Church. The very body of Christ is present and engaged in the climactic battle between good and evil.

As you continue through this chapter, you will watch the dispensational model slowly unravel. The plagues of Revelation are not indiscriminate acts of wrath, but they are God's vengeance on behalf of His persecuted people. Just as in Egypt, the judgments fall not on the faithful, but on those who oppress them. The prayers of the saint's trigger fire from the altar. The blood of the martyrs cries out for justice. And justice is what they receive.

Paul's tribulation paradigm confirms this. In 2 Thessalonians 1, he makes it clear that God will repay tribulation to those who trouble the Church. The saints endure affliction now, but it is the persecutors who will face divine wrath when Christ returns. This is not a pattern of escape but of vindication.

And let's not forget persecution through economic pressure is nothing new. Revelation 13's mark system is not a strange invention. The early Church faced similar exclusion under Rome. To refuse to burn incense to Caesar was to lose your place in the marketplace. Believers were pushed out of society not because they were lawless, but because they were loyal. That same pattern is returning in full force.

As the chapter unfolds, we will examine these patterns and prophetic truths in greater depth. But it begins with this: the Church is present. The saints are not spectators, they are targets. And through them, the glory of God will be revealed.

The Tribulation as a Time of Testing

The tribulation described in Scripture is not divine punishment against God's people, but a time of testing inflicted by the world upon the saints. Just as ancient Israel endured affliction from Egypt, yet was ultimately delivered, the Church, too, will be refined through trials and rescued by the Lord's return. Just as Pharaoh's heart hardened before the plagues fell on Egypt, the Beast's kingdom will rage against the faithful before divine judgment descends. The plagues of Revelation, mirroring those of Exodus, are not aimed at the people of God. They target those who reject Him, worship the Beast, and spill the blood of the saints. These judgments are not collateral, they are calculated. The saints cry out, and God answers with fire from the altar. This is divine vengeance, not indiscriminate wrath. It is justice in response to persecution.

The Beast will wage war on God's saints and utterly wear them out, but as you will see, this always ends with the vindication of the Church.

"And he shall speak great words against the most High, and shall wear out the saints of the most High…"
(Daniel 7:25)

But what follows this wearing out? Daniel is not silent. The very next verses paint a picture not of escape, but of judgment. The Son of Man comes. The Ancient of Days sits. The books are opened. The dominion of the Beast is taken away and consumed with fire. And the kingdom is handed not to a separate group but to the saints of the Most High.

*"I beheld till the thrones were cast down, and the Ancient of days
did sit... a fiery stream issued and came forth from before him... the
judgment was set, and the books were opened"*
(Daniel 7:9–10)
*"I saw in the night visions, and, behold, one like the Son of man
came with the clouds of heaven... and there was given him dominion,
and glory, and a kingdom..."*
(Daniel 7:13–14)

*"But the judgment shall sit, and they shall take away his dominion,
to consume and to destroy it unto the end. And the kingdom and
dominion... shall be given to the people of the saints of the most
High"*
(Daniel 7:26–27)

The fire that issues from the throne in Daniel's vision is
judgment. It is the consuming wrath of the Ancient of Days, and it
coincides precisely with the arrival of the Son of Man. This harmony
is echoed in Revelation 19, where the final judgment of the Beast
occurs not in isolation, but in the blazing light of Christ's return.

*"And the beast was taken, and with him the false prophet... These
both were cast alive into a lake of fire burning with brimstone."*
(Revelation 19:20)

Where is the escape? Where is the vanishing act that
dispensationalism demands? If these are the so-called tribulation
saints, why are they so highly exalted after supposedly being left
behind? Why are they the ones to inherit the kingdom while the
Church is nowhere to be seen? Why is the Bride absent from the
wedding and the guests ruling on thrones? If we are to take this
dispensational logic seriously, it raises a far more troubling question:
is the Church not worthy of the kingdom?

The text does not support that division. The dispensational
model does not rightly divide the Word of truth. It divides what God
has joined.

As you continue reading this book, you are going to find that
the way Scripture treats these so-called tribulation saints completely
contradicts the pretribulational narrative and could put the position

of the New Testament Church's role in the Kingdom of God into serious question because if that narrative were true.

The saints of Revelation and Daniel are not a second-tier class of believers. They are the redeemed. They are the Church.

The Antichrist's Agenda

The Antichrist's agenda extends far beyond mere persecution of Christians. His ambition encompasses complete global domination spiritually, politically, and economically. Scripture portrays him exalting himself "above all that is called God, or that is worshipped," and positioning himself "in the temple of God, shewing himself that he is God" (2 Thessalonians 2:4). This means he blasphemously tries to apply one of the Ten Commandments to himself, "thou shalt have no other gods before me." He will tolerate no competing allegiance, whether Jewish, Christian, or other. Some who do not take 2 Thessalonians 2:4 as literal prophecy ask why the Antichrist would desecrate a Jewish temple. The answer is plain in the Scripture: he exalts himself above anything that is called a god or is worshipped. His goal is not merely political superiority but divine exclusivity. He wants to be God with a capital G.

He will stop the sacrifices not because they save but because they threaten his status. He will sit in the temple not because it is holy but because it is a symbol of resistance. The Jews are a resilient people, and ethnoreligious identity has historically helped them survive dispersion and persecution. But above all, it is the Church that he hates. Why? Because we have the covenant. The Spirit of God dwells in us. And we are the visible proof that the kingdom belongs to another.

Relentless War Against the Saints

The Saints refuse allegiance to the Beast and expose his deceit, never taking the mark of the Beast but being sealed to the day of redemption by God. Consequently, the Antichrist wages relentless warfare against them. They will never worship the Beast, and since the Antichrist will never allow the saints to have allegiance to God the Father and the Lord Jesus Christ, he will make war with the saints and utterly wear them out, because this faith is a threat to his kingdom. The Antichrist wants to remove all traces of the true God from earth, and that includes His saints.

Revelation vividly depicts this war as systematic and ruthless, beginning with blasphemies and escalating into a regime of enforced worship. Those who resist are marked as enemies and systematically persecuted. Revelation 13 describes how the False Prophet deceives the masses into worshipping the Beast, executing those who refuse compliance and establishing an economic system that excludes nonparticipants:

"And he causeth all… to receive a mark… that no man might buy or sell, save he that had the mark, or the name of the beast…" *(Revelation 13:16–17)*

Historical Shadows of the Beast System

This persecution has historical precedent. Under Emperor Diocletian, Christians were expelled from commerce, their Scriptures banned, and loyalty was demanded through incense offerings to Caesar. Believers faced economic isolation, imprisonment, and execution if they refused. Those who complied were issued a libellus, a certificate proving they had sacrificed to the emperor, allowing them to buy, sell, and live unmolested. But for those who remained faithful to Christ, economic exclusion was just the beginning. They were marked as enemies of the empire.

Diocletian's persecution was only a shadow. The Beast embodies the full substance of this tyrannical vision. But it goes to show this system of exclusion from commerce can be done without technology. How much easier can it be enforced in a tech-savvy world?

The system under Diocletian is a typological foreshadowing of the Beast's economic tyranny. In a typological framework, such events serve as paradigms patterns that may repeat in smaller, local fulfillments but ultimately point to a greater, climactic reality in the future. Diocletian's rule represents a beast-like archetype, not the final fulfillment, but a warning for every generation.

His death, unlike the Beast of Revelation, came quietly in retirement and disillusionment. He withered in shame. But the Beast at the end of the age does not die quietly. His dominion is taken away and consumed alive with fire. Scripture is dramatic and deliberate in how it portrays this event:

"I beheld then because of the voice of the great words which the horn spake: I beheld even till the beast was slain, and his body destroyed, and given to the burning flame."
(Daniel 7:11)

"And the devil that deceived them was cast into the lake of fire and brimstone, where the beast and the false prophet are…"
(Revelation 20:10)

This contrast preempts historicist interpretations that flatten prophecy into past fulfillment. Diocletian's empire was a foreshadowing, not the final form. He will still face his judgment before the Great White Throne.

But where was the Church's escape in his day? Were not Christians starving? Were they not in need? Were they not refused access to the economy and livelihood? Would any modern pretribulation teachers dare to aim their emotional appeals here, invoking images of starving babies to dismiss posttrib theology? Did these believers not suffer imprisonment, torture, and death rather than offer incense to Caesar a pagan parody of allegiance eerily similar to the mark of the Beast?

Are these saints a separate group from the Church? Or are they our brothers and sisters, part of the same body, tested before us, now awaiting vindication?

Let the reader judge. The notion of a special category called "tribulation saints," conveniently created to preserve a faulty system of eschatology, cannot bear the weight of church history or prophetic fulfillment.

Yet Revelation identifies the Beast's main victims who provoke his ire clearly: those who keep God's commandments, hold the testimony of Jesus, and refuse compromise (Revelation 14:12; 12:11; 7:14). Far from defeated, these saints who live during the tribulation are promised eternal vindication and reign with Christ:

"And I saw thrones, and they sat upon them... and I saw the souls of them that were beheaded for the witness of Jesus... and they lived and reigned with Christ a thousand years."
(Revelation 20:4)

Daniel also confirms this ultimate vindication:

"But the judgment shall sit, and they shall take away his dominion... And the kingdom and dominion... shall be given to the people of the saints of the most High..."
(Daniel 7:26–27)

A Love Story in the Midst of War

God is the same today as He was yesterday and shows no signs of changing. His grace and love have always existed, and no dispensational system can alter this foundational truth. The full scope of God's love and grace is consistently revealed throughout Scripture, but it is often watered down in the dispensational model, which places more emphasis on the divisions of a man-made system than on the continuity of God's redemptive character. Dispensationalism erects theological walls between law and grace, Israel and the Church, old covenant and new, in ways that obscure the seamless thread of divine mercy. As Scofield himself admits, dispensations are "periods marked off in Scripture by some change in God's method of dealing with mankind, or a portion of mankind, in respect to the two questions of sin and of man's responsibility" (Scofield Reference Bible, Introduction). Yet, this approach mistakenly suggests that God's fundamental attributes or purposes shift significantly between these periods. But God is love, and we witness a perfect demonstration of His love extending beyond the limits of the law, crossing boundaries that dispensational charts deem impossible. His character remains steadfast and unchanged by theological systems constructed by men.

This drama unfolds against a deeper backdrop, vividly depicting the profound love story of redemption illustrated through prophetic imagery. Revelation 12 portrays a majestic woman clothed with the sun, the moon beneath her feet, and crowned with twelve stars. This depiction mirrors Joseph's prophetic dream in Genesis 37, where the sun symbolizes Jacob, the moon represents his wife, and the twelve stars denote his sons, thereby clearly identifying the woman as Israel.

Israel frequently appears as a rebellious wife in the Old Testament narratives. God, portrayed as her faithful husband, laments her repeated unfaithfulness, declaring, "Surely as a wife treacherously departeth from her husband, so have ye dealt treacherously with me..." (Jeremiah 3:20). According to the Mosaic Law, a man was explicitly forbidden to reconcile with an estranged wife once she had defiled herself:

"Her former husband... may not take her again to be his wife, after that she is defiled..." (Deuteronomy 24:4).

Yet, God, driven by His boundless mercy and relentless love, transcends these legal confines, not to compromise His holiness but to reveal the overwhelming depth of divine love and redemption that surpasses human expectations.

Remarkably, God Himself explicitly acknowledges this legal prohibition and compassionately calls Israel back to Him, as recorded in Jeremiah:

"They say, If a man put away his wife, and she go from him, and become another man's, shall he return unto her again? Shall not that land be greatly polluted? But thou hast played the harlot with many lovers; yet return again to me, saith the Lord." (Jeremiah 3:1)

God's readiness to reclaim Israel despite her infidelity forms the critical pivot point of redemption history. It is through this restored and grace-filled relationship that the miraculous fulfillment of prophecy emerges, captured beautifully in the declaration: "Unto us a child is born, unto us a son is given..." (Isaiah 9:6). Jesus, the Messiah, emerges from this extraordinary love story between God and His estranged wife. Out of Christ, who embodies God's immeasurable love and grace, arises the Church, the faithful remnant of Israel's seed, signifying the ultimate triumph of divine mercy over judgment.

This redeeming love is inseparable from grace. By God's mercy and grace, Israel bore God the Father many children in this redemptive motif. The dispensational model dissolves when we see how God's grace is not confined to supposed periods of dealing with mankind differently. While there are indeed different covenants throughout salvation history, the grace and love of God are never withheld. His mercy flows freely across all covenants, to all who believe. Grace flows through the cross past, present, and future. The blood of Christ is not diluted by covenant or "periods"in history. Jesus is the firstborn of many brethren from the land of Israel. It is through His name that the entire host of heaven is named, uniting believers of all ages and covenants under one spiritual family.

This connection is made explicit in Revelation 12:17:

"And the dragon was wroth with the woman, and went to make war with the remnant of her seed, which keep the commandments of God, and have the testimony of Jesus Christ."

As we've seen earlier in this chapter, both Daniel and Revelation speak in unison. The Beast makes war with the saints. This directly ties Israel's seed to the Church. Israel gave birth to both the Messiah and the Church. As it is written by Paul in Romans 8:29, Jesus is "the firstborn among many brethren."

Even more compelling, as mentioned earlier in this book the Codex Sinaiticus, one of the oldest complete manuscripts of the Bible, includes a colophon at the very end of Revelation which identifies the saints as the Church. This ancient scribal note reflects the earliest Christian understanding: there was no distinction between the tribulation saints and the Church. The earliest copyists saw what modern dispensationalism denies that those who endure persecution in Revelation are the very body of Christ.

This spiritual lineage enrages the dragon. What he believed was a broken covenant became fertile ground. What he thought was defiled became holy. The estranged wife bore not only the Messiah but also His brethren, the Church. And so, the Beast's fury is not only political or economic. It is personal, theological, and ancient.

The Prayers That Precede the Trumpets

The saints who feel pressure from the tribulation begin to cry out to God. And that is one more thing that is constantly overlooked, the fact that the trumpets, the heralds of each plague and the impending return of Christ, never sound before the prayers of the saints are offered up to God. This is not incidental. It is deliberate and theological. It is retribution on those who hurt His Church. Revelation portrays a divine order: the suffering of the saints precedes the judgments of God. Their cries ascend before His throne and are answered in kind, not with silence, not with removal, but with holy vengeance.

This aligns with Paul's Tribulation Paradigm, where tribulation is endured patiently by the saints, knowing that divine justice will eventually avenge their suffering. It parallels Moses and the Hebrew people in Egypt, where plagues targeted their oppressors while God's people remained under divine protection. We should not fear the very thing designed to avenge us. The dragon may rage, and so might the son of perdition, but the saints will be avenged. The plagues culminate in the return of Christ, where the wicked hide themselves, trembling at the wrath of the Lamb. The haughty will indeed be made low.

This pattern begins earlier, in the breaking of the fifth seal, where John sees under the altar "the souls of them that were slain for the word of God, and for the testimony which they held." These are not silent victims. They are conscious, vocal, and pleading for divine justice:

"And they cried with a loud voice, saying, How long, O Lord, holy and true, dost thou not judge and avenge our blood on them that dwell on the earth?"
(Revelation 6:10)

Here, the saints are not passively waiting for escape. They are boldly interceding for vindication. And God's response is not to dismiss them, nor to scold them for desiring justice. Instead, they are given white robes, told to rest a little while longer, and reassured that their number would be fulfilled. This implies that more of their brethren will suffer before judgment falls. This cry for vengeance in the fifth seal becomes the theological groundwork for what happens in the trumpet judgments.

Before a single trumpet sounds in judgment, something pivotal happens:

"And the smoke of the incense, which came with the prayers of the saints, ascended up before God out of the angel's hand. And the angel took the censer, and filled it with fire of the altar, and cast it into the earth..."
(Revelation 8:4–5)

Notice the careful sequence: the prayers of the saints rise before God's throne, followed immediately by heaven's response, fire cast to the earth. This heavenly act directly precedes the sounding of the trumpets, tying the saints' prayers explicitly to the onset of divine judgments:

"And the seven angels which had the seven trumpets prepared themselves to sound."
(Revelation 8:6)

Let's look at the first couple of trumpets. Their judgment clearly connects to the imagery of fire cast upon the earth:

"The first angel sounded, and there followed hail and fire mingled with blood, and they were cast upon the earth..."
(Revelation 8:7)

"And the second angel sounded, and as it were a great mountain burning with fire was cast into the sea: and the third part of the sea became blood."
(Revelation 8:8)

This isn't coincidence. This symbolic imagery is deliberate. The fire cast to earth in response to the saints' prayers in verse 5 directly corresponds to the fiery judgment of the first trumpet in verses 7 and 8. The prayers of persecuted saints trigger divine retribution against their oppressors.

Pretribulationism Undermined by the Trumpet Sequence

This critical detail undermines the logic of pretribulationism, which absurdly implies saints would be praying for their own judgment. If the Church is raptured before these events, who is praying for divine judgment in Revelation 8? And if these saints are newly converted believers, now termed "tribulation saints," why would they pray for fire and judgment upon themselves?

To be fair, I don't believe most adherents to dispensationalism have deeply considered the prayers of the saints ascending before the trumpets sound in Revelation 8. But they are still left with a vexing problem. Pretribulation doctrine then implies God removes His Church to protect them from wrath, saves a second group called tribulation saints, then inexplicably answers their prayers with judgment against them. These verses expose the incongruences of pretribulation rapture with the Scripture.

The only coherent interpretation is that these saints cry out to God against their persecutors. God's response, then, is not wrath poured on the saints but a precise and righteous judgment against their tormentors. Paul explicitly confirms this:

"Seeing it is a righteous thing with God to recompense tribulation to them that trouble you…"
(2 Thessalonians 1:6)

Revelation 8 clearly illustrates that God's wrath is targeted, deliberate, just, explicitly provoked by the persecution of the saints, and aimed solely at the ungodly. Far from removing His people, God hears their prayers and vindicates them, affirming the saints' essential role in Revelation's unfolding prophetic drama.

Rebuttal & Answer:
"What About Being Counted Worthy to Escape in Luke 21:36?"

Before we misunderstand the nature of this escape, we must step back and ask: what kind of escape is Jesus actually describing? Is it a supernatural removal from the world, or a faithful endurance through it, being sober and awake so the Second Coming doesn't catch us unaware?

"Watch ye therefore, and pray always, that ye may be accounted worthy to escape all these things that shall come to pass, and to stand before the Son of man."
(Luke 21:36)

This verse has become a staple in pretribulation proof-texting. Interestingly, when it appears to support their doctrine, dispensationalists suddenly stop assigning it to another dispensation. They claim this is Jesus teaching the Church how to escape the tribulation—by being accounted worthy. But here's where the logic begins to unravel. When verses contradict pretribulation theology, dispensationalists quickly reassign them to Israel. When verses seem useful to their position, they forget about the dispensational distinctions they themselves imposed.

So, we should pause and ask: does this verse belong to the Church or not? You can't have it both ways. If Jesus is speaking to the Church here, then we must take the whole chapter seriously including the parts that describe persecution, betrayal, endurance, and martyrdom. And if He's not speaking to the Church, then using this verse as a promise of rapture becomes inconsistent with their own system.

Because in the world of dispensationalism, every verse must be carefully chopped, sorted, and reassigned like parts in a warehouse. Maybe this verse doesn't apply to believers at all. Maybe it's just for "Israel," right? You've got to get your dispensations right! See how convenient that game is? But let's be honest—if every uncomfortable verse can be outsourced to another group based on a timeline chart, then maybe the problem isn't the passage. Maybe it's the prescription. Maybe they just haven't dispensed it correctly this time.

But sarcasm aside, the text refuses to cooperate with that logic. Jesus is plainly warning His followers—those who would face persecution, deception, tribulation, and judgment. And He commands vigilance, prayer, and strength. He's not outlining a disappearing act, but a faithful stand.

This is where context becomes everything. What does it mean to be accounted worthy to escape? And escape what, exactly? Jesus has just described signs in the heavens, distress of nations, men's hearts failing for fear, and the powers of heaven being shaken.

The escape is not from persecution or martyrdom because earlier in the same chapter, He warns that some of His followers will be betrayed, hated, and even put to death. So clearly, escape cannot mean exemption from suffering.

Rather, the escape in view is from the wrath of God that falls when Christ returns. It is not an escape from tribulation, but from being condemned with the wicked. To stand before the Son of Man is not to float away in safety—it is to be found faithful, unashamed, and prepared at His appearing. That's what Jesus is saying: be watchful, pray always, and live in such a way that you are not caught off guard when judgment falls.

This harmonizes beautifully with another passage that rarely appears in pretribulation proof texts:

"And they departed from the presence of the council, rejoicing that they were counted worthy to suffer shame for his name."
(Acts 5:41)

Is this a contradiction? Are we to be accounted worthy to escape or worthy to suffer? The answer is both. There is no contradiction when you rightly divide the Word. We are counted worthy to suffer with Christ now, and we are counted worthy to escape the wrath that falls upon the ungodly when He returns. These two realities are not in conflict—they are part of the same faithful walk.

The irony is sharp. Pretribulationists cherry-pick Luke 21:36 as if it supports a secret rapture, while ignoring the rest of the chapter where Jesus describes His people enduring tribulation. They grasp at the word "escape" without examining what is actually being escaped. They redefine the Church to exclude any reference to endurance or suffering, even though Scripture consistently honors those who overcome by faith.

In the end, the dispensational framework demands a theology of survival, not of faithfulness. It selectively assembles verses to support a doctrine that cannot survive the full context of Scripture. But the gospel calls us higher. We are not cowards running from the battlefield—we are soldiers standing firm, praying always, that we may be found worthy to stand before the King when He comes.

Biblical Usage of 'Escape' ἐκφεύγω

The Greek word for "escape" is ἐκφεύγω (ekpheugō): according to Thayer's Greek Lexicon, it means "to flee out of, flee forth, seek safety in flight; to escape." It denotes purposeful action taken to avoid peril, typically by moving away from danger under one's own initiative. It is used in verses like Matthew 10:23 and Luke 21:21 where believers are told to flee persecution, not be removed supernaturally. It implies human action under divine direction, not a secret rapture.

"But when they persecute you in this city, flee (ekpheugō) ye into another..."
(Matthew 10:23)

"Then let them which are in Judaea flee (ekpheugō) to the mountains..."
(Luke 21:21)

Even more support comes from additional uses of ekpheugō, which reinforce the idea of escaping by one's own strength and alertness and not by divine disappearance:

"And the keeper of the prison awaking out of his sleep, and seeing the prison doors open, he drew out his sword, and would have killed himself, supposing that the prisoners had been fled (ekpheugō)."
(Acts 16:27)

Here, ekpheugō clearly refers to a natural escape of prisoners fleeing the cell, not being raptured away. The jailer assumed they had run by human action, not vanished by divine removal. Another example comes during a violent confrontation in Ephesus:

"And the man in whom the evil spirit was leaped on them, and overcame them, and prevailed against them, so that they fled (ekpheugō) out of that house naked and wounded."
(Acts 19:16)

This reinforces a key distinction: the biblical concept of escape is not passive removal but active perseverance. It involves deliberate, obedient flight from danger and not an involuntary snatching away. The kind of escape Jesus speaks of in Luke 21:36 is not something that happens to someone without their participation. It is a call to vigilance, to readiness, and to faithful endurance. It is the kind of escape that comes through obeying God's warning and acting decisively in the face of approaching judgment.

Whether the command is to flee (ekpheugō) or to be counted worthy, the emphasis is on the believer's preparedness and response, not on being secretly extracted without suffering. The believer must be spiritually alert, watching, praying, and discerning the times. This is entirely consistent with the warnings Jesus gives throughout the Olivet Discourse, where endurance, not evacuation, is the mark of the faithful.

And this brings us to how the passage has been preserved and transmitted. The underlying manuscripts and the choices of the King James translators both confirm that Luke 21:36 was never intended to suggest a vanishing act. The focus remains where it always has been—faithful endurance unto the end. The call is not to vanish, but to stand. Not to escape from faithfulness, but to endure through tribulation until the Son of Man returns in glory.

The Strength to Endure

By what means do we flee? If Jesus is not describing an involuntary removal, such as being snatched away without warning in a secret rapture, then the flight He speaks of must involve spiritual fortitude. It must draw upon the believer's readiness, moral courage, and discernment. The question is not simply whether we flee, but how. And the answer Scripture provides is consistent: we flee through faithfulness, vigilance, and the ability to respond rightly in the midst of trial.

"Watch ye therefore, and pray always, that ye may be accounted worthy to escape all these things that shall come to pass, and to stand before the Son of man."
(Luke 21:36, KJV)

This verse aligns perfectly with the biblical pattern of flight seen throughout Scripture. It is not about being mysteriously removed without effort. It is about being accounted worthy to flee actively, consciously, and obediently. The context reinforces the themes of alertness, spiritual integrity, and endurance under pressure.

If we compare the King James Version to many modern translations, we notice that it does not include the phrase "that you may be strong" (κατισχύσητε), which is found in several Alexandrian manuscripts. This is because the KJV is based on the Textus Receptus, a manuscript tradition that renders Luke 21:36 as a call to be "accounted worthy." The distinction is more than textual, it is theological. The KJV preserves the moral and eschatological weight of Jesus' words by emphasizing worthiness rather than strength.

Both manuscript families ultimately affirm the same spiritual theme: preparedness in the face of trial. Yet many dispensationalists distort even the KJV wording, forcing it to imply a supernatural disappearance. They seize on the word "escape" as if it means removal from the battlefield, when the very verse speaks of standing. There is no promise of vanishing, only the urgent call to endure. The emphasis is not on being strong enough to disappear, but on being faithful enough to stand.

Turning to the Alexandrian manuscripts, we find that some include the word κατισχύσητε (katischuō)—a verb that means to be strong, to prevail, or to be able to withstand. Lexically, it is built from κατά (kata, meaning "down" or "according to") and (ἰσχύω ischuō, meaning "to be able," "to have strength"). It conveys the sense of prevailing strength or resilience under pressure. The word appears in passages like Matthew 16:18, where Jesus says, "the gates of hell shall not prevail (katischuō) against it," and Luke 23:23, describing the voices of the mob that prevailed in demanding Jesus' crucifixion.

In Luke 21:36, when this word appears in Alexandrian manuscripts, it strengthens the idea that the believer must not merely be morally upright but spiritually fortified. Even here, the message remains consistent. It is not about disappearance. It is about resilience. It speaks of a spiritual strength that meets the hour of testing. These manuscripts confirm the pattern we see throughout

Scripture: the believer flees by wisdom and alertness, not by being miraculously evacuated. There is no escape hatch. There is a call to overcome.

Modern translations make this even clearer:

· *"That you may have strength to escape..." (NASB, BLB, LEB)*
· *"That you may be strong enough to escape..." (Lexham)*
· *"To have strength to escape all these things..." (Holman CSB)*

These renderings help correct the misconception. The focus is not on vanishing but on standing firm. The believer is not promised exemption from suffering. They are exhorted to be unwavering when the hour comes.

Whether we read from the Textus Receptus or the Alexandrian text, the message is the same: the faithful must be spiritually equipped to flee. And that leads to the deeper question— why flee? Because what lies ahead is not simply hardship, but deception, lawlessness, and judgment. The purpose of this flight is not to escape discomfort, but to remain uncompromised in a world unraveling under divine indignation.

So, when Jesus says, "pray always, that ye may be accounted worthy to escape," He is not teaching evacuation. He is summoning His people to readiness. The call is to stand when others fall, to endure when others cave, and to flee sin, compromise, and fear by walking in truth. This is not a passive deliverance. It is a pursuit of holiness. It is not automatic. It is achieved through steadfast faithfulness, just as the early church was counted worthy to suffer for His name.

To Stand Before the Son of Man

What is the goal of having this spiritual fortitude? And what is the ultimate purpose of that endurance?

"...to stand before the Son of man."
(Luke 21:36)

This powerful phrase reappears at the opening of the sixth seal in Revelation, a scene of cosmic upheaval and divine judgment:

"And the kings of the earth... said to the mountains and rocks, Fall on us... for the great day of his wrath is come; and who shall be able to stand?"
(Revelation 6:15–17)

This is the very thing Jesus warned us to escape; not the earth itself, but the terror, shame, and unpreparedness that overtakes the ungodly at the unveiling of the Lamb's wrath. The warning is not about location, but condition, not about distance from the world, but about spiritual readiness before the face of divine judgment. The question thunders from the text: "Who shall be able to stand?" It is not a metaphor for ordinary hardship, but a declaration of final judgment at the climactic return of Christ. Once again, we find ourselves not at the beginning of the tribulation, but at its culmination the moment when wrath is poured out at the Second Coming.

Are you seeing the pattern yet? Many sincere believers within the dispensational tradition have read these verses through a framework that shifts key moments of judgment and deliverance to the beginning of the tribulation. In doing so, they often reinterpret verses meant to describe the Second Coming as if they speak of a prior, secret event. This rearranges the biblical sequence, flipping the prophetic structure and inadvertently diminishing the comfort and resolve these passages were meant to give the Church as it endures to the end.

Yet this interpretive pattern stands in direct tension with what Paul clearly affirmed: "For God hath not appointed us to wrath, but to obtain salvation by our Lord Jesus Christ" (1 Thessalonians 5:9). That wrath is not the tribulation in general, but the climactic outpouring of judgment at the return of Christ. Paul, like Jesus, grounds our hope not in early removal, but in final deliverance. Salvation is not appointed before tribulation but revealed after faithfulness. And once again, the pattern holds. The saints are not taken out before the fire. They are preserved in it, refined through it, and revealed after it.

And what follows this wrath? Let's go back to the book of Revelation. Who shall stand before Him? Isn't it striking that we find the same wording in Christ's warning in Luke: "...to stand before the Son of man." The very goal of being counted worthy to escape is to stand. The thunderous question imposed by Seal Six—"Who shall be able to stand?"—is not rhetorical. It is answered, soundly and gloriously.

The next chapter gives us the answer. A great multitude, vindicated, victorious, and visible.

"After this I beheld, and, lo, a great multitude, which no man could number, of all nations, and kindreds, and people, and tongues, stood before the throne, and before the Lamb, clothed with white robes, and palms in their hands... These are they which came out of great tribulation, and have washed their robes, and made them white in the blood of the Lamb."
(Revelation 7:9, 14)

This is the fulfillment of Luke 21:36. The faithful will stand before the Son of Man. And here they are—standing, not vanishing. These saints did not escape the tribulation by disappearance, but by perseverance. They endured. They were not spared the furnace, but they came through it refined, triumphant, and prepared to stand before the Lamb.

And how did they escape? Jesus tells us plainly in the verses leading up to His command to pray for escape:

"Take heed to yourselves, lest at any time your hearts be overcharged with surfeiting, and drunkenness, and cares of this life, and so that day come upon you unawares. For as a snare shall it come on all them that dwell on the face of the whole earth."
(Luke 21:34–35)

This is the real danger the thing Jesus calls us to escape. Not hardship. Not existence. But spiritual stupor. It is the danger of being lulled to sleep by the distractions of this world and caught off guard when the Day of the Lord springs like a snare. Jesus is not offering a trapdoor out of persecution. He is sounding the alarm to stay spiritually awake.

The faithful do not vanish. They endure. We flee by staying alert, resisting the intoxicating pull of the world, and anchoring ourselves in the hope of His return. This is what it means to be "accounted worthy" or "strong enough to escape." Not because we disappear, but because we are not overtaken like the world. While kings and captains cry out for the rocks to hide them, the saints stand. And why? Because we are not appointed to wrath, but to obtain salvation through our Lord Jesus Christ.

The faithful, watchful saints escape deception, avoid being entangled in worldly distractions, and flee compromise. They are preserved through trial, not removed from it. They are kept from falling, not kept from facing the storm. And in the end, they stand exactly where Jesus said they would: before the Son of Man, just like the great multitude in Revelation 7.

The pattern is clear. The saints will be present during the tribulation—opposed, persecuted, and worn down by the Antichrist. But the Lord is not unjust. He promises to recompense tribulation on those who trouble His people and to grant rest to the faithful at His coming. This cycle of endurance and divine justice echoes throughout Scripture.

Even when the law of Moses had no remedy for Israel's unfaithfulness, God broke through the boundaries of legal failure with a higher law of love, saying, "Return unto me." That same redemptive heart beats for the Church today. If you have felt overwhelmed or abandoned by the idea of suffering, know this: God does not abandon His own. He restores. He vindicates. He brings justice.

Next Revelation:
Interpreting Prophecy Properly

Some prophecies are rooted in a specific land or people. Others unfold on a global scale. When we overlook the difference, we risk misreading the entire prophetic landscape. Blurring the lines between regional and universal leads not to clarity, but confusion and we find ourselves drawing conclusions the text never intended to support.

Chapter 7:
Interpreting Prophecy Properly

When reading prophecy, one of the most important skills we can develop is discernment. Not every event in Scripture carries the same scope. Some are regional, affecting a specific land, people, or city. Others are global, impacting the entire world, or at least having widespread implications. Biblical prophecy often zooms in and out, shifting focus between the nations and Israel, between a single city and the entire inhabited earth. If we do not make this distinction, we end up forcing global meaning onto local texts, or worse, we overlook global warnings because we are too focused on national ones.

Let us begin with a few examples of global consequences:

"For God so loved the world, that he gave his only begotten Son..."
(John 3:16)

This is not a message confined to Israel. It is for every nation, every people, every person. The scope is universal and redemptive.

"And there went out another horse that was red: and power was given to him... to take peace from the earth, and that they should kill one another..."
(Revelation 6:4)

That is not a local disturbance. That is global war, civil breakdown, and widespread bloodshed. The context is apocalyptic in scope, not confined to a single region.

"A great multitude, which no man could number, of all nations, and kindreds, and people, and tongues..."
(Revelation 7:9)

This confirms that tribulation is not a regional issue. It spans the globe, targeting the faithful across every nation. The diversity of the redeemed shows that persecution will not be isolated to a single ethnic group or national border.

Now let us look at some examples of regional prophecy:

"And the sixth angel poured out his vial... and the water thereof was dried up, that the way of the kings of the east might be prepared."
(Revelation 16:12)

This refers to the Euphrates River—a literal, strategic location with specific military implications. This is clearly a regional event.

"There was a great earthquake, and the tenth part of the city fell"
(Revelation 11:13)

That is Jerusalem, one city experiencing an earthquake judgment. Again, a regional fulfillment.

Here is where dispensationalism often falters. It globalizes what is regional and isolates what is global, frequently based on arguments from silence. One of the clearest examples of this is the interpretation of Daniel 9:27. Many dispensationalists argue that this verse proves the Church is absent from the tribulation because the prophecy focuses on Israel and Jerusalem. But the text never says the Church is excluded.

This is where the logical fallacy of silence creeps in by inferring absence from a lack of mention. But silence is not a substitute for proof. Absence of evidence is not evidence of absence. The fact that the Church is not named in Daniel 9:27 does not mean it vanishes from God's plan during the tribulation. It simply means the lens of the prophecy, at that moment, is focused on Israel. The camera is zoomed in regionally, not because the rest of the world disappears, but because that particular sequence centers on Jerusalem.

Arguments from silence do not preclude the Church from the tribulation. The failure here is not due to lack of Scripture, but due to the lack of interpretive discipline. This is the difference between proof and evidence versus presupposition and conjecture. When doctrine is built on what a text does not say, instead of what it plainly declares, the result is a theological house of cards that is unstable and unable to stand under scrutiny.

To be fair, dispensationalism is not a monolith. While the majority of popular and classical dispensationalist teachers such as LaHaye and Lindsey promote the idea that the tribulation is exclusively for Israel, some within the camp, especially more nuanced or progressive voices, acknowledge that the tribulation has global ramifications. They recognize that while Daniel's prophecy is regionally centered, that does not imply the Church is absent from the global scene. However, these views remain minority positions, often overlooked in mainstream pretribulational teaching.

So yes, Daniel 9:27 is a regional prophecy. It concerns Jerusalem, the temple, and the people of Israel. But that does not mean the Church has vanished. It simply means the focus of that specific text is on Israel, just as other prophecies focus on the Church, the Gentiles, or the world at large. The prophetic lens zooms in and out, capturing different layers of God's redemptive plan. We will dig deeper into this tension in Chapter 8.

Even when we consider the temple in 2 Thessalonians 2, which certainly refers to a Jewish temple consistent with what we see in Revelation, the scope of the Antichrist's actions remains much broader. Paul writes that the man of sin "opposeth and exalteth himself above all that is called God, or that is worshipped" (2 Thessalonians 2:4). That is a claim to universal supremacy. And since the saints coming out of the tribulation are from every nation, it follows that his persecution is widespread, not limited to Israel or the Jewish people alone.

Let's be clear: regional conflicts in prophecy do not negate global ones, and global judgments do not cancel out local fulfillments. Sound interpretation does not force one to eclipse the other. It harmonizes them. And when we follow that principle, we begin to see a layered, consistent, and Spirit-breathed view of the end times, one that exposes the selectivity and escapism of much modern dispensationalism while restoring the plain power of what Scripture actually says.

Literalism and Its Limits

Then there are the overly literalistic interpretations. There is a difference between taking Scripture seriously and taking it simplistically. Wooden literalism, the habit of reading prophecy in a flat, surface-level way, ignores context, genre, audience, and authorial intent. And it is one of the easiest ways to fall into error. In contrast, natural literal interpretation recognizes figures of speech and literary devices while still affirming real fulfillment.

Consider Mark 1:5:

"And there went out unto him all the land of Judaea, and they of Jerusalem, and were all baptized of him in the river of Jordan..."

No one believes this means every single individual in Judea literally showed up. It is a figure of speech, a common way to emphasize how widespread the response was. Even the most rigid literalists will acknowledge that "all" in this passage does not mean every person without exception.

But somehow, when we arrive at Revelation 13:16, the same interpretive flexibility vanishes:

"And he causeth all, both small and great, rich and poor, free and bond, to receive a mark..."
(Revelation 13:16)

Here, the same teachers who rightly accept a rhetorical "all" in Mark 1:5 insist that the "all" in Revelation 13:16 must mean every man, woman, and child on earth without exception. This is where the inconsistency of interpretation becomes problematic. The pretribulational argument relies on an exhaustive reading of this passage to support a rigid doctrinal framework: namely, that every person on the planet—except for the 144,000 and a narrowly defined group of "tribulation saints"—takes the mark of the Beast. This creates an artificial dichotomy: the only categories allowed are the marked and the glorified. It leaves no room for any unaligned outliers, no nuance, no category for dissenters, no space for survivors who are neither sealed by God nor aligned with the Beast.

But the intent of Revelation 13:16 is not to declare absolute, mathematical totality. It is to communicate the sweeping reach of the Beast's edict across social strata. The phrase "small and great, rich and poor, free and bond" is a literary device an idiomatic construction meant to emphasize that no class of person will be exempt from the demand. The Antichrist's mandate will be socially comprehensive, not individually exhaustive. It will not matter whether someone is a peasant or a prince, a servant or a sovereign. The mark will be imposed wherever his political reach can extend. But that does not mean it will be universally received without exception.

This is not an abstract point. It has real interpretive weight. As we will explore in the Rebuttal and Answer section later in this chapter, the Beast's dominion falls short of total global assimilation when Christ returns. His kingdom, though immense, will not achieve absolute control. The Antichrist will rise as a dominating superpower and will exercise influence over many nations, but Scripture reveals that his empire will be contested, incomplete, and ultimately shattered by the appearing of the Lord.

Therefore, the point of Revelation 13:16 is not to present a binary without nuance. It is to declare that regardless of social standing, the Beast's command will be enforced within his immediate domain and under his sphere of influence. The wording does not preclude the existence of non-compliant outliers. In fact, Scripture explicitly affirms that there are those who refuse those whose names are written in the Lamb's book of life (Revelation 13:8), those who are beheaded for their faith (Revelation 20:4), and those who stand with the Lamb in victory (Revelation 14:1–5).

What the pretribulational system often ignores is that some of these refusers are not sealed saints, nor glorified martyrs. They are unnamed outliers unmarked, unexalted, and yet spared. These are the forgotten figures of prophetic narrative. They do not fit neatly into pretrib categories, so they are often left out of the discussion altogether. But we will return to them shortly in the Rebuttal and Answer section, where their presence is not only acknowledged, but elevated as a key to unlocking a more faithful, Spirit-led reading of the text.

And then comes the key verse:

"And all that dwell upon the earth shall worship him, whose names are not written in the book of life of the Lamb slain from the foundation of the world."
(Revelation 13:8)

This verse is crucial. It does not say every human being without exception worships the Beast. It gives a qualifier—those whose names are not written in the book of life. That is the exhaustive group in question. The determining factor is not universal participation, but covenantal exclusion. The mark is not imposed upon every last individual. It is given to those who are not recorded in the Lamb's book.

And that subtle distinction dismantles the pretrib argument that relies on a mathematically universal interpretation of Revelation 13. Because if the only ones who worship the Beast are those whose names are not written in the book of life, then by contrast, those who are written in the book do not. This means the "all" is conditional, not absolute.

This reveals a larger hermeneutical issue. The same dispensational teachers who acknowledge rhetorical language in one verse apply rigid literalism in another when it suits their framework. Scripture, however, is not to be selectively interpreted for convenience. The text governs the meaning, not the presupposition.

The Faulty Logic of the Literalistic Argument

The goal of this wooden literalistic interpretation is to undermine posttribulationism with a faulty logic chain. The argument goes like this:

- If everyone takes the mark except the so-called tribulation saints,
- And if the rapture happens at the end,
- Then no one would be left to populate the millennial reign.

Therefore, the rapture must happen before the tribulation, or else we are left with a millennial kingdom with no human survivors.

But this entire chain is built on a flawed premise. It assumes absolute literalism where the text uses rhetorical scope. It ignores the nuance that some will resist the mark, that remnants always remain, and that God knows how to preserve His own, even through wrath.

In reality, the "all" in Revelation 13:16 functions just like it does in Mark 1:5. It does not signal mathematical totality. The Beast's reach is vast, but not without exception. And when that logic threatens a doctrinal framework, the flexibility many dispensational teachers show elsewhere is conveniently absent.

The Olivet Discourse and Global Application

This same misreading occurs in the Olivet Discourse, where some claim Jesus was only addressing Jews, despite the fact that the discourse opens with the disciples asking about the sign of His coming and the end of the world (Matthew 24:3). Jesus' answer spans wars, tribulation, deception, and endurance, all culminating in "the coming of the Son of man" after the tribulation, when He sends His angels to gather His elect from the four winds (Matthew 24:29–31).

That is not limited to Judea. It is global. And the "elect" are gathered from across the earth, not from a single nation or group. If the coming of the Son of Man is at the end, and He gathers His elect from everywhere, then the Olivet Discourse is clearly meant for every believer, not just the Jewish remnant. Once again, rigid dispensational filters collapse under the weight of Jesus' own words.

A prime example of this interpretive inconsistency arises with the fig tree Matthew 24:32–34. Many pretribulationists insist the fig tree represents the modern nation of Israel. They argue that when Israel is gathered back into the land, that generation will not pass until all the events Jesus described are fulfilled. But the problem is what follows next. Jesus explicitly says the elect are gathered immediately after the tribulation.

So, which is it? Is the fulfillment of the fig tree parable before the tribulation, or after it? Is the gathering of the elect before the tribulation, or after? When is the reunification they claim the fig tree symbolizes? These contradictory timelines cannot be harmonized within the pretrib framework without severe interpretive contortions.

This is a textbook case of the ad hoc fallacy: explanations produced on the fly to defend a doctrine, rather than derived organically from a consistent reading of the text. To be fair, most people who employ these tactics do not realize they are doing so. They genuinely believe they are defending the truth, doing it with sincerity and to the best of their ability. But sincerity does not make a contradiction disappear. And when the interpretive structure breaks down, it often does so under the weight of contradictions introduced only to protect a preconceived system.

Many have been sold the idea that there is no hope without a pretribulational rapture. That to suffer is to be forsaken. But I am here to say the opposite. There is hope without it. Hope that is not built on escape, but on endurance. Christ will wipe away every tear. He will avenge His saints with His wrath. Even in the tribulation, Christ is for us and not against us. He is with us in the fire, not simply waiting for us on the other side of it.

Revelation's Structure and Symbolism

Real interpretation does not flatten Scripture to serve our theories. It submits to the shape of the text, even when that shape disrupts our comfort. The book of Revelation is not a neatly packaged, linear timeline. It is a prophetic tapestry woven with symbolism, spirals, and snapshots from heaven's perspective. When we impose a wooden or overly systematic framework onto this apocalyptic vision, we distort its meaning rather than unveil its message.

One of the most consistent mistakes in pretribulational interpretation is the assumption that Revelation unfolds in a strict, chapter-by-chapter sequence of end-time events. But this idea quickly crumbles under the text itself. Revelation employs a cyclical structure, in which the same time period is retold from multiple angles. Scholars refer to this as recapitulation.

Each cycle in Revelation emphasizes a different dimension of the end: the suffering of the saints, the judgment of the wicked, the wrath of God, the triumph of Christ, and the final vindication of His people. These overlapping visions do not confuse the timeline. They clarify it. Like multiple witnesses giving testimony to the same event, each pass through the prophetic vision adds another layer of depth and truth. Much like the four Gospels harmonize distinct yet united views of Christ's life, Revelation provides a multifaceted account of the final confrontation between good and evil. The difference is, Revelation accomplishes this layered storytelling within one book.

We see the pattern clearly in Revelation 6, where the sixth seal erupts in cosmic disturbance and the wrath of the Lamb. This moment of eschatological climax directly parallels Revelation 19, where Christ appears on a white horse to judge and make war.

"For the great day of his wrath is come; and who shall be able to stand?"
(Revelation 6:17)

This is not the beginning of wrath. It is the climax. Later chapters, such as Revelation 11, 14, and 16, circle back to this same endpoint. Each time, they add a new dimension to the final confrontation.

Revelation 11 ends with the temple of God opened in heaven, flashes of lightning, voices, thunderings, and a great hailstorm and a vision of divine judgment unleashed.

Revelation 14 gives us the image of the Son of Man on the clouds with a sharp sickle:

"Thrust in thy sickle, and reap: for the time is come for thee to reap; for the harvest of the earth is ripe."
(Revelation 14:15)

This echoes the harvest judgment described in Matthew 13 and the prophetic reaping in Joel 3.

Revelation 16 reaches a crescendo as a great voice from the temple declares:

"It is done."
(Revelation 16:17)

And immediately afterward, Babylon falls:

"And the great city was divided into three parts, and the cities of the nations fell... and great Babylon came in remembrance before God, to give unto her the cup of the wine of the fierceness of his wrath."
(Revelation 16:19)

Yet Babylon falls again in Revelation 17 and 18. Not because the event is happening a second time, but because the perspective shifts. Chapter 17 gives us Babylon's mystical identity, her spiritual adultery, and her alliance with kings. Chapter 18 then reveals her material downfall, the collapse of her economy, and the wailing of merchants and monarchs who benefited from her corruption.

These are not two Babylons. They are two camera angles on the same judgment. Two prophetic lenses capturing the same moment from different spiritual vantage points. If Revelation followed a strict linear timeline, we would be forced to believe that Babylon falls twice. But that would be both unnecessary and illogical. The cyclical structure resolves this tension beautifully.

Just as the Gospels give us four accounts of Christ's first coming, Revelation gives us multiple views of His second. Each cycle reinforces the others. Each repetition testifies again to the justice of God, the endurance of the saints, and the certainty of Christ's victory.

This is the Spirit's way of engraving the truth deeper with each pass. And it demands that we pay attention not just to the events, but to the pattern itself.

Daniel's Prophetic Pattern

This technique of layered cyclical prophecy is not unique to Revelation. The prophet Daniel employs the same method with striking consistency. He presents overlapping visions that reexamine the same prophetic period from different angles each cycle adding depth, clarity, and divine emphasis. These repetitions are not redundant; they function like multiple courtroom witnesses testifying to the same event, each revealing new details that confirm the bigger picture.

In Daniel 2, the prophet is shown a great metallic statue representing successive world kingdoms: Babylon, Medo-Persia, Greece, and Rome culminating in a final kingdom shattered by the stone cut without hands. This vision gives a sweeping, top-level political overview.

Then in Daniel 7, the same succession of empires is revealed again, but this time symbolized as beasts ferocious, unstable, and increasingly violent. This cycle offers a theological and moral perspective, exposing the spiritual nature of these kingdoms and the blasphemous rise of the final horn that persecutes the saints.

And again, in Daniel 8, the prophecy zooms in further, focusing more narrowly on specific conflicts between Medo-Persia and Greece, eventually zeroing in on a fierce king who defiles the sanctuary and magnifies himself against the Prince of princes.

These visions are not meant to be stacked sequentially like chapters in a novel. They are meant to be seen as cycles each run-through covering familiar territory with a new lens, reinforcing the same endpoint: a showdown between the saints of God and a final blasphemous ruler, followed by divine deliverance and the establishment of the everlasting kingdom.

To understand Revelation, we must recognize this same pattern at work. Revelation is not a linear scroll, but a divine spiral. Events are played out to their climax, and then the narrative backs up and runs through the cycle again from a fresh perspective. This is what I call in simple terms "cyclic chronology." Each layer peels back another veil, showing us not only what will happen, but how heaven views the unfolding drama. Just as Daniel's visions climax with the triumph of the saints and the defeat of the oppressor, so too does each cycle in Revelation end with the return of Christ, the fall of the wicked, and the vindication of those who remained faithful.

Far from confusing, this structure is clarifying. It highlights what matters most and reinforces the unshakable hope that no matter how intense the darkness becomes, the Lamb wins and His people share in that victory.

The Problem with Hyper-Literalistic Interpretations

Another flaw in the dispensational reading of Revelation is that the inconsistent literalism often applied to its symbols.
Take, for example, the locusts described in Revelation 9. In popular level pretrib circles, especially among televangelists, prophecy fiction authors, and YouTube ministries, these locusts are said to represent modern military helicopters. The idea is that John, lacking the vocabulary for advanced machinery, described what he saw in first-century terms: metallic wings, stinging tails, roaring sounds, and faces like men.

While this view attempts to bridge the gap between the ancient and the modern, it ultimately relies more on imaginative speculation than on biblical context or prophetic patterns. To be fair, not all dispensational scholars hold to this interpretation, but the method it represents remains problematic. It tries to force every symbol into a direct, one-to-one match with contemporary objects, while ignoring the layered spiritual realities the imagery was meant to convey.

Here is the inconsistency: if the locusts are helicopters, must we also imagine the sword from Christ's mouth as a sharpened weapon of steel? Is the sea of glass a physical ocean? Or is it something more? This is not simply a matter of literal versus symbolic interpretation. It is about understanding how apocalyptic language conveys both real judgment and transcendent meaning.

Furthermore, if such literalism were consistently applied, it would quickly become untenable. Symbolism in Revelation serves as a bridge, connecting tangible realities with spiritual truths. The consistent literalist approach collapses because it fails to recognize this vital hermeneutical principle.

Symbols Are Spiritually Real

Biblical symbolism is not empty poetry. It reveals eternal realities through visionary imagery. The Lamb represents the sacrificial authority of Christ. The sword represents the unstoppable power of His word. The locusts, terrifying as they are, represent real judgment and demonic torment unleashed upon the earth. They are not modern war machines, but spiritual agents described in symbolic form because their origin and impact are spiritual in nature, even as they convey literal consequences within symbolic language.

What we must avoid is turning Revelation into either a newspaper horoscope for end-time military tech or a purely mystical book divorced from real events. It is neither. It is prophetic literature, where symbols are vivid not to confuse, but to expose the spiritual forces behind political power, religious deception, and global persecution.

Endurance Reassigned and the Imbalance in Literalism

In dispensational frameworks there is often a dangerous imbalance. Some hopeful promises, such as the return of Christ and His reign on earth, are rightly taken literally. But the present call to endurance and overcoming is frequently reassigned to a future group called "tribulation saints." This leaves the Church expecting an escape instead of preparing for perseverance. Rather than encouraging believers to overcome in the face of trial, the focus shifts toward avoiding tribulation altogether.

You cannot take every frightening image hyper-literally while relocating the promises of endurance and victory to another group. That is not faithful interpretation; it is theological cherry-picking. When Revelation's judgments are magnified into looming terror but the Church's call to faithfulness is reassigned or minimized, Revelation ceases to be a book of living courage and becomes a manual of fear.

Revelation reveals Jesus Christ, not helicopter warfare or black ops conspiracies. The locusts represent something far more ancient and cosmic than modern weaponry: the opening of spiritual judgment upon a world in rebellion. And the Lamb, the Bride, the altar, and the New Jerusalem are not vague metaphors. They are spiritually real, eschatologically grounded, and destined to break into human history.

This is not escapism. It is a divine confrontation. The message of Revelation is not "you will be gone." It is:

"Be thou faithful unto death, and I will give thee a crown of life." *(Revelation 2:10)*

The Pattern of Revelation: Persecution and Vindication

The pattern throughout Revelation is unmistakable:
- **Revelation 6 (fifth seal):** the martyrs cry out, "How long, O Lord?"
- **Revelation 11:** the two witnesses are slain by the beast and then raised in glory.
- **Revelation 13:** the beast is given power to make war with the saints and to overcome them.
- **Revelation 14:** the 144,000 stands with the Lamb on Mount Zion, after His return, echoing the prophets who declared the Lord would roar from Zion (Joel 3:16 and Amos 1:2).
- **Revelation 19–20:** the beast and false prophet are cast into the lake of fire, and the saints reign with Christ.

This cyclical pattern acts like multiple witnesses testifying to the same event from different angles, adding new depth in layers, much like how the four Gospels present Christ's life and ministry from various perspectives. Revelation, though a single book, approaches its central events repeatedly from fresh vantage points, reinforcing the clarity and significance of its message.

The rhythm is clear: persecution, patience, power, and promise. That is the heartbeat of posttribulational theology, not exemption from tribulation, but vindication through endurance.

Rebuttal & Answer:
Who Survives to Enter the Millennium?

One objection frequently raised against a posttribulational return of Christ is the claim that some people must survive the tribulation in natural bodies to populate the millennium. The argument typically goes like this: if Jesus returns at the end, and the righteous are all resurrected or glorified, and the wicked are all judged, who remains to repopulate the earth? Many pretrib believers consider this the definitive argument against the posttrib position. However, upon closer inspection, this claim presents yet another false dichotomy. Pretribulationists must assert an absolute binary scenario, suggesting that everyone who is not among the glorified saints or tribulation saints must have taken the mark of the beast and been judged accordingly. In their framework, the saints who survive the tribulation repopulate the earth during the millennium precisely because they missed the rapture, while those who died during the tribulation gain immediate access to glory. This raises significant theological and logical questions. One might ask: does this not imply partiality on God's part? Scripture clearly states that God is not a respecter of persons (Acts 10:34). Unfortunately, this unintended consequence arises from classical dispensationalism's binary model.

This simplistic scenario is foundational to pretrib arguments, designed preemptively to discredit the posttrib model. However, this binary invention falls apart once we harmonize overlooked and often conveniently ignored scriptures, revealing a more complex and consistent biblical reality.

Scripture nowhere teaches that every single person on earth is slain at the Second Coming. Rather, it presents a nuanced, layered picture:

"And the kings of the earth, and the great men, and the rich men... hid themselves in the dens and in the rocks of the mountains... For the great day of his wrath is come; and who shall be able to stand?"
(Revelation 6:15–17)

"And I saw the beast, and the kings of the earth, and their armies, gathered together to make war... And the remnant were slain with the sword of him that sat upon the horse..."
(Revelation 19:19–21)

"And the beast was taken, and with him the false prophet... These both were cast alive into a lake of fire..."
(Revelation 19:20)

"And the third angel followed them, saying with a loud voice, If any man worship the beast and his image, and receive his mark in his forehead, or in his hand, the same shall drink of the wine of the wrath of God..."
(Revelation 14:9–10)

"And I saw the souls of them that were beheaded for the witness of Jesus... and they lived and reigned with Christ a thousand years."
(Revelation 20:4–6)

"And it shall come to pass, that every one that is left of all the nations which came against Jerusalem shall even go up... to worship the King, the Lord of hosts..."
(Zechariah 14:16)

These passages collectively show a more balanced judgment, distinguishing clearly between those who worshiped the beast and those who did not. Not everyone fits neatly into the categories prescribed by dispensational teaching. Revelation portrays various groups and outcomes, some judged severely, others given an opportunity to live under Christ's righteous rule during the millennial reign.

The complexity of biblical eschatology should caution against overly simplified binary frameworks. God's pattern of justice is always thorough yet nuanced, distinguishing between rebellious worshippers of the beast and those who, though involved in the conflict, did not align spiritually with the Antichrist. Scripture consistently demonstrates God's mercy alongside His judgment, preserving remnants even amid great upheaval.

Therefore, the pretribulation binary argument—intended to close the discussion—actually opens it wider when examined carefully. A balanced biblical interpretation shows that God's judgment is precise, redemptive, and consistent with His character, rather than arbitrary or partial.

The Distinction Between Combatants and Covenant Judgment & The Limits of the Beast's Dominion

Let's take a more nuanced look at some of these verses because naturally, detractors will interpret the verses previously listed through a dispensational lens. Pretribulationists often overlook the presence of enemy combatants and other outliers who do not take the mark. A critical point emerges here:

"And the remnant were slain with the sword of him that sat upon the horse…"
(Revelation 19:21)

This remnant is notably not cast into the lake of fire like the beast-worshipers. They are killed by Christ's judgment, but not consigned immediately to eternal torment. This indicates an important distinction. These individuals were military outliers who fought alongside the Antichrist's empire, yet did not spiritually align themselves with the beast through the mark. They were enemies of Christ but not loyal worshipers of the beast.
Daniel 7:12 supports this distinction:

"As concerning the rest of the beasts, they had their dominion taken away: yet their lives were prolonged for a season and time."

Daniel's vision explicitly reveals that, after the final beast is judged, other nations—symbolized by these beasts—remain alive for a time. Their political power is removed, but their existence continues. This is not a throwaway detail—it is a theological anchor. It tells us that divine judgment can be both sweeping and selective. Dispensational interpretations often overlook this nuanced reality, ignoring these national outliers who remain after Christ's return.

This aligns closely with Revelation 19:21, where the remnant is slain but not eternally condemned. This suggests they are not part of the covenantal judgment reserved exclusively for those marked by allegiance to the beast. They were opponents in war but lacked full spiritual alignment with the Antichrist's regime.

Even more importantly, Daniel 7 clarifies the symbolic framework:

"These great beasts, which are four, are four kings, which shall arise out of the earth."
(Daniel 7:17)

"The fourth beast shall be the fourth kingdom upon earth…"
(Daniel 7:23)

Daniel makes it unmistakably clear: the beasts represent kings and kingdoms. The final beast—clearly paralleled with the beast in Revelation—is destroyed entirely:

"But the judgment shall sit, and they shall take away his dominion, to consume and to destroy it unto the end."
(Daniel 7:26)

This is a stark contrast. The Antichrist and his kingdom are consumed and destroyed, while the other beasts—those representing prior or parallel kingdoms—have their dominion taken away but their lives prolonged. This contrast signals a crucial interpretive distinction. Unlike the beast's kingdom, which is obliterated, other nations survive the Second Coming. They are not annexed into the beast's regime, nor are they entirely faithful. They remain as subdued outliers who must now submit to Christ's rule.

If we harmonize these two passages—Daniel 7:12 and Revelation 19:21—it implies something even more profound: not every single individual from these nations was either a combatant who fought against Christ or a Beast-worshipper. Within these nations are those whose lives were prolonged for a time, people who may have been swept up in the tide of history without pledging loyalty to the Beast. They were not glorified saints, but neither were they eternally condemned. They occupy a space pretribulational theology rarely acknowledges a remnant spared from annihilation, yet unsealed and unglorified. Their survival stands as testimony that divine judgment is both precise and just, distinguishing between allegiance and circumstance, worship and warfare.

Revelation 13:7 offers further insight:

"And it was given unto him to make war with the saints, and to overcome them: and power was given him over all kindreds, and tongues, and nations."

Notice the language carefully: the Beast is given "power," but this does not imply absolute global conquest or total annexation. Power indicates significant influence or dominance without necessitating universal incorporation. Thus, his dominance, while extensive, remains partial. Nations may ally with him under coercion, deception, or fear, yet they retain distinct identities. Several motivations for national allegiance to the Antichrist are scripturally consistent:

- Political or ideological alliances.
- Economic dependency on the beast's global trade network (Babylon).
- Deceptive miracles performed by the false prophet.
- A desperate instinct for survival against perceived heavenly invasion.

This cumulative evidence dismantles the rigid binary required by pretribulationism. It paints a biblical picture of global complexity, spiritual discernment, and divine justice that is far more nuanced than the dispensational framework allows.

Survivors in Natural Bodies

Zechariah 14:16 explicitly references survivors after Christ's return:

"And it shall come to pass, that every one that is left of all the nations which came against Jerusalem shall even go up... to worship the King, the Lord of hosts..."

These individuals clearly survive in natural bodies, not glorified ones. They are Gentiles from nations subdued by Christ's victory, now brought under His rule. They represent remnants whose existence continues into the millennium. This group aligns with Revelation 21:24:

"And the nations of them which are saved shall walk in the light of it."

The critical nuance is this: Revelation 13:8 states that only those whose names are not written in the Lamb's book of life worship the beast. This does not imply universal participation from every individual in every nation. Not everyone living under the Antichrist's dominion aligns spiritually with him. As in any authoritarian system, many dissenters remain—some resisting openly, others refusing quietly. The remnant slain at Christ's return but not immediately burned in hell may have included conscripted soldiers or civilians coerced into conflict, judged for their opposition on the battlefield.

When we let Scripture interpret Scripture, it becomes evident that the outliers mentioned in Daniel and Revelation are the same outliers described in Zechariah. These survivors from the nations that came against the Lord are not glorified saints nor Beast worshippers. They are those whose nations had their dominion taken away but whose lives were prolonged for a season and time, as Daniel 7:12 reveals:

"As concerning the rest of the beasts, they had their dominion taken away: yet their lives were prolonged for a season and time."

This is a crucial insight. These kings and the citizens of their kingdoms have lost their autonomy as sovereign nations under

Christ's rule. However, because they neither received the mark nor actively fought as combatants, they were spared. This is how the world will be repopulated during the millennial reign not by tribulation saints forced to live in the shadow of a glorified Church and the shadow of the resurrected tribulation saints who died during the tribulation. It is not consistent with God's character to pour out indiscriminate plagues on His faithful people, only to elevate the dead and reduce the living saints to second-class status. That portrait makes God appear inconsistent.

To be clear, most pretribulationists who raise this objection are sincere believers doing their best to make sense of complex texts. They are not setting out to twist Scripture. They are trying to organize passages from a framework they were taught to trust. However, the structure of the pretribulation model unintentionally forces this binary when applied to posttribulationism: either a person is glorified, or they took the mark. The tribulation saints, according to many adherents of the pretrib view, are the only ones permitted to survive in the millennium in natural bodies. So, when evaluating the posttrib model, they argue that no such group of outliers could exist because all believers have been raptured and glorified, and all unbelievers took the mark. The middle category, the surviving remnant who neither took the mark nor were glorified is rarely acknowledged, and when it is, it is inconsistently applied.

It should be evident by now that the pretribulational system of interpretation does not allow one to cut a straight path through Scripture concerning the repopulation of the millennium. The false dichotomy it pushes between the saints and total destruction leaving no room for outliers: this cannot withstand the weight of harmonized biblical evidence. The internal contradictions of the system, built upon binaries and assumptions, unravel when tested against the full counsel of Scripture.

This reality strengthens the posttribulational interpretation. God's judgment pattern is not indiscriminate extermination, but selective justice tempered with mercy. Some individuals face instant eternal judgment because they took the mark. Others are slain as combatants. Still others are preserved and taught righteousness in Christ's millennial kingdom.

Therefore, the original objection collapses because it presumes a false binary that is pushed on to the posttribulation model. Scripture presents a richer, more complex picture, reflecting God's consistent approach: wrath for rebellion, mercy for the remnant, and renewal through Christ's righteous reign.

When interpreting prophecy, precision matters. The Bible does not trade in ambiguity when rightly divided—it presents layered truth, often through cycles, symbols, and selective focus. By distinguishing regional from global, symbolic from literal, rhetorical scope from mathematical totality, we begin to hear Scripture on its own terms rather than through the lens of man-made systems. We have seen how dispensationalism often imposes rigidity where the text flows organically, inserts binaries where Scripture leaves nuance, and flattens apocalyptic language into modern speculation. But God's prophetic word is not confused—it is cohesive. Its patterns echo across Daniel, Zechariah, Revelation, and the Gospels with unified intent: to warn, to reveal, and to prepare the faithful.

You have nothing to fear—not the plagues, not the wrath, and certainly not the idea of becoming some second-class saint. God is not partial in His love. He does not elevate the dead over the living, nor does He forget the faithful who endure. At the sound of the last trumpet, we shall all be changed, glorified together before the eyes of a trembling world. The same Jesus who bore our shame will crown us with honor in the presence of our enemies.

Next Revelation:
The Time of Jacob's Trouble: Is It Only for Israel?

The patterns we have traced through Revelation and Daniel lead us to a deeper question: what role does Israel play in the final conflict? As the nations rage and the Beast rises, the prophetic spotlight returns to a time of unparalleled distress known as Jacob's trouble. Is this a separate story, or part of the same redemptive arc? Chapter 8 will take us into the heart of this question—where covenant, crisis, and restoration converge. What we find is that Jacob's Trouble doesn't exempt the church from being present during the tribulation.

Chapter 8:
The Time of Jacob's Trouble:
Is It Only for Israel?

When we hear the phrase "Jacob's trouble," it often conjures images of a distant, cataclysmic tribulation period strictly reserved for national Israel. It is frequently portrayed as a final chapter for ethnic Jews, disconnected from the Church and rooted solely in Old Testament covenantal identity. Yet a careful and honest reading of Jeremiah 30 reveals a far more nuanced and layered reality. This passage must first be understood in its historical context before it can be rightly applied with theological integrity to future prophecy. To read it only through a futuristic or dispensational lens is to risk divorcing the passage from the covenantal framework in which it was originally delivered.

Jeremiah wrote during the final years before the Babylonian exile. Judah the surviving southern kingdom of Israel was facing imminent judgment for its long-standing rebellion against God. Generations of covenant-breaking, idolatry, and social injustice had provoked divine correction. Yet even in the midst of Jeremiah's piercing prophecies of coming disaster, God repeatedly inserted messages of mercy and promises of ultimate restoration. The people would indeed be chastised, but they would not be annihilated. In fact, in the very fabric of Jeremiah's prophecy, we find a divine pattern of death and rebirth: a period of affliction followed by deliverance, sorrow followed by renewal. This structure hints at a deeper spiritual typology one that is ultimately fulfilled in Christ and His Church.

Just as Jacob once wrestled with God through the night and was transformed into Israel, so too would Judah pass through the crucible of affliction and emerge with a renewed identity. This moment in Jacob's life was not just personal—it was prophetic. Jacob, though the second born, laid hold of his brother's heel and ultimately inherited the covenantal blessing. He contended with both man and God and prevailed, not by power, but through desperate dependence on the promise. In like manner, Jesus—the true Seed— wrestled not with flesh and blood, but with sin, death, and the grave.

He prevailed through obedience unto death, and through His triumph, He made us spiritual Israel in Himself.

Was there a separate covenant prepared for Esau when Jacob was blessed by Isaac? No, the birthright was singular. It passed not to both brothers, but to one—the one chosen by grace. So too, the covenant of promise has not been divided into two inheritances, one for Israel and one for the Church. The second has become the inheritor of the first. The New Covenant does not supplement the Old—it fulfills it.

This is why you must be born again. Fleshly birth is not sufficient. You are born again through water and Spirit into the kingdom of God (John 3:5). And there is no alternative entrance. Scripture declares that anyone who tries to enter the sheepfold by another way is a thief and a robber (John 10:1). There is only one door, one Shepherd, and one flock.

The seed of Israel's suffering would, in time, give birth to something greater than the nation itself: a redeemed people, defined not by ethnicity but by covenantal faithfulness, whose scope extends beyond the natural lineage of Abraham to include all who believe. This is the pattern of redemptive history where judgment serves a restorative purpose and where tribulation paves the way for transformation.

Jeremiah 30–31 is one such restoration passage. It speaks of a terrifying time a "time of Jacob's trouble," but it is framed not as final ruin, but as a precursor to redemption. Consider the foundational verse:

"Alas! for that day is great, so that none is like it: it is even the time of Jacob's trouble; but he shall be saved out of it."
(Jeremiah 30:7)

Notice the emphasis: he shall be saved out of it. This was not a death sentence, but a deliverance promise. It was a message of hope wrapped in warning. Judah would indeed suffer under the crushing weight of Babylon's power, but their covenant with God would not be extinguished. Restoration would follow chastisement. And yet, we must also observe that the language Jeremiah uses is richly symbolic and prophetically expansive. It is not confined to the moment. Much of the imagery in these chapters the labor pains, exile, deliverance, covenant renewal resonates far beyond the sixth century BC. These motifs echo into the realm of eschatology, whispering of final judgment and ultimate restoration on a global scale.

The language Jeremiah employs, both poetic and prophetic, finds its ultimate flowering not only in Israel's historical experience but also in the birth of the New Covenant community. The Church, born out of the travail of Israel's history, stands as the spiritual offspring of the promises made to the patriarchs. Christ Himself is the firstborn among many brethren, and the remnant He gathers includes both Jew and Gentile those brought forth through travail into the fullness of covenantal life.

This dual-layered fulfillment in both historical and future is not an interpretive stretch. It is entirely consistent with the literary and prophetic style of Jeremiah, who often spoke in patterns that transcended their immediate circumstances. Therefore, when we approach the concept of "Jacob's trouble," we must resist the temptation to isolate it as a time of wrath uniquely reserved for ethnic Israel, disconnected from the wider covenantal story. While it unquestionably referred in the first instance to Judah's suffering under Babylon, it also foreshadowed a greater time of tribulation at the end of the age a time in which all of God's people, both natural and grafted branches, pass through affliction in anticipation of ultimate redemption.

To interpret Jacob's trouble rightly, we must allow Scripture's covenantal continuity to guide our understanding. The pattern Jeremiah introduces the chastisement of God's people followed by redemptive deliverance is not locked within the confines of a single generation or nation. It reverberates through redemptive history. It culminates not in the survival of an ethnic remnant alone, but in the full and glorious redemption of all who are counted as the true seed of promise: those who walk in the faith of Abraham and are united in Christ, in whom all the promises of God.

God's Dealings with One People:
Jew and Gentile United in Christ

The New Testament radically transforms the categories through which we understand God's covenant people. No longer are His promises segregated along ethnic lines. Through the work of Christ, Jew and Gentile have been fused into one new humanity a single people defined not by fleshly descent, but by faith in the true Seed of promise.

Paul declares in Ephesians 2:

"For he is our peace, who hath made both one, and hath broken down the middle wall of partition between us."
(Ephesians 2:14)

And again:

"Now therefore ye are no more strangers and foreigners, but fellowcitizens with the saints, and of the household of God."
(Ephesians 2:19)

There is no longer a two-covenant system one for the physical descendants of Abraham and another for Gentile believers. The blood of Christ has forged a single people of God. To suggest, then, that Jacob's Trouble applies only to ethnic Israel while the Church remains uninvolved is to fundamentally misunderstand the nature of the New Covenant.

The cross did not merely offer Gentiles a parallel blessing; it incorporated them into the root promises given to Israel. It is no longer about physical lineage, but about belonging to Christ. Paul drives this point home when he proclaims:

"There is neither Jew nor Greek, there is neither bond nor free, there is neither male nor female: for ye are all one in Christ Jesus."
(Galatians 3:28)

And immediately prior, he grounds this unity in the identity of the true Seed:

"Now to Abraham and his seed were the promises made. He saith not, 'And to seeds,' as of many; but as of one, 'And to thy seed,' which is Christ."
(Galatians 3:16)

It is not multiple seeds, but one Seed—Christ—and only those who are in Him are heirs of the covenant. This is the core of the New Covenant reality. The author of Hebrews echoes this very principle, identifying Jesus as the fulfillment of all the promises made to Abraham. It is not biological descent that determines covenant status, but spiritual union with the Son of God.

This truth was embedded from the beginning. In Genesis 17:4–5, God declares:

"As for me, behold, my covenant is with thee, and thou shalt be a father of many nations. Neither shall thy name any more be called Abram, but thy name shall be Abraham; for a father of many nations have I made thee."

God never intended for Abraham's family tree to be limited to native Israelites alone. The covenantal promise pointed forward to a day when, through the Seed—Christ—Abraham would become the spiritual father of many nations. Gentiles were not an afterthought. They were always included in the divine plan, to be grafted into the family of faith through the righteousness that comes by believing God.

Paul's own teaching in Romans 9 reinforces this reality, declaring that not all who are born of Israel are truly Israel:

"Neither, because they are the seed of Abraham, are they all children: but, In Isaac shall thy seed be called. That is, They which are the children of the flesh, these are not the children of God: but the children of the promise are counted for the seed."
(Romans 9:7–8)

Physical descent guarantees nothing. The covenantal promises belong to those who are reckoned according to the promise, not merely according to the flesh. Christ is the true Seed, and only those who belong to Him whether Jew or Gentile constitute the covenant family.

Paul's Teaching on the One Olive Tree (Romans 11)

Paul reinforces this unified vision in Romans 11, using the metaphor of an olive tree. Natural branches being ethnic Israel were broken off because of unbelief, and wild branches being Gentile believers were grafted in. But notice carefully: there is only one tree.

"And if some of the branches be broken off, and thou, being a wild olive tree, wert grafted in among them, and with them partakest of the root and fatness of the olive tree..."
(Romans 11:17)

Paul does not present a vision of two trees growing side by side—one for Israel and another for the Church. He declares one tree, one root, one shared inheritance. All who believe, regardless of origin, are nourished by the same covenantal sap. The dividing wall has been removed, not rearranged.

The only distinction that remains is not between Jew and Gentile, but between belief and unbelief. The root is holy, but only those joined to it by faith remain. This is why the dispensational framework collapses under the weight of Scripture. It proposes separate trees, separate programs, separate destinies. Yet Paul sees one body formed through grace, not two peoples managed through chronology.

Jacob's Trouble, if it points forward to an eschatological distress, cannot concern ethnic Israel alone. To claim so is to sever the very tree into which the Gentiles have been grafted. If we share the promises, we also share in the testing. The time of trouble comes upon all who are counted among the people of God, for the true Israel of God is composed of those who are in Christ—the one Seed, the one Body, the one Tree.

Dispensationalism proposes an elaborate framework by necessity in which God has two distinct peoples: Israel and the Church. Israel's promises are earthly; the Church's promises are heavenly. Israel inherits land; the Church inherits heaven. And therefore, they argue, the tribulation—especially the Time of Jacob's Trouble—is intended only for Israel.

But this model is a theological fiction. It fractures what God has united in Christ. It denies the clear and repeated testimony of Ephesians, Romans, and Galatians. Worse still, it creates contradictions that compromise the integrity of the New Testament witness.

If Jew and Gentile are one new man, one body, and one tree, how can they be subjected to separate end-times programs? The entire premise of a Church raptured early so that God can turn His attention back to Israel is built upon a disunity that the cross has abolished.

Here lies the deeper issue: dispensationalism needs this division by design. The system requires a dual-covenant framework in order to survive. When confronted with Scripture that clearly contradict the system, dispensationalists must delegate those "difficult" verses to a different group. If a passage speaks of the elect being gathered by the angels immediately after the tribulation, it must be "Israel." If another passage speaks of deliverance or escape, it belongs to "the Church," unless the timing of the escape appears to be posttribulational. And when contradictions arise such as saints existing during the tribulation despite a supposed pretrib rapture, they introduce an entirely new category: "tribulation saints." These are theological placeholders, not clearly defined groups derived from Scripture, but interpretive necessities invented to patch the holes in a divided system.

It is a consistent pattern of behavior. Rather than adjusting the framework to fit the text, the text is reclassified to preserve the framework. Yet Scripture itself refuses to cooperate with such compartmentalization. Paul's teaching in Romans 9 drives the point home with clarity and force:

"For they are not all Israel, which are of Israel."
(Romans 9:6)

This simple but profound statement clarifies two realities. First, it acknowledges the visible, earthly existence of national Israel a people tied to a physical land and a historic identity. Second, it reveals that true covenantal Israel—the Israel of promise—is a spiritual body comprised only of those who are united to Christ, the true Seed.

In other words, while a nation called Israel may exist politically and geographically, covenantal status does not rest on ethnic lineage or national borders. It rests solely on union with Christ. Paul continues:

"That is, they which are the children of the flesh, these are not the children of God: but the children of the promise are counted for the seed."
(Romans 9:8)

There is one Seed, and there is one covenant people—those who belong to Christ, whether Jew or Gentile. Physical birth offers no guarantee of inheritance. Only spiritual rebirth through faith in the promised Seed grants entrance into the covenant family.

This understanding does not erase national Israel's prophetic role in the last days. As we will see later in this chapter, God has a plan to save a remnant of Jewish people living in the land of Israel at the time of Christ's return. But they will not be saved because of their nationality. They will be saved because they turn to the Lord in repentance and faith, becoming the firstfruits of a millennial harvest. Their national existence provides the stage, but only their spiritual rebirth will grant them participation in the covenant blessings.

Thus, the idea of a dual-covenant system collapses under the weight of Scripture. There is not one plan for the Church and another for ethnic Israel. There is only one covenant, one Seed, one people and all who are grafted into Christ partake of the promises made to Abraham.

Refuting Dispensational Use of Daniel 9:27

One of dispensationalism's cornerstone arguments is that Daniel 9:27—the famous "70th week" prophecy—concerns only Israel. Because the Church is not explicitly named, they insist it must be absent from the tribulation period. I call this the 70th week assumption because their entire interpretation is based on assumption.

This is an argument from silence, and a fallacious one. The absence of a name does not imply the absence of presence. Scripture often speaks broadly to events that encompass both Jew and Gentile without always spelling it out explicitly. To build an entire eschatological framework on what a text does not say is theological conjecture, not exegesis. It reveals more about dispensationalism's assumptions than it does about the actual words of Scripture.

Just as their argument for a missing Church after Revelation chapter 3 collapses under scrutiny, the same flawed reasoning reappears here. The Church is not absent from the tribulation—it is present, faithful, and enduring. Revelation consistently describes saints who suffer, overcome, and reign with Christ. These saints are drawn from every nation, tongue, and tribe, an unmistakable sign that God's covenant people are not limited to ethnic Israel during the final upheaval.

The book of Revelation makes this reality plain. Believers those who keep the commandments of God and the testimony of Jesus are present throughout the tribulation:

"And it was given unto him to make war with the saints, and to overcome them…"
(Revelation 13:7)

These saints are not a different body, invented to preserve a theological system. They are the Church, the very same Church that Christ declared would endure until His return (Matthew 16:18).

And notice the global composition of this body:

"After this I beheld, and, lo, a great multitude, which no man could number, of all nations, and kindreds, and people, and tongues, stood before the throne, and before the Lamb…"
(Revelation 7:9)

This is not an assembly limited to national Israel. It is a redeemed multitude from the whole world emerging victorious from "great tribulation" (Revelation 7:14). If the tribulation were solely Jacob's Trouble, reserved for ethnic Israel, then what are all these Gentiles doing standing faithful before the Lamb?

Exposing the Contradiction in the "Only for Israel" Claim

There is another glaring inconsistency. If Jacob's Trouble truly concerns only Israel, then why are Gentile Christians warned not to be "left behind"? The pretribulationist marketing engine thrives on fear— "You do not want to be here during the tribulation." But if the tribulation is reserved exclusively for Jews, what danger threatens the Gentile believer? According to their own logic, none. And yet the urgency remains.

This reveals the internal incoherence of the system. Dispensationalism maintains that the tribulation is exclusively about Israel when arguing for a pretrib rapture but turns around and leverages that same period to issue global warnings, sell books, and fill conferences. It cannot be both.

This results in an inescapable catch-22:

- If the tribulation is only for Israel, then Gentile Christians have nothing to fear.
- If Gentile Christians are warned about it, then the tribulation involves more than Israel.

Both claims cannot be true. Dispensationalism finds itself trapped by its own marketing slogans and a theology that tries to sell a crisis to one group while insisting the crisis belongs to another.

And if somehow, we are expected to believe this is not a contradiction, then perhaps we are also meant to believe that the saints in Revelation 8 are praying for their own torment. But that is precisely what the text would imply if we followed dispensational logic.

"And another angel came and stood at the altar, having a golden censer... and the smoke of the incense, which came with the prayers of the saints, ascended up before God... and the angel took the censer, and filled it with fire of the altar, and cast it into the earth...And the seven angels which had the seven trumpets prepared themselves to sound."
(Revelation 8:3–6)

The saints cry out to God, and their prayers trigger judgment. Are we to believe that the faithful are calling down plagues upon themselves? Of course not. The saints are praying for justice, and God responds by sending judgment upon the ungodly. Likewise, the warnings about the tribulation are given to the Church—not because it will escape, but because it must endure. Vindication comes through endurance, not exemption.

The absurdities required to maintain the dispensational framework multiply quickly. Logical fallacy gives way to theological inconsistency, and inconsistency is papered over with slogans. But the house of cards collapses the moment Scripture is allowed to speak plainly.

And even if we were generous—even if we granted their premise for argument's sake—their framework still fails. Suppose for a moment that Jacob's Trouble applies strictly to Israel. Even then, not all Israel are the children of promise. Paul says it plainly:

"They are not all Israel, which are of Israel..."
(Romans 9:6)

There is a remnant! A spiritual Israel! Those who are counted as heirs by faith. Ethnic descent does not guarantee covenant inheritance. Paul continues:

"That is, they which are the children of the flesh, these are not the children of God: but the children of the promise are counted for the seed."
(Romans 9:8)

Even under dispensationalism's own assumptions, the claim that all of ethnic Israel is the object of God's special dealing during the tribulation unravels. The weakness of their position is evident in the fact that even under favorable conditions, it crumbles—logically, theologically, and exegetically.

Ultimately, we must look to the harvest scene in Revelation. The final multitude gathered from the tribulation is drawn from every nation, kindred, tongue, and people. Any mention of a faithful remnant outside national Israel—whether saint or survivor—overturns the misuse of Daniel 9:27 and dismantles the exclusivity of their interpretation of Jacob's Trouble.

In this book, I address both: a remnant of Jews who turn in faith, and a multitude of saints from the nations who pass through tribulation. This unified witness undermines the idea that Jacob's Trouble is reserved exclusively for ethnic Jews. That interpretation not only misreads Daniel 9:27, but it also ignores the global reality of Revelation 7.

The covenant people of God are no longer defined by race, but by relationship to Christ. Those who endure the tribulation are not a fragmented cast with separate destinies, but they are one body, one people, and one bride, waiting for the appearing of their King.

Regional vs. Global Consequences

One final nail in the coffin of the "only for Israel" argument is the global scope of the tribulation itself and not just the wrath poured out at Christ's return.

We already demonstrated in Chapter 7 that the seals, trumpets, and bowls unleash consequences that affect the entire world, not just Israel. Revelation does not present a neatly confined regional crisis, but a shaking of all nations. For example, during the opening of the second seal:

"And there went out another horse that was red: and power was given to him that sat thereon to take peace from the earth, and that they should kill one another: and there was given unto him a great sword."
(Revelation 6:4)

Peace is not removed merely from the land of Israel—it is stripped from the earth (Greek: γῆ). According to Thayer's Greek Lexicon, γῆ (gē) can refer to (1) the whole earth, (2) the entire inhabited world, or (3) a region of the world when limited by context. But in Revelation 6, there is no qualifier restricting the scope. The result is worldwide instability and bloodshed. The context demands the universal sense of the word: a global escalation of violence and lawlessness during the tribulation.

Later, when describing the rise of the beast:

"And it was given unto him to make war with the saints, and to overcome them: and power was given him over all kindreds, and tongues, and nations."
(Revelation 13:7)

The Beast's authority and influence are not limited to one region but extend over every ethnic group, language, and nation proving that the tribulation impacts the entire world.

The fallout of the tribulation touches every corner of the globe. Nations far removed from Israel are depicted as suffering from famine, plague, war, and judgment. The sun is darkened. The waters are poisoned. The economies collapse. Kings and captains hide in fear. This is not a local disaster—it is a cosmic reckoning.

Yet mainstream pretribulation teachers consistently refuse to harmonize these regional and global narratives. They isolate regional prophecies while ignoring the comprehensive scope of Revelation. They cherry-pick passages and insert artificial divisions, interjecting unbiblical concepts to defend an untenable system.

This interpretive imbalance stems from classical dispensationalism's need to divide Israel and the Church into separate prophetic destinies. In their model, Israel receives judgment on earth while the Church enjoys bliss in heaven. But this entire framework is built upon theological presuppositions rather than the plain teaching of Scripture.

And as more progressive and nuanced versions of dispensationalism emerge, we are not witnessing a clearer refinement but a slow dilution. When foundational pillars such as the dual-people model and the Israel-only tribulation are removed, the system begins to fall apart without its foundation. The structure may survive in name for a time, but its internal logic erodes. Each exposed contradiction brings it closer to theological bankruptcy.

When the full picture is embraced the global scale of the tribulation, the unified body of Christ, the shared inheritance of the saints—the error of dispensational interpretation becomes painfully obvious.

Continuity from Daniel 11–12:
Regional Tribulation, Global Resurrection

Daniel 11 outlines regional conflicts with wars between the kings of the north and south, political turmoil centered around Israel, and intense struggles for territorial dominance. At first glance, the focus appears local. Yet this regional spotlight is not isolated from the broader end-time scenario. As the chapter draws to its climax, a darker figure emerges: the Antichrist, who rises above these local struggles to become the central aggressor on a global scale.

This is where Revelation provides vital commentary. The Antichrist, exercises authority not merely over the Middle East, but over "all kindreds, and tongues, and nations" (Revelation 13:7). His influence and authority as the leading superpower encompass the whole earth, not just Israel and her surrounding neighbors. Thus, even though Daniel 11 narrates regional battles, Scripture zooms out to show that the Antichrist's influence spirals into a worldwide crisis.

Far from being contradictory, this telescoping between regional conflict and global chaos perfectly harmonizes the prophetic record. It mirrors how biblical prophecy often moves between local and universal scopes—highlighting the epicenter of God's covenant dealings through Israel, which find their fulfillment in Christ and extend ramifications to every nation.

This sets the stage for Daniel 12, where the perspective dramatically expands:

"And at that time shall Michael stand up, the great prince which standeth for the children of thy people: and there shall be a time of trouble, such as never was since there was a nation even to that same time: and at that time thy people shall be delivered, every one that shall be found written in the book."
(Daniel 12:1)

The phrase "at that time" explicitly connects the violent culmination of Daniel 11 with the unprecedented "time of trouble" in Daniel 12. In the Greek Septuagint (LXX), this "time of trouble" is rendered with the word thlipsis—the very same word used in the New Testament to describe tribulation.

Importantly, the deliverance described is not based on ethnicity alone but on spiritual faithfulness: "every one that shall be found written in the book." This points to those identified by divine inscription, not mere physical descent.

This precise linguistic and narrative link reveals a consistent posttribulational framework. The tribulation (thlipsis) immediately precedes the deliverance of God's faithful people, and that deliverance is not a secret or partial rescue but the global resurrection of the dead:

"And many of them that sleep in the dust of the earth shall awake, some to everlasting life, and some to shame and everlasting contempt."
(Daniel 12:2)

Here, the prophetic sequence is undeniable. Regional turmoil intensifies into the global authority and influence of the Antichrist. This provokes the final tribulation, which climaxes in the return of Christ and the resurrection of the righteous.

This pattern harmonizes seamlessly with Revelation 7, where a multitude "out of every nation, and kindred, and people, and tongue" emerges victorious "out of great tribulation" (Revelation 7:9, 14). It also aligns with Revelation 20, where the first resurrection occurs after the Beast's defeat.

Rather than presenting a fragmented, dispensational view of separate plans for Israel and the Church, Daniel 11 and 12 portray a unified prophetic panorama: one tribulation, one global judgment, and one victorious deliverance for the redeemed.

The tribulation is not merely a Jewish national crisis; it is the final global confrontation between the kingdom of God and the kingdoms of this world.

So, when we let Scripture interpret Scripture, the continuity from Daniel 11 to Daniel 12 destroys the dispensational framework and affirms the singular, glorious hope of a posttribulational resurrection and victory.

A Note on the 144,000: Redemption, Not Covenant

Some might object by appealing to the 144,000 sealed from the tribes of Israel (Revelation 7; 14). Are they not a separate group, proving the tribulation is only about Israel? No. Their sealing represents God's redemptive mercy, not the reestablishment of an old covenant.

Dispensational interpreters often assert that the 144,000 are a distinct class of ethnic Jews who function separately from the Church during the tribulation. John Walvoord, for example, describes them as "a special group of Israel's representatives on earth" during a period in which the Church is absent. Tim LaHaye echoes this view in Are We Living in the End Times?, claiming that they are evangelists who convert others during the tribulation but remain disconnected from the Body of Christ. These interpretations rely heavily on a rigid Israel–Church distinction that Revelation itself does not support.

These 144,000 are described as "the firstfruits unto God and to the Lamb" (Revelation 14:4). They are redeemed from among men and not by the law, but through the finished work of Christ. They are firstfruits not as a replacement for the Church, but as the first visible converts among the faithful Jewish remnant, sealed for redemption at Christ's return to establish His millennial kingdom.

They are the initial spiritual harvest of the new millennial age. Just as Christ was the "firstfruits" of the resurrection, so too the 144,000 represent the beginning of the restored Israel at the dawn of the Kingdom. They do not inherit by law; they inherit by redemption through the blood of the Lamb.

They are the living demonstration that God's covenant with Abraham's bloodline, though broken nationally, still finds fulfillment through the Son, not through the Mosaic law.

It is vital to recognize that Jesus is not returning to rescue the modern Israeli government or to validate secular Zionism. He is coming to bring Israel and all the nations under His righteous reign:

"And out of his mouth goeth a sharp sword, that with it he should smite the nations: and he shall rule them with a rod of iron…"
(Revelation 19:15)

This is not new. The Old Testament had already declared this same reality:

"But with righteousness shall he judge the poor, and reprove with equity for the meek of the earth: and he shall smite the earth with the rod of his mouth, and with the breath of his lips shall he slay the wicked."
(Isaiah 11:4)

Christ's kingship over the nations was always the plan. The kings of the earth, including the rulers of Jerusalem, will be brought into subjection. Yet within Israel, as prophesied, there will be a faithful remnant—144,000 sealed from the twelve tribes—who will look upon the Messiah they once rejected and believe.

This redemption parallels the apostolic pattern established at the beginning of the Church:

"To the Jew first, and also to the Greek."
(Romans 1:16)

The initial outpouring of the Spirit fell upon Jews in Jerusalem before extending to the Gentiles. Likewise, when Christ returns, the first visible fruits of the millennial Kingdom will be the redeemed Jewish remnant, followed by the ingathering of the surviving Gentile nations, whose dominion was taken away but whose lives were prolonged for a season (Daniel 7:12).

Moreover, the ancient Jewish expectation of the Lion of Judah will find its ultimate fulfillment at the Second Advent. The Jews who survive the tribulation and particularly the sealed 144,000 will no longer look for a suffering servant, but for the conquering King. Their eyes will be fixed on the Mount of Olives, in direct fulfillment of prophecy:

"And ye shall flee to the valley of the mountains; for the valley of the mountains shall reach unto Azal: yea, ye shall flee, like as ye fled from before the earthquake in the days of Uzziah king of Judah: and the Lord my God shall come, and all the saints with thee."
(Zechariah 14:5)

As the Mount of Olives splits in two at Christ's descent, the faithful remnant of Israel will recognize Him. Unlike His first coming, when some believed and others scoffed, the sealed tribes will submit unanimously.

No division. No debate. No rebellion. The twelve tribes, once scattered and estranged, will be unified in their acknowledgment of the Messiah. They will believe in the Lion of Judah, and their collective submission will mark them as the firstfruits of the millennial reign of Christ.

Therefore, the presence of the 144,000 is not evidence of two separate peoples of God. Rather, it is the prophesied redemption of a faithful remnant, integrated into the universal reign of Christ over all the earth.

Rebuttal & Answer:
"But The 144,000 Are Evangelists During the Tribulation."

One argument frequently raised by pretribulationists is based on this verse:

"And I saw another angel fly in the midst of heaven, having the everlasting gospel to preach unto them that dwell on the earth, and to every nation, and kindred, and tongue, and people."
(Revelation 14:6)

They claim this proves that the 144,000 sealed from the tribes of Israel (Revelation 7; 14) are evangelists during the tribulation period. The idea is that these Jewish witnesses replace the Church, spreading the gospel while the Church is absent from the earth.

However, this interpretation doesn't add up upon closer examination of the context.

First, the 144,000 are not roaming the earth preaching. They are standing victoriously with the Lamb on Mount Zion:

"And I looked, and, lo, a Lamb stood on the mount Sion, and with him an hundred forty and four thousand, having his Father's name written in their foreheads."
(Revelation 14:1)

This scene is not depicting tribulation evangelism but victory after Christ has returned. Mount Zion is symbolic of Jerusalem restored and redeemed. As the prophets Joel and Amos foretold, the Lord will "roar out of Zion" at the climactic day of judgment:

"The Lord also shall roar out of Zion, and utter his voice from Jerusalem; and the heavens and the earth shall shake: but the Lord will be the hope of his people, and the strength of the children of Israel."
(Joel 3:16)

Why does the Lord roar? Because the Lion of Judah has triumphed. Jesus, the risen King, has returned to claim what is His. The roar is not the cry of warning. It is the shout of conquest! He roars because the war is over. The King has come. It is the very voice of victory reverberating from Mount Zion after the great battle has been won. It is the sound of final justice, not ongoing chaos.

Revelation 14 shows Christ standing as King in Zion after defeating the Antichrist, not during the tribulation while evil still reigns.

Second, the angel preaching the everlasting gospel in Revelation 14:6 is not describing the start of the tribulation or an ongoing missionary effort. It occurs after the fall of Babylon:

"And there followed another angel, saying, Babylon is fallen, is fallen, that great city, because she made all nations drink of the wine of the wrath of her fornication."
(Revelation 14:8)

The fall of Babylon represents the destruction of the Beast's kingdom and the great system of apostasy and rebellion. But that is not all. The gospel is not only declared after Babylon's collapse; it is also declared after the Lord Himself has returned to Mount Zion and crushed the nations that resisted Him. The Lamb is not hidden—He stands revealed in glory.

This moment parallels Isaiah's powerful vision of Christ returning from Edom after treading the winepress of judgment:

"Wherefore art thou red in thine apparel, and thy garments like him that treadeth in the winefat? I have trodden the winepress alone... For the day of vengeance is in mine heart, and the year of my redeemed is come... And I looked, and there was none to help... therefore mine own arm brought salvation unto me."
(Isaiah 63:2–6)

This is not wrath aimed at the faithful, but vengeance executed on the wicked. The year of His redeemed has come. The same Christ who tramples the nations also lifts His voice to redeem and rule. This balances both judgment and mercy, it's the reason the saints are not appointed to wrath, but to salvation through the victorious One who now reigns.

The "everlasting gospel" proclaimed in this context is not an altar call amid widespread rebellion, but a sovereign announcement of Christ's triumph. It is the good news of a conquered earth being brought under His righteous rule a call for the surviving nations to submit to the King.

This angelic announcement echoes the words of Jeremiah:

"Babylon is suddenly fallen and destroyed: howl for her; take balm for her pain, if so be she may be healed."
(Jeremiah 51:8)

It is a proclamation of final judgment and the dawning of Christ's kingdom, not a second-chance evangelistic campaign during the tribulation.

Third, the context of Revelation 14 points forward to the millennial reign of Christ. The storm of tribulation has passed. The Beast's dominion is broken. Christ has come to establish His government on the earth. The everlasting gospel continues to spread in this new era of restoration—not through human missionaries dodging Antichrist's armies, but through the sovereign rule of Christ Himself.

The redemptive work of Christ does not end at His return—it continues into the Millennium. Those who survive into the millennial age, including the Jewish remnant and peoples of various nations, will experience a worldwide revival under Christ's direct rule, as foretold in the prophets:

"For the earth shall be full of the knowledge of the Lord, as the waters cover the sea."
(Isaiah 11:9)

Now, we can see the picture in Revelation 14 is not the Church being replaced by Jewish evangelists during the tribulation.

It is the triumphant aftermath of Christ's return, the vindication of the righteous, the downfall of the wicked, and the global spread of divine restoration. The Jewish remnant, sealed by God, stands in victory as the firstfruits of the millennium, and the gospel spreads throughout the world to the outliers from every nation making one flock under one Shepherd.

Isn't it amazing that God would save both Jew and Gentile and not Jew alone? That sounds like the Church, my friend. The blood hasn't lost its power to save.

The claim that Jacob's Trouble or Daniel 9:27 excludes the Church is not just an argument from silence—it is a misreading of covenant theology itself. Scripture does not teach two redemptive programs running side by side, but one everlasting covenant fulfilled in Christ. As it was with Jacob and Esau, so it is now: Esau was born first, but Jacob, the second-born who clung to his brother's heel, received the inheritance. The greater came after. Likewise, the New Covenant surpasses the old—not by abolishing it, but by fulfilling it in the true Seed, Jesus Christ. In Him, the faithful remnant of Israel and the grafted-in Gentiles become one people. Jacob's Trouble is not about reverting to an old system, but about bringing forth the fullness of God's plan through judgment and redemption. And when Christ returns, the 144,000—sealed from the tribes of Israel—will not stand apart from the Church, but as the firstfruits of a new age. They are not evidence of separation, but the beginning of restoration. They are the visible sign that God's promises to Israel have been fulfilled in the One who rules from Mount Zion—King of all, Lord of both Jew and Gentile, Redeemer of the one true Israel.

The Next Revelation:
When Jesus Comes as a Thief

The unity of God's people demands both vigilance and readiness—not complacency or false security. In the next chapter, we will uncover the true meaning of Christ coming "as a thief"—and why the Church must be awake, sober, and prepared when that day overtakes the world.

Chapter 9:
When Jesus Comes as a Thief

As we have already seen in this book, the Bible often describes the return of Christ using the imagery of a thief. Yet how many have misunderstood, or even inverted, this metaphor? The thief imagery is not about a stealthy rescue. It is about sudden, devastating judgment upon the unprepared. It is crucial to reclaim the biblical meaning of this symbol. The thief does not sneak away treasure while the world sleeps undisturbed. The thief strikes without warning, leaving devastation in his wake. This is the force behind the warnings of Christ and His apostles. Let us revisit this topic with a fresh perspective.

To grasp the full weight of this symbol, we must move carefully through Scripture, allowing the consistent pattern to emerge. Jesus is not returning secretly to whisk believers away. He is returning abruptly, publicly, and destructively, catching the world off guard and overwhelming the unready. This is not the story of an invisible disappearance, but of an unstoppable interruption. When Christ comes as a thief, the world will be shaken to its foundations. Those who have built their lives on sand will find their false security swept away in an instant.

Jesus gives us a vivid picture of this in Matthew 24:

"But as the days of Noah were, so shall also the coming of the Son of man be. For as in the days that were before the flood they were eating and drinking, marrying and giving in marriage, until the day that Noah entered into the ark, and knew not until the flood came, and took them all away; so shall also the coming of the Son of man be."
(Matthew 24:37–39)

The people in Noah's day were not watching, not waiting, and not warning one another. They were living their ordinary lives, indulging in daily routines, laughing and feasting, right up until the flood swept them all away. It was not a gentle removal. It was sudden, comprehensive destruction. And Jesus explicitly says His coming will be just like that.

When the Son of Man returns, those who have aligned themselves spiritually with the Antichrist, who have persecuted the saints and taken the mark of the beast, will be caught off guard and swept away in the same manner. The day will come suddenly. The judgment will be inescapable. But for the Church, those who are spiritually awake, this day will not overtake them as a thief. They will not be surprised, because they have been watching the signs and discerning the season. As Jesus said just moments earlier in Matthew 24:

"Now learn a parable of the fig tree; When his branch is yet tender, and putteth forth leaves, ye know that summer is nigh."
(Matthew 24:32)

The faithful do not know the exact day or hour, but they know the season. They are not blind to the convergence of signs. They are not sleeping in the darkness of apathy or deception. They are alert, sober, and prepared for the return of their King.

This sweeping judgment, likened to the days of Noah, provides the perfect transition into the next aspect of Christ's return: His sudden and unmistakable appearance in glory, like lightning flashing from east to west.

Thief in the Night: Suddenness and Judgment, Not Secrecy

The first step is to understand clearly what a thief represents in biblical language. A thief does not announce his coming. He strikes suddenly, without warning, and to the great loss of those who are unprepared. The unwatchful, the complacent, and the spiritually numb are the ones overtaken. The thief's coming is not merely inconvenient; it is catastrophic. It brings irreversible consequences.

It is important to clarify that within pretribulation rapture teachings, there are at least three distinct views regarding the imagery of Christ coming as a thief. Some pretribulation teachers interpret the "thief in the night" imagery as referring exclusively to an imminent, secret rapture. Others agree with the posttribulation position, acknowledging that this imagery refers specifically to the visible Second Coming in judgment. Still others adopt a hybrid approach, asserting that the "thief" imagery applies to both an imminent rapture event and the later Second Coming. Clearly, opinions vary widely within the pretribulation camp. However, for the purposes of this chapter, we are specifically addressing the dispensational idea, often emphasized in popular prophecy teaching, that Christ's coming as a thief is something believers should eagerly anticipate as an imminent, secret deliverance.

With this clarified, let us consider carefully the biblical tone surrounding the thief imagery. This tone is clearly set in Revelation 3:3, where Jesus warns the compromising church of Sardis:

"Remember therefore how thou hast received and heard, and hold fast, and repent. If therefore thou shalt not watch, I will come on thee as a thief, and thou shalt not know what hour I will come upon thee."
(Revelation 3:3)

Notice the warning here is not presented as a celebration but explicitly as a threat directed toward a church in a sorry spiritual state. Pretribulation teachers often spiritualize the seven churches of Asia, citing Philadelphia as the ideal church model. Interestingly, while many dispensationalists insist on a strictly linear chronology throughout Revelation, they suddenly abandon this approach when dealing with the seven churches. This inconsistency appears to be by design because applying a linear chronology to the churches would place Laodicea, the lukewarm church, as the last in the sequence, rather than Philadelphia. How many sermons on Laodicea have you heard? It is preached often yet rarely acknowledged as the final church in a sequence. Ironically, recognizing Laodicea as the final church would align typologically with the posttribulational interpretation of 2 Thessalonians 2:1–3, further challenging the pretribulational timeline.

When we look at how this aligns precisely with the apostolic warning in 2 Thessalonians 2:3, where Paul declares that the day of Christ will not come "except there come a falling away first." The Laodicean rebuke embodies that very apostasy as a church that thinks it is rich and in need of nothing, yet is wretched, poor, blind, and naked. What Revelation depicts typologically, Paul affirms doctrinally: before the return of Christ, the visible Church will be marked not by fervent holiness, but by widespread spiritual decay.

The lesson from Revelation 3:3 remains clear: coming as a thief is depicted negatively as a severe consequence for those spiritually asleep. It is not about joyful deliverance; rather, it portrays an unexpected visitation resulting in judgment. The thief imagery here demands vigilance. Those who are not awake will suffer loss when Christ arrives.

The same tone emerges again in Revelation 16:15:

"Behold, I come as a thief. Blessed is he that watcheth, and keepeth his garments, lest he walk naked, and they see his shame."
(Revelation 16:15)

This warning, placed amid the unfolding judgments of Revelation, explicitly ties the thief imagery to urgency, readiness, and the threat of exposure. Christ's coming strips away pretense. It lays bare the true condition of every soul. Those found clothed in righteousness will be vindicated. Those found naked, stripped of true faith and holiness, will suffer public shame and irreversible loss.

Revelation 16:15 closely aligns with another crucial verse:

"And I heard a voice from heaven saying unto me, Write, <u>Blessed are the dead which die in the Lord from henceforth</u>: Yea, saith the Spirit, that they may rest from their labours; and their works do follow them."
(Revelation 14:13)

Interestingly, this verse harmonizes clearly with the teachings found in the pseudo-Ephraim texts (both the Syriac and Latin versions), which—the Latin version—is often cited by pretribulation proponents as early historical proof of their doctrine. Yet upon closer inspection, these ancient texts explicitly describe escape through death and martyrdom during tribulation, not through a secret pretribulational rapture. We will fully address pseudo-Ephraim's texts in a forthcoming rebuttal section in chapter 12. However, this example highlights a consistent pattern in pretribulation presentations: nothing is straightforward or cut and dry. Contextomy and selective cherry-picking lie at the heart and soul of the dispensational doctrine itself.

Scripture consistently frames the thief motif as a sobering call to spiritual readiness rather than an encouragement toward complacency or anticipation of a hidden escape. The emphasis throughout the biblical narrative remains on the devastating consequences of spiritual unpreparedness, underscoring the importance of constant vigilance. Paul encapsulates this urgent call clearly in 1 Thessalonians 5:4–6:

"But ye, brethren, are not in darkness, that that day should overtake you as a thief. Ye are all the children of light, and the children of the day: we are not of the night, nor of darkness. Therefore let us not sleep, as do others; but let us watch and be sober."

Believers must remain spiritually awake, alert, and prepared. Christ's coming as a thief will devastate the unprepared, but for the faithful, sober-minded believer, it will signal glorious deliverance and vindication.

The Day of the Lord: Destruction for the Unready

Building on the thief motif and the language of sudden destruction, we now turn to another aspect of Christ's return that is often misunderstood particularly by amillennial and postmillennial interpreters. Having seen that the Day of the Lord is characterized by abrupt cosmic judgment and the unveiling of Christ in glory, it is important to clarify what Jesus meant when He said the kingdom "comes not with observation." This phrase is sometimes used to support the idea of a purely spiritual or gradual reign. But does it really deny a visible, millennial kingdom?

Some amillennial and postmillennial interpreters appeal to Jesus' statement in Luke 17:20 "The kingdom of God cometh not with observation" to argue that the kingdom's arrival is entirely spiritual, invisible, or gradual. But this is a misreading of the text's intent. The Greek word translated "observation" is παρατηρήσεως (paratērēseōs), which refers to careful watching or visible signs of a coming event.[8]Jesus was not denying the reality of His future reign. Rather, He was emphasizing that when His kingdom comes in its final, visible form, it will not be preceded by visible signs announced in the way earthly kings are welcomed. It will not be heralded by emissaries or marching processions.

This is why Jesus immediately follows the statement in Luke 17:20–21 with a warning about the days of Noah and the days of Lot, culminating in the declaration that His return will be like lightning flashing from one end of the sky to the other (Luke 17:24). The kingdom does not come with advance human fanfare. It arrives suddenly, decisively, and universally. This is not an argument against a future visible kingdom but a warning against expecting a gradual or observable buildup that allows for preparation at the last moment. The point is not invisibility, but it is abruptness.

This harmonizes perfectly with the pattern we see throughout Scripture. Joel describes the Day of the Lord in vivid cosmic terms:

"The sun shall be turned into darkness, and the moon into blood, before the great and terrible day of the Lord come."
(Joel 2:31)

Peter quotes this exact passage in Acts 2 and later echoes the same apocalyptic imagery in his epistle:

"But the day of the Lord will come as a thief in the night; in the which the heavens shall pass away with a great noise…"
(2 Peter 3:10)

Likewise, Paul warns:

---

[8] παρατήρησις, εως, ἡ — 1. observing, careful observation — in a negative sense: "watching for something from a critical perspective," "hostile observation" (cf. παρατηρέω). 2. observable phenomenon, visible display — "the kingdom of God is not coming with observable signs" (Luke 17:20). The meaning is debated; it may either refer to a hostile watching (surveillance) or an observable display of external phenomena (cf. Plutarch, Caes. 5.6; Appian, Bell. Civ. 2.110 §459). A Greek-English Lexicon of the New Testament and Other Early Christian Literature, 3rd ed., s.v. "παρατήρησις." —BDAG

"For when they shall say, Peace and safety; then sudden destruction cometh upon them, as travail upon a woman with child…"
(1 Thessalonians 5:3)

In each of these cases Joel, Peter, and Paul the Day of the Lord is marked by sudden cosmic disruption, not subtle transition. There is no sense of gradual enthronement, no delay between Christ's return and the collapse of this present world order. It is the crisis moment that initiates the kingdom in power.

When Jesus declares in Revelation, "Behold, I come quickly" (ταχύ)—as in Revelation 3:11, 22:7, 22:12, and 22:20—He is not suggesting that His return will happen soon in calendar terms, but that when it happens, it will be without delay. The standard Greek lexicon BDAG (3rd edition) defines ταχύ in this context as:

"quickly, without delay, suddenly, in a short time, with speed"
(BDAG, s.v. ταχύ, entry 2)

This reinforces the consistent biblical theme: the return of Christ is not a stealth extraction or a spiritual abstraction. It is a sudden, visible, and decisive interruption of human history. The thief motif, the Day of the Lord, and the kingdom language converge around this one reality—a sudden and observable return of Christ that shatters false peace and ushers in both judgment and reign.

Therefore, the phrase "the kingdom of God cometh not with observation" cannot be used to deny a future millennial kingdom. It means no one will be able to anticipate or control its arrival. The Son of Man will not be announced by human voices in advance. When He appears, it will be too late to prepare. His lightning-flash return will separate the faithful from the unfaithful in a single moment of apocalyptic unveiling.

Days of Noah and Days of Lot: Illustrations of Sudden Judgment

Jesus Himself drew upon vivid historical examples to illustrate the suddenness of His coming: the days of Noah and the days of Lot.

"But as the days of Noah were, so shall also the coming of the Son of man be. For as in the days that were before the flood they were eating and drinking, marrying and giving in marriage, until the day that Noah entered into the ark, and knew not until the flood came, and took them all away; so shall also the coming of the Son of man be."
(Matthew 24:37–39)

In Noah's day, life appeared normal. Society continued in its routines eating, drinking, marrying with no sense of impending doom. Yet judgment fell suddenly, catching the unready off guard and sweeping them away.

Likewise, Jesus said:

"Likewise also as it was in the days of Lot; they did eat, they drank, they bought, they sold, they planted, they builded. But the same day that Lot went out of Sodom it rained fire and brimstone from heaven, and destroyed them all. Even thus shall it be in the day when the Son of man is revealed."
(Luke 17:28–30)

Again, ordinary life lulled the people into false security. But on the very day Lot left, destruction fell without warning. In both examples, it is clear: the faithful are preserved through vigilance, while the unready perish through complacency. Christ's return will mirror this pattern. Life will seem stable, but destruction will break forth in an instant.

Jesus' teaching is consistent with many other biblical accounts of sudden judgment upon the unprepared. Consider Belshazzar, king of Babylon. While he and his lords were eating and drinking from the holy vessels taken from the temple, the harbinger of the handwriting on the wall appeared. In a single night, judgment fell. The king was killed, and his kingdom was given to another. Yet Daniel was not removed years before the event; he was preserved through the crisis because of his faithfulness.

Similarly, the people of Jericho went about their daily lives behind seemingly impregnable walls, thinking they were safe and that Joshua—Yeshua[9]—would never come for them. Yet at the shout and the sound of the last trumpet, sudden judgment descended. Only Rahab was saved, and her deliverance came by a scarlet cord, a symbol of the blood of Jesus—Yeshua—Christ. In each case, those who watched and trusted in God were not overtaken by destruction, while the unprepared were swept away without warning.

This completely dismantles the pretribulational notion that Christ comes secretly for His Church long before judgment falls. The pattern Jesus describes is unified: rescue and judgment are simultaneous. Noah was not raptured years before the flood; he was preserved through it. Lot was not removed from the earth and sent to heaven; he was protected as judgment fell. Daniel was not whisked away in advance but delivered from within Babylon. Rahab was not transported out of Jericho but shielded by the sign of faith.

Christ's return will not be secret or invisible. It will be as visible and undeniable as a lightning strike across the heavens:

"For as the lightning cometh out of the east, and shineth even unto the west; so shall also the coming of the Son of man be."
(Matthew 24:27)

The thief metaphor must be read in light of this broader context. It is not about Christ sneaking into the world and sneaking back out with His Church. It is about Christ appearing so suddenly and overwhelmingly that there is no time left for the unprepared to react. His coming is not partial, not localized, and certainly not hidden. It is universal and final, shattering the false peace of the ungodly in one decisive moment.

Those who have been lulled into complacency by false assurances will be like the occupants of a house robbed in the night stripped, exposed, and destroyed before they can even call for help. Their worldly securities, their imagined fortresses, their treaties and technologies, will offer no protection when the true King returns to claim His kingdom.

---

[9] Joshua (Yeshua) and Jesus (Iēsous) are the same name in different languages. Yeshua is the Hebrew/Aramaic form. Iēsous is the Greek transliteration, adjusted because Greek lacks the "Y" and "Sh" sounds and requires a masculine ending.

Jesus Himself emphasized that His coming would catch the unready like a snare:

"And take heed to yourselves, lest at any time your hearts be overcharged with surfeiting, and drunkenness, and cares of this life, and so that day come upon you unawares. For as a snare shall it come on all them that dwell on the face of the whole earth."
(Luke 21:34–35)

The snare falls upon "all them that dwell on the face of the whole earth." This matches precisely the sudden destruction Paul described, and the cosmic upheaval Peter foresaw. Yet for the faithful, there is no fear of this sudden destruction. Those who watch and remain awake will not be overtaken as by a thief.

The Wise Goodman: Watching for the Thief

Jesus also gave a crucial parable that deepens our understanding of how to prepare for His coming:

"But know this, that if the goodman of the house had known in what watch the thief would come, he would have watched, and would not have suffered his house to be broken up."
(Matthew 24:43)

The goodman, the wise master of the house is not taken by surprise. He is vigilant. He watches through the night, knowing the thief will come unexpectedly, but being ready for his arrival. This is the posture of the faithful Church. We are not sleeping but watching. We are not intoxicated with the world's illusions, but sober and clear-eyed.

This spiritual sobriety is exactly what Paul exhorted in 1 Thessalonians 5. He warns that at the Day of the Lord, the unprepared will be overtaken like those drunken in the night, while the faithful remain awake and alert:

"Therefore let us not sleep, as do others; but let us watch and be sober. For they that sleep sleep in the night; and they that be drunken are drunken in the night. But let us, who are of the day, be

sober, putting on the breastplate of faith and love; and for an helmet, the hope of salvation."
(1 Thessalonians 5:6–8)

In the last days, many will be spiritually intoxicated by the pleasures, comforts, and distractions of this present world. They will give their allegiance to the Beast in order to maintain their luxuries and avoid hardship. Yet not everyone gathered to Armageddon will be there because of conscious worship or devotion to the Beast. Many will be driven by fear, confusion, or a desperate instinct for self-preservation. As the supernatural signs unfold and the world descends into chaos, countless individuals, rulers, and commoners alike will perceive the return of Christ and His hosts not as the long-promised hope, but as a cosmic threat to their own dominion and survival. They will cling to the only powers left standing, aligning with the Beast not out of faith, but out of panic and a last effort to defend their kingdoms and way of life.

Their spiritual stupor, the drunkenness of worldly cares, and the darkness of unbelief will leave them blind to the true nature of the conflict. Peter foretold this hardening: "There shall come in the last days scoffers, walking after their own lusts, and saying, where is the promise of his coming?" (2 Peter 3:3–4). Their love for ease and their trust in worldly power will blind them to the danger until it is too late.

Jesus also likened the final separation at the end of the age to the harvest, when the wheat and the tares are gathered and distinguished:

"Let both grow together until the harvest: and in the time of harvest I will say to the reapers, Gather ye together first the tares, and bind them in bundles to burn them: but gather the wheat into my barn"
(Matthew 13:30).

This gathering of the tares for judgment parallels the mustering of God's enemies to Armageddon. Just as the wicked are bound together for destruction, so the armies of the earth are assembled for their final reckoning.

When the Son of Man appears, it is the faithful who are gathered to Him, and the wicked who are exposed, uprooted, and judged. The thief comes not for the righteous, but for those who have defied His warnings and persisted in rebellion.

The thief imagery reaches its climax in the events of Armageddon. Revelation paints the final confrontation clearly:

"And he gathered them together into a place called in the Hebrew tongue Armageddon."
(Revelation 16:16)

The unrepentant kings of the earth, the armies of the Beast, and the deceived multitudes are all mustered for war against the Lamb. Some are hardened idolaters, others are simply swept up in the storm, fighting for their own dominion, convinced they must resist a threat from above. They have mobilized their might, their technologies, and their false prophet's signs and wonders. But at the very moment they feel most emboldened, the true King returns. He does not come to negotiate. He comes as a thief to strip, to destroy, and to reclaim what is rightfully His. This sudden, violent overthrow of the wicked fulfills Paul's warning:

"For when they shall say, Peace and safety; then sudden destruction cometh upon them, as travail upon a woman with child; and they shall not escape."
(1 Thessalonians 5:3)

The armies assembled at Armageddon will not escape. They will be swallowed by the sword of Christ's mouth (Revelation 19:21), slain by the brightness of His coming (2 Thessalonians 2:8). The spiritual stupor that kept them blind until the very end will prove to be their ruin.

But the goodman, the one who watches and remains sober will not suffer his house to be broken into. He is a child of the day, awake and ready. While the world is overtaken in darkness, the faithful are preserved, vindicated, and gathered safely to Christ.

The Time of Rewarding the Saints

But for the faithful, this same moment is not terror but triumph. It is the time of reward, the fulfillment of every promise.

The 7th and final trumpet of Revelation declares:

"And the nations were angry, and thy wrath is come, and the time of the dead, that they should be judged, and that thou shouldest give reward unto thy servants the prophets, and to the saints, and them that fear thy name, small and great; and shouldest destroy them which destroy the earth."
(Revelation 11:18)

Notice how the wrath of God comes at the end, when Christ returns and judges the nations. As we have already seen, Christ says He comes as a thief at the very moment when the armies are gathered at Armageddon. This is the thief in the night, the sudden appearance of Christ to break the nations in His judgment. The wrath is not poured out piecemeal throughout the tribulation, nor is it dispensed in secret while the world goes on oblivious. It comes at the climactic return of the King, when all the nations are assembled and face Him together.

At this same hour, the rewarding of the saints takes place, not seven years before the tribulation, but at the second coming itself. Scripture is clear that the faithful receive their reward when Christ appears in glory, not in some secret, prior event. Those who are awake do not fall victim to the thief, because we are not appointed to wrath. We have obtained salvation through Him who will tread out the winepress of the wrath of God. We have nothing to fear. Stay awake. Stay sober. Stay vigilant.

Blessed is that servant, whom his lord when he cometh shall find so doing.
(Luke 12:43; see also Matthew 24:46)

When Christ returns as a thief, it is the hour of both vengeance and vindication. The wicked are destroyed. The faithful are crowned.

As Paul assures the Church:

"Henceforth there is laid up for me a crown of righteousness, which the Lord, the righteous judge, shall give me at that day: and not to me only, but unto all them also that love his appearing."

(2 Timothy 4:8)

It is not wrath that awaits the watching saints. It is reward! Paul seals this hope in 1 Thessalonians 5:9, a verse that must be heard afresh in its full force:

"For God hath not appointed us to wrath, but to obtain salvation by our Lord Jesus Christ."
(1 Thessalonians 5:9)

The day of the Lord is indeed coming as a thief. The destruction will be real, global, and inescapable for those who are asleep, who are drunken with the world. But for those who are awake, sober, and faithful, this day is not appointed for wrath. It is appointed for salvation. It is the day when our Lord will gather us to Himself. It is the day when every tear will be wiped away. It is the day when the saints will inherit the kingdom prepared for them from the foundation of the world. While the world reels under the sudden judgment of the thief, the faithful will rejoice in the appearing of their King.

Rebuttal & Answer:
"But Don't You Know The Return of Christ is Imminent."

One of the most common objections raised against the posttribulational understanding of Christ's return is the claim of "imminency," the belief that Jesus could return at any moment without any preceding signs. Many insist that this doctrine is clear and essential, yet a careful and honest reading of Scripture repeatedly challenges such a notion. Scripture consistently presents the return of Christ as being preceded by distinct prophetic events. If certain prophesied signs must occur first, then the idea of an "any-moment" return becomes fundamentally unsustainable.

Paul's Explicit Refutation of Imminency

The Apostle Paul directly addresses the question of imminency in his second letter to the Thessalonians, confronting the idea of an any-moment return of Christ with exceptional clarity. He writes:

"Now we beseech you, brethren, by the coming of our Lord Jesus Christ, and by our gathering together unto him, that ye be not soon shaken in mind, or be troubled... Let no man deceive you by any means: for that day shall not come, except there come a falling away first, and that man of sin be revealed, the son of perdition."
(2 Thessalonians 2:1–3)

Paul's language could not be more emphatic. Before the Church is gathered to Christ, two unmistakable events must take place: a widespread apostasy and the revealing of the Antichrist. The necessity of these precursors completely destroys the concept of an imminent, signless rapture. Any event that must occur first, by definition, renders an any-moment return impossible.

This same pattern of prophecy given, and then fulfillment runs throughout Scripture. Consider the messages to the seven churches in Asia Minor (Revelation 2–3). Each church received a prophecy tailored to its circumstances, often including warnings about impending persecution, slander, and tribulation. For example, to the church in Smyrna, Christ declares:

"Fear none of those things which thou shalt suffer: behold, the devil shall cast some of you into prison, that ye may be tried; and ye shall have tribulation ten days: be thou faithful unto death, and I will give thee a crown of life."
(Revelation 2:10)

Here, believers are specifically warned of imminent imprisonment and trial at the hands of their persecutors, including hostility from those "who say they are Jews, and are not, but are the synagogue of Satan" (Revelation 2:9). The church in Pergamum is told to hold fast amid martyrdom (Revelation 2:13).

If the churches in Asia Minor had truly believed in an imminent rapture, these detailed prophecies of persecution and deliverance would have been perplexing. There was no promise of sudden removal before tribulation; rather, the prophetic warnings pointed to events that had to unfold. The recipients of these letters would not have expected Christ's return at any moment but instead would have watched for the fulfillment of prophecy in their own lives and communities.

The Death Blow:
The Gathering and the End-Time Sequence

The argument is devastatingly reinforced in 2 Thessalonians 2:1–3. Paul specifically ties the coming of the Lord to "our gathering together unto him." The Greek word for gathering, ἐπισυναγωγή (episynagōgē), is rich in meaning. Thayer's Greek Lexicon defines it as "a gathering together in one place, the assembling of the faithful." This is not a vague or spiritualized event; it is a concrete, visible gathering of the redeemed at Christ's return.

This same word is used by Jesus in Matthew 24:31: "And he shall send his angels with a great sound of a trumpet, and they shall gather together (episynagōgē) his elect from the four winds, from one end of heaven to the other." The linguistic and thematic connection between 2 Thessalonians 2:1 and Matthew 24:31 is unmistakable. Both passages describe the Church being gathered to Christ—not in secret, but at the visible Second Coming, after the tribulation and after the sign of the Son of Man appears in heaven.

Yet many pretribulationists, even when admitting that 2 Thessalonians 2:1–3 describes the Second Coming, sidestep the force of the passage by separating the gathering from the actual event. But Paul links them inseparably. Our gathering to Christ cannot occur before the falling away and the revelation of the Antichrist. This is why I call 2 Thessalonians 2:1–3 the death blow to the doctrine of an imminent pretribulational rapture. The plain reading, reinforced by the lexical meaning of episynagōgē, locks it together with the gathering described by Jesus in Matthew 24.

Paul's teaching could not be more decisive. He declares that the coming of Christ, and our gathering to Him, will only take place after a recognizable falling away and after the Antichrist is revealed.

This sequence shatters the entire foundation of imminency. It draws a direct line between the tribulation events, the gathering of the elect, and the visible return of Christ.

Any honest reading of these passages forces us to reject the notion of an any-moment return and to embrace the scriptural order of prophecy, fulfillment, and the final gathering of the saints at Christ's glorious appearing.

The Day and Hour: The Real Context

Many pretribulationists appeal to Jesus' statement, "But of that day and hour knoweth no man" (Matthew 24:36), arguing that this supports an imminent, secret pre-tribulational rapture. Yet the broader context clarifies otherwise. Jesus explicitly timestamps the event in Matthew 24:

"Immediately after the tribulation of those days… then shall appear the sign of the Son of man in heaven…"
(Matthew 24:29–30)

Christ clearly places His visible return immediately after—not before—the tribulation. Therefore, the unknowable "day and hour" refers specifically to the precise timing of the visible Second Coming itself. This passage provides no support for a secret or imminent event years prior; rather, it emphasizes the suddenness and unpredictability of Christ's posttribulational return.

At this juncture, pretribulationists often attempt to counter by appealing to Daniel 9:27, arguing that if any signs must precede Christ's return, then the exact day and hour would become mathematically calculable. However, this line of reasoning is deeply flawed. The only way the pretribulational critique of the posttribulational rapture could work is if the Second Coming were guaranteed to happen exactly seven years—to the day and hour— from the signing of the covenant with many in Daniel 9:27. Even then, their logic could be applied to any event of their choosing, but it remains speculative at best.

Yet, biblical prophecy is not constructed as a stopwatch exercise. Scripture consistently emphasizes recognizable seasons and significant redemptive events, not rigid countdowns to the exact moment. The idea that the Second Coming is measurable to the precise day and hour from any single prophetic event is a stretch that finds no support in the actual language of prophecy.

This kind of hyper-literal approach is also seen in another common misinterpretation involving the sign of Jonah. Jesus said, "For as Jonas was three days and three nights in the whale's belly; so shall the Son of man be three days and three nights in the heart of the earth" (Matthew 12:40). Some interpreters insist this requires a precise seventy-two-hour period, even advocating for a Wednesday crucifixion to fit the timeline. However, Scripture plainly states that Jesus rose "on the third day" (Luke 24:7; 1 Corinthians 15:4), not after exactly three full days and nights. The emphasis was not on an exact mathematical interval, but on the fulfillment of prophecy and the redemptive reality of Christ's presence in the realm of the dead.

Peter confirms this on the Day of Pentecost by citing Psalm 16:10:

"Because thou wilt not leave my soul in hell, neither wilt thou suffer thine Holy One to see corruption."
(Acts 2:27)

Peter's emphasis is on Christ's descent and deliverance from Sheol,[10] not a precise ticking clock.

In summary, the critique that posttribulationism undermines the unknowability of Christ's return simply does not hold up. Jesus Himself declared that we cannot know the precise day or hour of His return, but He just as clearly taught that His coming will be "immediately after the tribulation of those days." Any other argument not only ignores the clear timing Jesus gave, but replaces the wisdom of Scripture with unnecessary speculation.

Discerning the True Season of Christ's Return

---

[10] Sheol (שְׁאוֹל) in Hebrew and Hades (ᾅδης) in Greek both refer to the realm of the dead—a temporary place where souls await judgment. In the Old Testament, Sheol is the general abode of the dead, both righteous and wicked. In the New Testament, Hades continues this meaning as the unseen place of the departed prior to the final resurrection and judgment (cf. Acts 2:27,31; Revelation 20:13–14).

Returning to Jesus' fig tree parable, we see the same principle at work. Rather than teaching imminency, Jesus instructs His followers to discern clear signs signaling the nearness of His return:

"When ye shall see all these things, know that it is near, even at the doors."
(Matthew 24:33)

This parable does not support a pretribulational interpretation of "no one knows the day or hour." Instead, it decisively crushes the pretribulation narrative. Jesus is clear: His followers will know the season of the end and of His coming. If the rapture were truly imminent, there would be no measurable signs or prophetic indicators. Yet Christ teaches the opposite, there will be observable events that mark the approach of His return.

This reality exposes a deep inconsistency in pretribulation teaching. Instead of properly exegeting the passage, pretribulationists often shift from hyper-literalism to hyper-symbolism when interpreting the fig tree parable. Under the pressure of defending a pretribulational and dual covenant system, they reinterpret the fig tree as a symbolic reference to the modern state of Israel, rather than the clear signs Jesus describes. This move allows them to sidestep the devastating contradiction between their doctrine of imminency and Jesus' actual teaching.

It is important to recognize that this interpretive strategy is not accidental. The system itself demands it. Many who make these arguments do so because they have been taught through sermons, popular books, and media to defend these inconsistencies. Instead of letting Scripture speak plainly, they are instructed to find ways around passages that would otherwise dismantle the pretribulational framework.

Jesus explicitly distinguishes between preliminary global crises—such as wars, earthquakes, and pestilences—and the definitive signs of His coming. He warns specifically that initial upheavals alone do not mark the end:

"Ye shall hear of wars and rumours of wars... but the end is not yet"
(Matthew 24:6).

Wars, disasters, and hardships have characterized every era of history; these alone cannot signal the final season.

Instead, Jesus offers an unmistakable prophetic marker: the Abomination of Desolation standing in the holy place (Matthew 24:15). The Apostle Paul echoes this clearly, describing the Antichrist exalting himself above God in the temple (2 Thessalonians 2:4). John confirms this timeline in Revelation 13:5–7, describing the beast's forty-two-month dominion and persecution of the saints. These are clear, recognizable signs that Christ's return is truly near—not earthquakes, plagues, or political upheavals alone.

In light of the biblical context, it becomes clear that the common pretribulation criticism simply lacks merit. The arguments for an imminent, signless rapture dissolve when we let Scripture speak for itself. Jesus and the apostles consistently anchor the hope of His coming in discernible, prophetic milestones—not in hidden schedules or secret events. The fig tree parable, far from supporting imminency, instructs believers to watch for visible signs. The true return of Christ is never presented as an unannounced, unpredictable event, but as the long-awaited climax of redemptive history, revealed at the appointed time. When weighed honestly against the full witness of the New Testament, the pretribulation critique cannot withstand careful exegesis. Instead, the Church is called to sober vigilance and to patient endurance, knowing that the signs will be unmistakable when the season of His appearing finally arrives.

Given these biblical realities, how should believers respond? Rather than waiting for an invisible rescue, believers are called to endure faithfully, soberly watching for the signs Jesus Himself provided. The Church is summoned not to passive escapism but to active, vigilant preparation. Jesus issues a clear command:

"And what I say unto you I say unto all, Watch." (Mark 13:37)

The Church must remain awake, sober, and vigilant. Christ's return will be sudden and decisive, bringing judgment upon the unprepared, but glory and reward to the faithful.

Therefore, let us cast aside myths and conjectures about imminency. Let us hold fast to the clear teachings of Scripture, discerning the signs of the season Jesus Himself provided. The Church was never called to watch for an invisible escape, but rather to stand firm until the sky splits open and the Son of Man returns visibly, gloriously, and triumphantly—immediately after the tribulation of those days.

Next Revelation:
Restoring the Blessed Hope

Are we truly left without hope if there isn't an imminent pretribulation rapture? Many pretrib teachers certainly believe so, often claiming that removing their doctrine leaves believers with nothing but fear and dread. In the next chapter, we'll take a closer look at the often quoted—and often misunderstood—blessed hope. But we're not just correcting pretrib errors. We're also going to confront something that many of my fellow posttrib teachers tend to overlook—the fact that our hope is not merely survival, but vindication, glory, and the righteous deliverance that comes with the visible, triumphant return of Jesus Christ.

Chapter 10:
Restoring the Blessed Hope

One of the most common emotional appeals leveled against the posttribulational return of Christ is the accusation that we are "stealing the blessed hope." Pretribulationists argue that by teaching the Church must endure the tribulation, we rob believers of their comfort and expectation. But this argument is not grounded in Scripture. It is a classic appeal to emotion—a logical fallacy designed to provoke fear and pity rather than reasoned reflection. Fear of suffering, fear of loss, and fear of shattered assumptions are powerful motivators, but they are not valid substitutes for truth. The question is not what feels hopeful, but what is written.

It has become increasingly clear throughout this study that pretribulationist interpretations of Scripture are built on a foundation of presupposition. The doctrine of the pretrib rapture does not arise from a careful synthesis of biblical passages, but from a series of assumed conclusions that are imposed on the text. The "blessed hope" is no exception. This verse is frequently offered as a proof text for the pretrib rapture. Yet an unbiased reading ought to prompt us to ask, "Why would anyone assume that?" Is assumption really the bedrock of doctrine?

In truth, this Scripture, when read in isolation and stripped of context, does not prove a pretribulational rapture. Yet this is precisely the sort of environment where the doctrine thrives in isolated verses, suffocated by assumptions. The argument relies not on careful exegesis, but on knee-jerk reactions from our flesh, which instinctively seeks comfort and ease over hardship or inconvenience. I understand why this is a natural human reaction. Everyone desires relief, not tribulation. But we must recognize that an appeal to emotion is not truth, nor is it evidence.

For many who read Scripture through a biased lens, the "blessed hope" becomes synonymous with escape from persecution, discomfort, and testing. But the real hope of the Church is not flight from trouble, but the glorious revelation of Christ in the clouds, the One who will avenge His bride, brutalized by the enemy, and lift up and exonerate His Church before the eyes of her oppressors. The true blessed hope is the appearing of Jesus Christ in majesty, coming to reward the faithful and to bring righteous retribution against the powers of darkness.

Let us be honest in our reading, resisting the temptation to embrace what feels easiest. Let us refuse to build our faith on assumptions or on arguments that appeal only to our longing for comfort. The "blessed hope" is not about escaping tribulation, but about beholding the glory of our returning King—who comes not to snatch us away from trial, but to bring justice, restoration, and public honor to those who have endured for His name.

Comfort Each Other With These Words

Not only is the blessed hope interpreted through assumptive reasoning, but the comforting words that Paul instructs the Thessalonians to share with one another are also distorted by sentimental presupposition. Pretribulationists often raise the question, "How can we comfort one another with Paul's words if God intends to pour out His wrath upon us?" As we have already thoroughly explored, this argument is fundamentally flawed. The posttribulation view faithfully maintains the biblical stance that plagues and judgments during the tribulation are God's instruments of vengeance directed explicitly toward those persecuting the Church. Believers, therefore, are not brutalized by this judgment—but it is God's just judgement upon the wicked who did the brutalizing of God's Bride.

We have already established that Paul's exhortation, "comfort one another with these words" (1 Thessalonians 4:18), does not stand in isolation; rather, it bookends a continuous flow of thought encompassing the resurrection of the dead in Christ, the catching away of the living, and the arrival of the Day of the Lord (1 Thessalonians 5:2). Despite modern chapter divisions, Paul's message is unified: the Second Coming, the gathering of the saints, and the judgment upon the world constitute a single coherent event. The pastoral directive to "comfort one another" occurs twice (4:18 and 5:11), clearly framing Paul's overarching vision of Christ's return.

This brings forth a critical reflection: Why would the Church require ongoing encouragement if Paul's message promised an immediate, effortless escape from tribulation? If the apostle's message truly indicated a pretribulational rapture, the command to repeatedly encourage one another would seem redundant and unnecessary. An assured escape would eliminate the need for perseverance, watchfulness, and patient endurance. However, the Greek verb Paul uses, παρακαλέω (parakaleō), translated as "comfort" or "encourage." Paul is not issuing a one-time reassurance but an ongoing command to continuously strengthen one another.[11]This comfort is not mere sentimental consolation; rather, it is an active encouragement intended to steady wavering souls, embolden fearful hearts, and fortify believers amidst adversity.

Examining the lexical breadth of παρακαλέω (parakaleō), we find meanings such as "to comfort," "to exhort," "to call near," and "to urge forward." The term often appears in contexts where individuals face significant trials, dangers, or discouragements. Paul's intentional use of this word indicates that the Church would inevitably encounter tribulation, grief, fear, and perhaps martyrdom. True biblical comfort does not arise from avoidance of suffering but from divine empowerment to endure and ultimately overcome it through the hope of resurrection and divine vindication. Paul explicitly conveys this understanding in 2 Thessalonians 1, assuring believers that while they currently suffer, Christ Himself will recompense tribulation upon their persecutors at His visible return (2 Thessalonians 1:6–8). Biblical comfort is not escape from adversity but the assurance of divine justice and ultimate deliverance.

At this juncture, we clearly discern where pretribulationists fundamentally misinterpret the meaning of "comfort." Their

---

[11] The verb παρακαλεῖτε (parakaleite) in 1 Thessalonians 5:11 is a present active imperative, second person plural, conveying the sense of continuous or habitual action. Paul is not merely issuing a one-time command but urging the Thessalonian believers to engage in ongoing mutual encouragement as a habitual part of their community life. The root παρακαλέω carries the semantic range of to comfort, exhort, encourage, or strengthen, depending on context. Here, it links back to the eschatological hope in the preceding verses, showing that understanding the return of Christ should produce a continual ministry of comfort and strengthening among believers (cf. 1 Thessalonians 4:18, where the same verb in the present imperative, παρακαλεῖτε, appears). This grammatical form underscores that biblical comfort is not a passive sentiment but an active, ongoing ministry within the body of Christ. See BDAG, s.v. "παρακαλέω"; Thayer, Greek-English Lexicon, s.v. "παρακαλέω."

emotional argument is constructed not from the explicit statements of Scripture but from the demands of their theological system. They insist enduring tribulation contradicts the idea of comfort, wrongly equating comfort with removal rather than strength through endurance. Yet this is not the gospel's promise. Christ never assured His followers exemption from trials but promised enduring peace amidst them: "In the world ye shall have tribulation: but be of good cheer; I have overcome the world" (John 16:33).

We must ask ourselves candidly: Does the blessed hope signify escape from suffering, or is it the assurance of triumph despite it? Pretribulationism offers a counterfeit comfort requiring no perseverance, watchfulness, or cross-bearing. The apostolic comfort Paul insists believers share is centered explicitly on the climactic, visible return of Jesus Christ—bringing resurrection, the gathering of the saints, and judgment upon the world. This is the genuine blessed hope, and it abundantly suffices to sustain believers through every hardship.

Scripture never bases doctrine upon human fear or emotional avoidance but firmly grounds our hope in the incontrovertible reality of Christ's victory even through suffering. Believers must test all doctrinal claims carefully, particularly those anchored more in emotional reasoning than the explicit testimony of Scripture.

The words Paul instructs believers to comfort each other with are words of resolute encouragement. In God's holy army, no believer is left behind. We exhort one another continually with the assurance that Christ will return, resurrect the dead, and gather together the living saints. The persecutions and hardships are temporary, but the kingdom we inherit is eternal.

This chapter is more than merely a rebuttal of an erroneous doctrine; it is a profound restoration of the true biblical hope. What has been distorted, concealed, and redefined as escapism is here rightly reclaimed as the triumphant, unifying promise of Christ's glorious return. The blessed hope is not a quiet disappearance; it is divine vindication. It is not passive retreat but active rescue. It is not selective salvation; it is total, glorious redemption.

Restoring the True Meaning of the Blessed Hope

Far from stealing the blessed hope, we are restoring it to its original meaning. The "blessed hope" is not an escape hatch from tribulation. It is the visible, triumphant return of Jesus Christ and the glorification of His saints at His appearing. As Paul wrote:

"Looking for that blessed hope, and the glorious appearing of the great God and our Saviour Jesus Christ."
(Titus 2:13)

The blessed hope is Christ Himself, not a secret event, and certainly not a detached phase. It is the glorious appearing of the Lord Jesus, raising the dead, gathering the living, and establishing His reign in power. Hope is not defined by the absence of hardship but by the assurance of victory through it.

Paul uses the word "appearing" (Greek: ἐπιφάνεια[12]epiphaneia), a powerful term indicating a visible, unmistakable manifestation. This same Greek word appears in 2 Thessalonians 2:8, where Paul describes Christ's return as follows:

"And then shall that Wicked be revealed, whom the Lord shall consume with the spirit of his mouth, and shall destroy with the brightness [epiphaneia] of his coming."
(2 Thessalonians 2:8)

Paul explicitly ties the destruction of the Antichrist and the glorious appearance of Christ together as one simultaneous event. This appearing is not hidden or secretive; it is a shining forth in

---

[12] The Greek word ἐπιφάνεια (epiphaneia) is a feminine singular noun meaning "appearance, manifestation, or glorious appearing." Derived from the verb ἐπιφαίνω ("to appear, shine upon"), it was commonly used in Hellenistic culture for the visible appearance of a deity or a royal visit. In the New Testament, Paul adopts this word with eschatological significance, referring explicitly to the visible, glorious return of Christ. It appears in key Second Coming texts such as 2 Thessalonians 2:8 ("the brightness of his coming") and 2 Timothy 4:8 ("unto all them also that love his appearing"). Grammatically, its use as a concrete noun emphasizes the objective, observable nature of Christ's return. It does not denote a secret or invisible event but a public manifestation that aligns with the apocalyptic expectations found throughout Scripture. See BDAG, s.v. "ἐπιφάνεια"; Thayer, Greek-English Lexicon, s.v. "ἐπιφάνεια."

power, a visible, undeniable event witnessed by all nations. Truly, this is the blessed hope.

To teach otherwise diminishes the very hope Scripture commands us to uphold. Paul gives no indication that this "hope" occurs apart from Christ's appearing. He assumes the reader understands that this appearing is the moment of glorification, resurrection, and deliverance. The dispensational interpretation of this verse as referring to a pretribulational rapture has no foundation. There is no textual basis for separating "the blessed hope" from "the glorious appearing." That separation is imposed by theological presupposition, not drawn from Scripture itself.

The implications of this misreading are devastating. By shifting the hope of the Church to an invisible, selective escape, pretribulationism inadvertently excludes the very saints who most need this assurance. What becomes of the faithful believers who endure tribulation, refuse the mark, suffer persecution, and cry out day and night for deliverance? Pretribulationism has no place for them within its definition of the blessed hope.

This doctrine inadvertently renders Christ's return irrelevant to their present suffering, pushes their resurrection into ambiguity, or leaves it entirely undefined. However, Scripture offers no such uncertainty. The blessed hope belongs especially to those saints enduring tribulation. It is their prayers ascending before the throne; it is their endurance that moves God to avenge, and it is their unwavering faith that will be justified when the heavens open and the Son of Man returns in His glory.

There are no second-class saints. There is no alternate resurrection or delayed rapture for faithful survivors. Scripture clearly reveals one Church, one return, and one blessed hope. Whether awake or asleep, first-century believers or end-time saints, we shall all live together with Him. This unity of hope must not be fractured by artificial divisions.

Once again, by imposing presuppositions onto Scripture, dispensational teaching diverts attention from the victorious return of Christ, replacing the defeat of His enemies, the judgment upon Babylon, and the public vindication of His saints with a private escape. Yet the Scriptures point us directly to the day when oppressors are swept away, and we stand before the Son of Man, who will wipe every tear from our eyes.

Our hope is the assurance of salvation in its fullest form: the resurrection of our bodies, glorification at Christ's visible coming, and the inheritance of the kingdom prepared for us from the foundation of the world. This is not merely the avoidance of suffering; it is the reception of the eternal promise.

The Blessed Hope Is Not Escape, But Relief

The blessed hope is not a private evacuation reserved for a privileged group of believers. Rather, it is the public unveiling of Christ from heaven, bringing relief to His saints and retribution upon His enemies.

"And to you who are troubled rest with us, when the Lord Jesus shall be revealed from heaven with his mighty angels."
(2 Thessalonians 1:7)

This promised "rest" is not an escape from trials, but relief through divine judgment. It is God's definitive response to the cries of His saints. It is the moment when the hunted are honored, the oppressed are exalted, and the One who bore our afflictions returns to reign in glory.

Moreover, the blessed hope does not imply avoidance of plagues; it signifies vindication through them. Revelation 8 vividly demonstrates that these plagues fall directly in response to the prayers of the saints. Fire from the heavenly altar is cast upon the earth, initiating judgments—not upon the Church, but upon those who persecuted her.

To assert that the Church is removed before the tribulation is to imply that the saints' prayers for justice have no meaningful role in the climactic unfolding of events. Yet Scripture explicitly contradicts this notion. The saints' prayers initiate divine judgments; their perseverance culminates in victory. Thus, the blessed hope is not escape from the storm. It is the reward bestowed upon those who have endured it faithfully.

One Resurrection, One Hope, One Gathering

The rapture is not a fragmented event; it is the visible climax of the first resurrection, the singular gathering of the righteous at the coming of Christ. Revelation 20 explicitly positions the resurrection of the saints after the tribulation, occurring at the defeat of the Beast. Similarly, Paul, writing in 1 Thessalonians 4, situates the rapture precisely at the resurrection of the dead in Christ. These are not distinct events. Rather, they are the same moment viewed from different perspectives.

To separate the resurrection described in 1 Thessalonians 4 from that in Revelation 20 would require a second rapture, a concept that Scripture never affirms. The apostles preached a singular, unified hope:

"There is one body, and one Spirit, even as ye are called in one hope of your calling."
(Ephesians 4:4)

Pretribulation theology fractures this unity. It suggests one rapture event for the Church, a separate resurrection for the martyrs, and an uncertain fate for surviving saints. Yet Paul is unequivocal:

"Whether we wake or sleep, we should live together with him."
(1 Thessalonians 5:10)

Scripture allows no division among the saints, no alternate destinies. All believers are raised together, gathered together, and glorified together at Christ's return.

Furthermore, consider why pretribulationism creates the necessity for a second rapture. If, according to pretribulational teaching, the dead in Christ and living believers are caught up together just before the tribulation, what then becomes of the saints described in Revelation who endure martyrdom during the tribulation for rejecting the mark of the beast? Revelation 20 explicitly includes these martyred saints as participants in the "first resurrection" (Revelation 20:4-5). By logical necessity, this demands yet another rapture or catching away of these tribulation martyrs after the initial pretribulation event. Here we observe how necessity becomes the mother of invention. The requirement for multiple stages of resurrection arises directly from the assumptions embedded within pretribulationism, not from explicit scriptural affirmation. This demonstrates how a single erroneous presupposition, such as an earlier secret rapture, inevitably demands further theological adjustments that Scripture simply does not support. The biblical model, in contrast, remains consistent: one singular resurrection and one singular rapture event, unified in the visible return of Christ.

Who's Really Stealing the Blessed Hope?

Pretribulation adherents often accuse posttribulation believers of stealing the blessed hope. Yet, in reality, it is they who commit the greater theft. By reserving the hope of Christ's appearing for a secret, privileged group, they withhold from the suffering saints of the end times the very promise meant to carry them through the fire. Their message robs the persecuted and the faithful of their anchor in the storm, their song in the night, and their assurance in tribulation.

Imagine the believer who has been fed on this doctrine every Sunday: "The Lord might rapture us right now." He has not been prepared to endure with patience, to persevere through trial, or to lay hold of faith when all seems lost. That is for another group, he is told—those "tribulation saints" who missed their chance. But when the hour of tribulation comes, what will sustain him? If his hope has been built on the promise of sudden escape, not the call to endure, will he not stumble? As Jesus warned, he becomes like seed on stony ground:

"When tribulation or persecution ariseth because of the word, by and by he is offended"
(Matthew 13:21).

In this way, pretribulation teaching itself steals the blessed hope from those who need it most, depriving them of roots deep enough to withstand the storm.

The blessed hope is not a hidden reward for a select few. It belongs especially to the suffering, the persecuted, the overlooked—those whose cry rises from prison cells, refugee camps, and forsaken places. "How long, O Lord?" they ask, and the answer is not escape into the heavens. The answer is the appearing of Christ in glory.

"Looking for that blessed hope, and the glorious appearing of the great God and our Saviour Jesus Christ."
(Titus 2:13)

Christ is not ashamed to call them brethren. He will not abandon His own in their hour of need. The blessed hope is their inheritance as much as any other. It is the strength that carries them through the fire and the anchor that holds in the wilderness.

Jesus Himself said it plainly:

"But he that shall endure unto the end, the same shall be saved."
(Matthew 24:13)

This is not salvation by works, but salvation by faith that perseveres—the same faith Paul commended when he wrote, "I have fought a good fight, I have finished my course, I have kept the faith" (2 Timothy 4:7). The blessed hope is not the prize of those who fear the trial, but of those who endure it—not because they are strong, but because they trust in the One who is.

From Genesis to Revelation, God's pattern is clear. Never does He promise a premature removal from tribulation. Rather, He promises sustaining grace, overcoming faith, and resurrection glory. Noah was saved through the flood, not from it. The Hebrews were preserved in the fire. Daniel was delivered in the lion's den. The Israelites passed through the plagues and crossed the Red Sea. God's method has never been to whisk His people away, but to bring them through—to protect, to purify, and to restore.

So, it will be again. The true blessed hope is not escape from the tribulation, but triumph in it. It is the vindication and exaltation of all who have trusted in Him, as He returns, not in secret, but in splendor for all His saints.

Appeal to Confidence, Not Fear

Jesus warned that in this world we would have tribulation, but He did not end there.

"These things I have spoken unto you, that in me ye might have peace. In the world ye shall have tribulation: but be of good cheer; I have overcome the world."
(John 16:33)

The hope of the Church is not built on exemption. It is built on victory. To fear tribulation more than we trust Christ is to give fear the final word. But the final word belongs to the Lamb.

"For God hath not given us the spirit of fear; but of power, and of love, and of a sound mind."
(2 Timothy 1:7)

Pretribulationists often appeal to fear. They paint images of saints tormented by plagues, left behind to suffer God's wrath. But this vision ignores the testimony of Revelation itself.

The plagues are not for the saints. They are judgments against those who persecute the saints. The bowls are poured out on Babylon, not the Church. The trumpet blasts are the answer to the prayers of the martyrs. The wrath of God is a precise judgment. It falls on the beast and his followers, not the Lamb and His bride.

To preach otherwise is to doubt the justice of God and to teach believers to dread the appearing of Christ rather than long for it.

Pretrib Misses the Point of the Blessed Hope

If you believe the blessed hope is about pretribulation escape, then you are missing the point entirely.

The blessed hope is not about fleeing tribulation but about entering glory. It is not about escaping oppression but about overcoming through the promise of resurrection. It is not about avoiding death but about rising in victory to live again forever with the King of kings.

Paul called it "that blessed hope, and the glorious appearing of the great God and our Saviour Jesus Christ" (Titus 2:13). The focus is on His appearing, not our disappearing. The hope is not evacuation but revelation, the unveiling of the One who reigns.

The tragedy of the pretribulation interpretation is that it diminishes this glory. It trades the triumphant return of Christ for a secret extraction. It replaces the thrill of His appearing with a fear of being left behind. It detaches the blessed hope from its anchor in resurrection, justice, and kingdom inheritance, and makes it about personal escape from hardship.

But Peter said we are "a royal priesthood" (1 Peter 2:9)—royalty now hidden, with no crown in this world, no honor among men. Because the kingdom we belong to is not of this world, but it is coming. And when it comes, "the kingdoms of this world [shall] become the kingdoms of our Lord, and of His Christ" (Revelation 11:15). We, as co-heirs with Christ, will reign with Him. That is the blessed hope.

The blessed hope is the glorious return of the one true King, bringing with Him eternal life, eternal glory, and eternal communion with Him who loved us, washed us in His own blood, and made us kings and priests unto God forever and ever.

Rebuttal & Answer: "The Restrainer Must be Removed Before the Antichrist Is Revealed!"

One of the most frequently cited proof texts for a pretribulational rapture is found in 2 Thessalonians 2:7, where Paul writes, "he who now letteth will let, until he be taken out of the way." Pretribulationists often conclude that the restraining force holding back the Antichrist must be the Holy Spirit operating through the Church. On this basis, they argue that the Church must be removed before the man of sin can be revealed.

However, this interpretation is not built upon the text itself, but on a set of theological assumptions that are read into it. Rather than following Paul's actual flow of thought, it effectively reverses his intent. The idea that the Church must be "taken out of the way" is not directly stated; it is inferred through circular reasoning and imposed on the passage.

The reason this verse is so frequently cited in isolation is precisely because, by itself, it is vague enough to accommodate nearly any theological bias. Removed from its immediate context, verse 7 becomes a blank canvas for doctrinal speculation. But when it is read within the full argument of 2 Thessalonians 2—especially the opening three verses—the meaning becomes much clearer, and far less accommodating to a pretribulational rapture. In fact, Paul's introduction makes it plain that he expects the Church to endure through the time of testing, not to be absent from it.

A careful reading of the entire passage reveals that Paul gives every reason to expect the perseverance and endurance of the Church during these last days, not its sudden removal. Instead of isolating an ambiguous phrase, we must allow the full sweep of Paul's teaching; his sequence of apostasy, revelation of the man of sin, and the visible coming of Christ to speak for itself. When context is restored, the argument for a pretribulational rapture simply falls away.

The standard pretribulational argument goes something like this: the restrainer is the Holy Spirit working through the Church. Once the Church is removed via the rapture, the Antichrist can then rise. But this reasoning is deeply flawed, based entirely on a theological presumption that is never actually proven. First, they assume the restrainer is the Church. Then, they argue the Church must be removed, and finally, they use this assumption to establish the timing of the rapture—all without ever demonstrating from the passage itself that the restrainer is the Church.

Again, this is classic circular reasoning, dressed in doctrinal language. Instead of engaging Paul's explicit teaching in the rest of the chapter, this argument seizes upon a single ambiguous phrase to construct an entire eschatological system. In truth, this is building a towering doctrine of escape on a vague clause, while neglecting the plain and direct statements Paul already made in the preceding verses.

Paul's Tribulation Paradigm and the True Sequence

To interpret 2 Thessalonians 2 rightly, we must first recognize that it is not a disconnected aside, but a continuation of Paul's established thought from chapter 1—a thought pattern that may rightly be called his "tribulation paradigm." There, Paul assures the church:

"It is a righteous thing with God to recompense tribulation to them that trouble you; and to you who are troubled rest with us, when the Lord Jesus shall be revealed from heaven with his mighty angels."

(2 Thessalonians 1:6–7)

This is a stunningly clear statement of timing and sequence. The Church is experiencing tribulation now and will continue to do so until Christ is revealed from heaven. It is at that moment, not before, that rest and relief are given to the saints, and vengeance is poured out on the persecutors.

Yet, despite the clarity of this sequence, pretribulation teachers have never been able to mount a solid exegetical defense for their position in 2 Thessalonians 2. In order to protect the system, they are committed to, some resort to redefining "apostasy" as the rapture itself, or they simply gloss over the broader context of the chapter in favor of forcing their narrative on a single isolated verse. The continuity between chapters—Paul's flow of thought about tribulation, rest, and the timing of Christ's coming—is often ignored. This breaks the natural connection that Paul intended his audience to follow.

Admission from a Pretribulation Scholar

Few passages in the rapture debate are as hotly contested as 2 Thessalonians 2. Here, we find a shocking admission from leading pretribulational authority John F. Walvoord—one that reveals the very cracks in the pretribulationist argument. Walvoord openly acknowledges:

"The exegesis of 2 Thessalonians 2:1–12 is a crucial aspect of the debate between posttribulationists and pretribulationists…" [13]

He even concedes the posttribulational reading "seems plausible" on the surface:

"Those who hold to a posttribulational rapture propose that the Thessalonians will be delivered at the end of the Tribulation by the coming of the Lord and that this is a contradiction of the pretribulational view. On the surface this seems plausible…"

---

[13] Sources: John F. Walvoord, The Rapture Question (Revised & Enlarged, 1979), pp. 231, 237, 242.

Yet, if you read the entirety of his discourse on 2 Thessalonians 2, you'll notice that Walvoord predictably stops at the second verse, distracting his audience with verse 2 and glossing over the context of verses 1 and 3. Instead of dealing plainly with Paul's argument in verses 1 and 3—where the coming of the Lord and our gathering to Him are explicitly said to occur only after the apostasy and the revealing of the man of sin—he diverts attention to verse 7. There, he identifies the "restrainer" as the Holy Spirit and asserts:

"Pretribulationists, who generally identify the restrainer as the Holy Spirit... This is the point of view that is precisely held by pretribulationists and is usually rejected by posttribulationists because it refutes posttribulationism.

This maneuver allows Walvoord to gloss over the "elephant in the room"—the plain context of verses 1–3—and distract his audience first with verse 2, then with speculative interpretations of the restrainer in verse 7. In doing so, he never fully addresses the posttribulational challenge presented at the very outset of the chapter, instead relying on his own framework to subvert Paul's explicit argument. The controversy over 2 Thessalonians remains, at its heart, a contest between clear context and convenient reinterpretation.

This tacit admission reveals that the straightforward meaning of verses 1–3 does not support their system. Instead, the argument is built by isolating verse 7 from its context and assigning it a meaning that can override the earlier, plain statements of Paul.

The second chapter continues the same thought: Paul beseeches the believers "by the coming of our Lord Jesus Christ, and by our gathering together unto him" not to be shaken or deceived. He is emphatic: "That day shall not come, except there come a falling away first, and that man of sin be revealed" (2 Thessalonians 2:3). This sequence utterly dismantles the notion of an imminent, signless rapture. Paul plainly states that two events—the apostasy and the revelation of the man of sin—must occur before Christ's coming and our gathering to Him.

The Nature of Apostasy and the Identity of the Restrainer

The Greek word Paul uses for "falling away"—ἀποστασία (apostasía)—means defection, rebellion, or spiritual departure. It does not refer to a spatial or physical removal, as pretribulationists sometimes claim, but rather to a moral and religious collapse. The root of ἀποστασία is the preposition ἀπό (apó), meaning "from" or "away from." While ἀπό can sometimes refer to a spatial departure ("to go away from a place"), its use in ἀποστασία is always abstract or figurative, especially in religious and ethical contexts.

For example, in Acts 21:21, Paul is accused of teaching "ἀποστασίαν διδάσκεις ἀπὸ Μωϋσέως" (apostasían disaskō apò Mōyseōs), meaning "teaching departure from Moses." This does not mean leaving a physical location but rather abandoning the Mosaic law or tradition. The usage here is clearly abstract a turning away from a religious position, not a physical exit. This demonstrates that the presence of ἀπό in ἀποστασία supports the understanding of a spiritual or doctrinal departure rather than any sort of literal departure.

The apostasy, then, is not the rapture; it is the abandonment of truth. Paul's other epistles reinforce this pattern:

"Now the Spirit speaketh expressly, that in the latter times some shall depart from the faith, giving heed to seducing spirits, and doctrines of devils"
(1 Timothy 4:1).

Elsewhere, "They will not endure sound doctrine... they shall turn away their ears from the truth and shall be turned unto fables" (2 Timothy 4:3–4). This is not private spiritual backsliding, but a systemic and visible collapse of fidelity to the truth.

The restraining influence is not removed through a supernatural rapture but nullified by spiritual compromise. When pulpits grow silent and holiness is sacrificed on the altar of cultural acceptance, the Church ceases to restrain evil. That is the hour when the man of sin rises.

Verse 6 serves as a tip-off that the real context for understanding the restrainer is found in the preceding verses. Paul writes, "And now ye know what withholdeth that he might be revealed in his time... only he who now letteth will let, until he be taken out of the way" (2 Thessalonians 2:6–7). Paul does not name the restrainer, but he does indicate that the Thessalonians already knew its identity—implying it was visible and familiar to them. If we trace Paul's logic from chapters 1 to 2, the most natural reading is that the restraint is the Church's spiritual effectiveness, not its presence or absence. When the Church is strong, holy, and united in truth, it stands as a bulwark against darkness. But when the Church falls into apostasy, the barrier is gone and evil surges forward. The Antichrist does not rise because the Church has vanished; he rises because the Church has become ineffective.

Early Church Witness and the Larger Canon

This understanding is not a novel interpretation. The earliest generations of Christians understood the rise of evil not as the result of the Church's disappearance, but its decline through apostasy. Ignatius of Antioch, writing to the Ephesians, clearly testifies to this principle:

"When you frequently come together, the powers of Satan are destroyed, and his destructive force is annihilated by the unity of your faith."
(Ignatius, Epistle to the Ephesians 13)

For Ignatius, it was not the absence of the Church that held back evil, but the Church's unity, spiritual fervor, and faithfulness. Apostasy—turning away from the faith—was what allowed evil to break forth, not the physical removal of believers.

This theme appears repeatedly in the early Church. In Revelation chapters 2 and 3, Christ warns His churches to repent or risk having their lampstand—their spiritual influence—removed from its place. He addresses real congregations with real warnings, showing that spiritual compromise would lead to a loss of power and protection, not a supernatural extraction from the earth. In Revelation 12:17, the dragon makes war on the faithful remnant, and in 13:7, the beast is permitted "to make war with the saints, and to overcome them." The saints are not absent; they are present, resisting, and suffering for the testimony of Jesus.

Tertullian, writing in the late second and early third centuries, affirms this same pattern. In his Apology (32), he writes:
"There is also another and a greater necessity for our offering prayer on behalf of the emperors... For we know that a mighty shock impending over the whole earth in fact, the very end of all things threatening dreadful woes is only delayed by the continued existence of the Roman empire."
(Tertullian, Apology 32)

And in On the Resurrection of the Flesh (24), Tertullian again connects the "withholding" of the Antichrist to the restraint provided by the existing world order and the prayers of the faithful:

"What obstacle is there but the Roman state, the falling away of which, by being scattered into ten kingdoms, shall introduce Antichrist upon its own ruins?"
(Tertullian, On the Resurrection of the Flesh 24)

In the context of the ancient world, Rome was the dominant superpower, the main force of law and order. Yet, as Tertullian's own writings suggest, it was not merely Roman political power but the prayers of the faithful saints that were understood to sustain this order and to restrain lawlessness. It was the intercession and the spiritual presence of the Church that "delayed" the impending chaos. The rise of the man of sin was not attributed to the absence or removal of the Church, but to the erosion of righteousness and the weakening of Christian witness through apostasy.

It is important to note that later traditions, centuries removed from Tertullian and Ignatius, sometimes shifted the conversation to focus on ecclesiastical offices or institutions. But in the earliest Christian tradition, the emphasis remained clear: as righteousness wanes and the Church falls into apostasy, the way is cleared for evil's rise. This is not about a secret rapture or the sudden removal of the Church, but the inevitable consequence of spiritual decline a pattern well known to both the apostles and the apostolic fathers.

The sequence is not disappearance, but decline: collapse, apostasy, and only then the revelation of the Antichrist.

It was not political power or military might that held back the man of sin. It was the faithful presence of the saints—their prayers, their endurance, their witness—that restrained the tide of lawlessness. As long as they stood in covenant with the Lord, their spiritual authority served as a preserving force. This is why Paul spoke of "what withholdeth" and "he who now letteth" (2 Thessalonians 2:6–7)—not in reference to some abstract force, but to the Church itself, indwelt by the Spirit, upholding the testimony of Jesus in the face of apostasy.

But herein lies a tragic irony: many today believe that the Church must be removed in order for evil to rise. They see tribulation as a thing to flee from, not to endure through. And in doing so, they have misunderstood the very heart of the blessed hope.

Next Revelation:
The Harmony of Jesus and Paul: No Secret Return

The blessed hope does not rest on escape from hardship but on the revealed glory of Christ at His return. Yet many have mistaken the Church's role in the last days, imagining our removal instead of our endurance. This error is compounded by the claim that Jesus and Paul spoke of different events one for Israel, one for the Church. But Scripture does not support this division. The same trumpet, the same return, and the same gathering appear in the words of both Jesus and Paul, not as separate plans but as a single, unified promise. In the next chapter, we will expose the false dichotomy and show that there is no secret return but only one glorious appearing of the King, seen by all and longed for by the saints.

Chapter 11:
The Harmony of Jesus and Paul:
No Secret Return

Many dispensational teachers claim that Jesus and Paul spoke of different events Jesus to Israel, and Paul to the Church. They argue that Matthew 24 describes a Jewish tribulation scenario, while 1 Thessalonians 4–5 introduces a separate mystery event called the rapture. But this division is artificial and unbiblical. Both Jesus and Paul describe the same future return of Christ, using identical language, signs, and sequence. There is no secret coming and no doctrinal contradiction. There is only one unified message: the glorious return of the Lord to gather His people.

The appropriate method in handling these passages is to harmonize them naturally, allowing Scripture to interpret Scripture in one cohesive narrative. This approach reflects the practice of the early church and the instincts of most believers who read the Bible without systematic presuppositions. Dispensationalism, by contrast, compartmentalizes these scriptures out of necessity in order to support its unique doctrinal system. Rather than following the plain and contextual flow of the text, dispensationalists artificially separate what is clearly intended to be a unified event.

It is not only in academic circles that this compartmentalization is promoted. Anyone who spends time in comment sections on social media will find dispensational rapture believers routinely repeating the same talking points: that those who see the rapture and second coming as a single, unified event are "confused" or "mixing up Israel and the Church." This is not just an internet phenomenon. It is rooted in the direct teaching of dispensational leaders. For example, J. Dwight Pentecost, Walvroord, and LaHaye[14] agree that "confusion" arises when Bible teachers mix up the rapture with the second coming and do not distinguish between the two.

---

[14] John F. Walvoord, The Rapture Question (Grand Rapids: Zondervan, 1979), Tim LaHaye, Rapture Under Attack (Eugene, OR: Harvest House, 1998), J. Dwight Pentecost, Things to Come (Grand Rapids: Zondervan, 1958).

Such claims are not isolated but reverberated throughout dispensational literature and pulpits. The accusation of "confusion" is commonly leveled against those who attempt to harmonize the Olivet Discourse with Paul's teaching on the resurrection and rapture. This charge serves as a defensive measure to protect the system rather than a reflection of sound biblical interpretation.

The irony is that dispensationalism and atheism, though they differ radically in their ends, employ a similar method: both compartmentalize scripture, isolating passages to create the perception of contradiction. For the atheist, the goal is to undermine the authority of the Bible by highlighting supposed inconsistencies. For the dispensationalist, it is to generate the illusion of separate and sequential events between the resurrection, rapture, and second coming dividing what the text itself keeps united.

Without the influence of complex doctrinal systems or institutional indoctrination, most sincere readers of Scripture instinctively harmonize the relevant passages. They see Jesus and Paul as speaking about the same climactic event the triumphant return of Christ, the resurrection of the dead, and the gathering of the saints rather than two unrelated or staggered comings. A straightforward, holistic reading of the New Testament naturally produces a unified hope, not a fractured one.

Parallel Passages: Matthew 24, Thessalonians, and Revelation

Matthew 24 and 1 Thessalonians 4–5 present unmistakably parallel descriptions of the return of Christ. Jesus declares in Matthew 24:30–31:

"They shall see the Son of man coming in the clouds of heaven with power and great glory. And he shall send his angels with a great sound of a trumpet, and they shall gather together his elect from the four winds, from one end of heaven to the other."
Paul affirms the same sequence in 1 Thessalonians 4:16–17:

"The Lord himself shall descend from heaven with a shout, with the voice of the archangel, and with the trump of God: and the dead in Christ shall rise first: then we which are alive and remain shall be

caught up together with them in the clouds, to meet the Lord in the air."

Both passages describe the visible descent of Christ, the unmistakable sound of the final trumpet, a supernatural gathering of God's people, and a glorious meeting in the clouds. These are not isolated motifs, but recurring, integrated elements of a single biblical storyline.

Paul continues without interruption in 1 Thessalonians 5:2, warning that "the day of the Lord so cometh as a thief in the night," a phrase drawn directly from Jesus' warning in Matthew 24:43. This seamless transition underlines that the same climactic event is in view for both Jesus and Paul. The parallel structure does not stop there but finds its apex in the Book of Revelation. At the seventh trumpet (Revelation 11:15–18), we read that "the kingdoms of this world are become the kingdoms of our Lord, and of his Christ; and he shall reign for ever and ever." This seventh and final trumpet marks the consummation of the age—the unleashing of wrath upon the wicked, the rewarding of the righteous, and the final judgment of the dead. Significantly, the seventh trumpet is also the point when the mystery of God is said to be finished, as Revelation 10:7 affirms:

"In the days of the voice of the seventh angel, when he shall begin to sound, the mystery of God should be finished, as he hath declared to his servants the prophets."

In the flow of the text, this is the precise moment when God's redemptive plan comes to completion—the resurrection, the gathering, the judgment, and the inauguration of Christ's kingdom.

A key term that unites these passages is parousia (παρουσία), meaning "coming" or "presence." In Matthew 24:27, Jesus declares, "as the lightning cometh out of the east, and shineth even unto the west; so shall also the coming (parousia) of the Son of man be." Paul uses the same word in 1 Thessalonians 4:15: "we which are alive and remain unto the coming (parousia) of the Lord shall not prevent them which are asleep." In the New Testament, parousia is never used of a hidden or secret event. Its entire meaning carries the sense of an open, manifest arrival.

Thayer's Greek Lexicon, παρουσία (parousía):

"In the N.T., especially of the advent, i.e., the future, <u>visible return from heaven of Jesus, to raise the dead,</u> hold the last judgment, and set up formally and gloriously the kingdom of God."

So, every usage of parousia in the New Testament, whether for ordinary arrivals or for the Second Coming, refers to a real, present, and visible arrival never a hidden or symbolic one.

Equally significant is the term episynagōgē (ἐπισυναγωγή), meaning "gathering together" or "assembly." In Matthew 24:31, Jesus promises that His angels will "gather together (episynagōgē) his elect from the four winds." Paul picks up this exact term in 2 Thessalonians 2:1: "by our gathering together (episynagōgē) unto him."[15]The use of the same Greek word, transliterated identically here for clarity, removes all doubt: both Jesus and Paul speak of a single, supernatural assembly of believers at Christ's coming, not two distinct or staggered events.

This "gathering" is the final harvest, echoing Jesus' parables. In Matthew 13:30, the angels gather the tares first for destruction, then the wheat into the barn. The sequence is consistent across the Gospels and Epistles: the wicked are bundled for judgment culminating in the final battle while the saints are gathered as the precious harvest. There is no need to invent a "secret" gathering; the narrative is one unified event.

When we turn to Revelation, the connection is cemented at the sounding of the seventh trumpet. Not only does this trumpet signal the transfer of kingdoms to Christ and the rewarding of the

---

[15] The Greek word ἐπισυναγωγή (episynagōgē, "gathering together") refers to a complete, collective assembling into one place or person. All major lexicons agree that in 2 Thessalonians 2:1, it signifies the final eschatological gathering of believers to Christ at His coming (parousia). Thayer defines it as "a gathering together in one place... the gathering of believers to Christ at His coming" (Thayer, Greek-English Lexicon, s.v. ἐπισυναγωγή). BDAG affirms it as "the eschatological gathering of Christians to the Lord at His return." Louw-Nida categorizes it as a definitive "gathering for a specific purpose" directly tied to the Second Coming. Strong similarly defines it as a "complete collection... the assembling of believers at the end of this age." This noun is directly related to the verb ἐπισυνάγω, used in Matthew 24:31 to describe the gathering of the elect "after the tribulation." The shared word family demonstrates that Paul and Jesus refer to the same post-tribulational event, further confirmed by Paul's explicit statement that this gathering cannot occur until after the apostasy and the revealing of the man of sin (2 Thessalonians 2:3).

saints, but it is also the very moment when, as Revelation 10:7 says, "the mystery of God is finished." In other words, all that was foretold—the resurrection, the gathering (episynagōgē), the judgment, and the kingdom—reaches its culmination at this trumpet. No mysteries remain to be fulfilled after this point.

For readers who feel some of these passages and themes are revisited often, this is deliberate. As noted in the preface, biblical prophecy is deeply interconnected. Its major events and motifs overlap repeatedly across different books, requiring that we return to foundational verses from several angles. This ensures the reader grasps not just individual proof texts, but the unified, sweeping narrative of Christ's return.

Unified Mission: No Divide Between Jesus and Paul

This harmony reflects the very mission of Christ, who was sent not only to Israel but to be "a light to lighten the Gentiles" (Luke 2:32). From the very beginning, God's redemptive plan was global in scope. Jesus' final words to His disciples were not a command to remain within the boundaries of Jerusalem, but rather to "go therefore, and teach all nations" (Matthew 28:19). Paul, called as the apostle to the Gentiles, declared that the Gospel is "to the Jew first, and also to the Greek" (Romans 1:16). Peter, too, was divinely sent to the house of Cornelius, a Roman centurion, demonstrating that the Gospel's reach shattered ethnic boundaries from the outset. The notion that Jesus' eschatological teaching was only for Jews is an affront to the very mission He launched—a mission that the apostles faithfully carried forward across all nations. This same mission unites the eschatology of Jesus and Paul into one seamless message.

Jesus and Paul are not speaking past each other, nor are they offering separate hopes for separate peoples. Rather, they present a single, cohesive expectation—the gathering of God's people—episynagōgē—at the visible, victorious—parousia—of the Lord. Attempts to divide their teaching are not rooted in Scripture, but in later systems that compartmentalize the text for doctrinal reasons. The hope of the Church is not fractured, secret, or staggered, but singular and climactic: the glorious return of Christ and the revelation of all God's redemptive mysteries at the seventh trumpet.

Dispensationalists often attempt to divide Jesus' words from Paul's letters by claiming that Jesus was speaking only to Jews under the Law, while Paul was revealing hidden mysteries to the Church. However, this division cannot withstand careful examination. The disciples were not simply representatives of Israel; they were chosen as the very foundation of the Church. Jesus Himself commissioned them with a mission that extends to the whole world:

"And he said unto them, Go ye into all the world, and preach the gospel to every creature."
(Mark 16:15)

This commission is universal in scope, carrying forward every promise and instruction—including those regarding His return—not merely for Israel, but for all who would enter the covenant.

Paul, likewise, does not undermine or detach himself from Jesus' teaching. On the contrary, he repeatedly points believers back to the words of Christ, building on the same foundation and fulfilling the same redemptive plan. The message that went first "to the Jew, and also to the Greek" (Romans 1:16) is a singular hope, grounded in one gospel and one Lord. Throughout his epistles, Paul draws no line of separation between Jewish believers and Gentile believers in terms of the blessed hope, the return of Christ, or participation in the promises. As he writes in Ephesians 2:14–16, Christ "hath made both one, and hath broken down the middle wall of partition between us... that he might reconcile both unto God in one body by the cross."

The notion of a divided message or a split destiny is entirely foreign to the New Testament. There is one people of God, one covenant body, and one glorious hope for all who are in Christ—Jew and Gentile alike. The unity between the Gospels and the Epistles is both consistent and deliberate, affirming that all the promises of God are "yea, and in him Amen, unto the glory of God by us" (2 Corinthians 1:20).

The True People of God and the Resurrection Hope

There is no scriptural basis for two returns of Christ. Nowhere in the Bible do we find a "pretribulational" phase distinct from the Second Coming. Every passage about Christ's return presents a singular, glorious, visible event. The resurrection of the righteous is always connected to "the last day"—never to some preliminary, secret coming.

Consider Daniel 12, where the Septuagint (LXX) renders "the time of trouble" as "tribulation." The context is unmistakable:

"And at that time shall Michael stand up, the great prince which standeth for the children of thy people: and there shall be a time of trouble [θλῖψις, 'tribulation' in the LXX], such as never was since there was a nation even to that same time: and at that time thy people shall be delivered, every one that shall be found written in the book. And many of them that sleep in the dust of the earth shall awake, some to everlasting life, and some to shame and everlasting contempt."
(Daniel 12:1–2)

But what is this "book" in which God's people are written? Daniel does not leave us with an ethnic, geographic Israel as the answer. Instead, the New Testament reveals this book to be the "book of life." The book of life is mentioned repeatedly in Revelation and is the definitive record of those who belong to Christ. As Revelation 21:27 declares:

"And there shall in no wise enter into it any thing that defileth, neither whatsoever worketh abomination, or maketh a lie: but they which are written in the Lamb's book of life."

This is confirmed in Revelation 20:12, 15, which speaks of the final judgment:

"And I saw the dead, small and great, stand before God; and the books were opened: and another book was opened, which is the book of life… And whosoever was not found written in the book of life was cast into the lake of fire."

The promise in Daniel is for those found written in the book of life—those who belong to Christ, regardless of national descent. This is the Church, the assembly of all who have been redeemed by the blood of the Lamb.

To insist that Daniel 12 refers only to geographic or ethnic Israel ignores the broader biblical narrative. Throughout the New Testament, God's people are defined not by genealogy or geography, but by faith in Christ. As Paul wrote in Philippians 4:3, the true laborers in the Gospel are "whose names are in the book of life." In Hebrews 12:23, the Church is described as "the general assembly and church of the firstborn, which are written in heaven." The Church—not ethnic Israel—is the people delivered at the resurrection.

This same order is affirmed in Revelation 20:4–6:

"And I saw thrones, and they sat upon them, and judgment was given unto them: and I saw the souls of them that were beheaded for the witness of Jesus, and for the word of God, and which had not worshipped the beast, neither his image, neither had received his mark upon their foreheads, or in their hands; and they lived and reigned with Christ a thousand years... This is the first resurrection. Blessed and holy is he that hath part in the first resurrection: on such the second death hath no power, but they shall be priests of God and of Christ, and shall reign with him a thousand years."
(Revelation 20:4–6)

This "first resurrection" explicitly includes those who endured the great tribulation and overcame the Beast. They rise and reign with Christ—the very fulfillment of the Danielic promise for those found "written in the book."

This harmonizes with Zechariah 14, which describes the climactic Day of the Lord. The nations gather against Jerusalem, and Christ returns with His saints:

"Then shall the Lord go forth, and fight against those nations, as when he fought in the day of battle. And his feet shall stand in that day upon the mount of Olives... and the Lord my God shall come, and all the saints with thee."
(Zechariah 14:3–5)

There is no hint of a secret, prior coming. Instead, Christ returns with all His saints at the very moment the nations are arrayed for battle. The prophecy continues:

"And it shall come to pass, that every one that is left of all the nations which came against Jerusalem shall even go up from year to year to worship the King, the Lord of hosts, and to keep the feast of tabernacles."
(Zechariah 14:16)

Those who survive the judgment—nations once arrayed against Christ—will now acknowledge His reign and worship Him in Jerusalem. This matches the vision of Revelation 19, where Christ appears in power, the armies of earth are defeated, and the saints return with Him:

"And the armies which were in heaven followed him upon white horses, clothed in fine linen, white and clean."
(Revelation 19:14)

All of these events—the gathering for battle, the visible descent of Christ, the resurrection, and the reign with the saints—occur at a single, public parousia (coming). As Paul writes:

"For as in Adam all die, even so in Christ shall all be made alive. But every man in his own order: Christ the firstfruits; afterward they that are Christ's at his coming."
(1 Corinthians 15:22–23)

Notice carefully: the text says, "at his coming," not "at his comings." The resurrection and rapture are one singular moment, not scattered across a secret coming and then a public advent. There is not a single verse that teaches another coming of Christ between the first and second advent. Even the passages used to defend a multistage resurrection speak only of a single, climactic event. It would appear that the pretribulational narrative lacks true biblical support.

Both Paul and Jesus issue the same warnings. They speak of deception, tribulation, and a great falling away; they promise vindication at Christ's return, not before. Jesus, in Matthew 24:10–12, declares:

"Then shall many be offended, and shall betray one another, and shall hate one another. And many false prophets shall rise, and shall deceive many. And because iniquity shall abound, the love of many shall wax cold."

This warning is not limited to a separate group of Jews. It is a sobering prophecy for the entire Church, for all who follow Christ. Paul echoes this in 2 Thessalonians 2:3:

"Let no man deceive you by any means: for that day shall not come, except there come a falling away first, and that man of sin be revealed…"

The same themes deception, apostasy, endurance appear in both passages. Jesus and Paul describe the same future, the same sequence, the same final hope. Their message is unified, urgent, and given by the same Spirit.

Scripture harmonizes the timing of the resurrection, the rapture, and the visible return of Christ as one unified event—the blessed hope of the Church and the appointed day of the world's judgment. All who are "found written in the book"—the book of life—are those who belong to Christ, the true Church delivered at His return.

The Call to Endurance: Not Escape, But Perseverance

And they call us to the same response: endurance. Jesus told His disciples in Matthew 24:13, "But he that shall endure unto the end, the same shall be saved." He was not promising an exemption from hardship; He was commanding perseverance through it. Paul, too, charted the same path. In Romans 5:3–4, he wrote, "We glory in tribulations also: knowing that tribulation worketh patience; and patience, experience; and experience, hope." And again in 2 Timothy 2:12, he exhorted, "If we suffer, we shall also reign with him." This is the consistent call of the New Testament Church—not escape, but endurance. Not removal from suffering, but perseverance through it, until the Lord is revealed from heaven and vindicates His saints in power and glory.

It is worth reflecting again on the testimony of those who have gone before us, especially during the time of the Diocletian persecution—a period already discussed earlier in this book. Those Christians did not receive an easy escape from tribulation. They faced imprisonment, torture, and martyrdom with patience and faith. They were not second-class Christians but were saints of God, true believers whose lives became a sweet savor offered up to God the Father.

Consider also the example of Ignatius of Antioch, who was devoured by wild animals in the Roman arena, and Polycarp, another disciple of the Apostle John, who was executed for his steadfast confession of Christ. What of the apostles themselves, nearly all of whom sealed their testimony with martyrdom? It is misguided—and frankly offensive—to dismiss their endurance as unique to Jews, as some pretribulational writers have argued. To do so is not only inaccurate but risks veering into antisemitism by relegating suffering solely to Jewish believers. While not every dispensationalist holds to this view, it is an unavoidable implication within some strands of classic dispensationalism, which claims the tribulation is for the Jews only and the Church will be removed beforehand. History, however, bears witness to a more radical reality: God's true saints—Jew and Gentile alike—have always been called to endure.

Let us then remember the ancient words from Job:

"For I know that my redeemer liveth, and that he shall stand at the latter day upon the earth"
(Job 19:25).

Even Job's hope was not in a secret return to heaven, but in the visible, glorious appearing of God our Redeemer standing upon the earth. That hope has always been the anchor of God's people. Let it be your comfort as well.

The Elect Are the Church: Not a Separate Jewish Remnant

Some claim the "elect" in Matthew 24 must refer exclusively to Israel. But this creates a theological contradiction: it demands two elect peoples with two separate destinies and, by extension, two different plans of salvation. This notion stands in direct opposition to Paul's argument in Romans 9:6–8:

"For they are not all Israel, which are of Israel... That is, They which are the children of the flesh, these are not the children of God: but the children of the promise are counted for the seed."

Scripture never offers parallel salvation programs one for the Church and another for ethnic Israel. The New Covenant in Christ is the fulfillment of all of God's promises and is open to all who believe, Jew or Gentile. The elect are not defined by ethnicity but by faith in Christ and reception of the promise of eternal life.

To address the 144,000 and the wider claims of dual covenant theology, it must be said: there is only one people of God who truly hold the promise of salvation. Nowhere in Scripture is there another covenant that brings salvation outside of Christ. Jesus Himself is emphatic:

"I am the way, the truth, and the life: no man cometh unto the Father, but by me."
(John 14:6)

He further warns,

"He that entereth not by the door into the sheepfold, but climbeth up some other way, the same is a thief and a robber."
(John 10:1)

These statements are exclusive, not harsh. The gospel offers a single, uncompromising way: salvation is found only in the Messiah, Jesus Christ.

John echoes this in his epistle, stating:

"Who is a liar but he that denieth that Jesus is the Christ? He is antichrist, that denieth the Father and the Son."
(1 John 2:22)

This does not mean every unbeliever is the Antichrist, but it does make clear that opposition to the Son is opposition to God's only way of salvation and makes such a person an antichrist by John's definition. No one enters the salvific covenant apart from the blood of the Lamb. Any theology that suggests otherwise is not only flawed but stands against the testimony of Scripture and the entire apostolic witness.

Therefore, to claim the elect in Matthew 24 are a distinct class of ethnic Jews, awaiting a separate return or a parallel salvation program, is to fundamentally deny the unity and exclusivity of the New Covenant. The Church, comprised of all who are in Christ, is "the Israel of God" (Galatians 6:16), the true seed of Abraham (Galatians 3:28–29):

"There is neither Jew nor Greek... for ye are all one in Christ Jesus. And if ye be Christ's, then are ye Abraham's seed, and heirs according to the promise."

When the angels gather the elect, they gather all who belong to Christ and not because they are Jewish, but because they are His.

For a deeper treatment of dual covenant theology its history, biblical critique, and implications see Chapter 12: "Grace Was Always the Way: Exposing the False Gospel of Dispensationalism." This chapter addresses in detail the claim that God offers salvation to Israel by a different means, demonstrating from both Old and New Testaments that there is always only one covenant, one Redeemer, and one people of promise.

The unity of the redeemed is not a minor point. It is the heartbeat of New Testament eschatology and soteriology. There is one flock, one Shepherd, and one blessed hope for all who are in Christ.

Clarifying the 144,000: Not the Elect Gathered by Angels

It is sometimes argued that the 144,000 Jews sealed in Revelation 7—and seen again with the Lamb in Revelation 14—are the very elect of Matthew 24. This interpretation suggests that Jesus' return is still primarily focused on a national Jewish remnant gathered after the tribulation. However, this argument not only conflates two entirely different prophetic portraits but also introduces significant theological and narrative problems.

First, the 144,000 are never described as being gathered by angels from the four winds. Their location and preservation are already established: Revelation 14:1 shows them standing with the Lamb on Mount Zion, not scattered among the nations. Their sealing takes place before the plagues begin (Revelation 7:3–4), and they are kept safe throughout the tribulation by divine decree. They are a preserved remnant, not a group supernaturally harvested at the Second Advent.

This distinction is reinforced by the prophetic instructions of Joel 2:32 and Zechariah 14:5, which call the faithful to flee to the mountains, specifically the Mount of Olives, at the time of the Lord's coming:

"...ye shall flee to the valley of the mountains; for the valley of the mountains shall reach unto Azal: yea, ye shall flee, like as ye fled from before the earthquake in the days of Uzziah king of Judah: and the Lord my God shall come, and all the saints with thee."
(Zechariah 14:5)

Why would this remnant be told to flee to the Mount of Olives during the Second Advent if they are the very elect to be gathered by angels from the four winds immediately after the tribulation? This question exposes a serious complication for the dispensational interpretation of both the fig tree parable and the "restoration" of Israel. It presses us to ask: When, exactly, is unified Israel restored—before or after the tribulation? The dispensational doctrine's foundation cracks under the pressure of proper exegesis.

At this point, we must pause and ask a crucial question—one that is often missed by pretribulation rapture teachers: What are the 144,000 the firstfruits of? As discussed earlier in Chapter 8, this is a pivotal issue that clarifies their prophetic identity. Revelation 14:4 describes them as "the firstfruits unto God and to the Lamb." Firstfruits, by definition, are not the whole harvest; they are a consecrated beginning, a sign of the fuller ingathering to come—namely, the millennial reign. The 144,000 serve as the firstfruits of the millennium, representing a restored, believing remnant within Israel who are preserved through the tribulation and given a unique role at the dawn of Christ's earthly kingdom.

By contrast, Jesus uses the language of a global harvest for the elect:

"The harvest is the end of the world; and the reapers are the angels. As therefore the tares are gathered and burned in the fire; so shall it be in the end of this world. The Son of man shall send forth his angels, and they shall gather out of his kingdom all things that offend... Then shall the righteous shine forth as the sun in the kingdom of their Father."
(Matthew 13:39–43)

And again, in Matthew 24:31:

"And he shall send his angels with a great sound of a trumpet, and they shall gather together his elect from the four winds, from one end of heaven to the other."

These images are distinct and should not be confused. The 144,000 are a symbolic remnant—firstfruits within Israel, sealed and protected through the tribulation as a testimony to God's faithfulness and the opening of the millennial age. The elect gathered by the angels are the Church universal—the full harvest, drawn from every tribe, tongue, and nation, brought together at the return of Christ.

To conflate these distinct prophetic images is to create confusion where Scripture offers clarity. The Church is the harvest gathered by angels at the end of the age. The 144,000 are the firstfruits—the sign that God's covenant faithfulness to Israel is not forgotten, but their role is distinct from the global gathering of the elect.

Understanding what the 144,000 are the firstfruits of the millennium gives us a cleaner, more cohesive prophetic timeline. It resolves ambiguity, avoids theological stretching, and sheds light on the specific role of Israel's remnant in the millennium. This topic, already addressed in detail in Chapter 8, stands as a vital reference point as we move forward.

In the next section, we turn to another widely used pretribulational argument: the claim that the twenty-four elders in Revelation represent the raptured Church. We will examine this claim in its context, seeking once again to let Scripture speak for itself rather than forcing it to serve any doctrinal system.

Rebuttal & Answer:
"The 24 Elders the Raptured Church."

One of the more persistent claims in pretribulational theology is that the twenty-four elders seated around the throne in Revelation 4–5 represent the raptured Church, already in heaven before the tribulation begins. But this assertion is built not on solid exegesis, but on theological assumption imposed upon a visionary text. A closer examination of the passage—lexically, contextually, narratively, and canonically—reveals that this interpretation not only fails under scrutiny but obscures the very structure and flow of Revelation's message. The elders are not a secret identity code for the Church. They are symbolic representatives of divine government, serving in a heavenly vision that frames the throne of God—not as a calendar cue, but as a theological reality.

To begin with, the scene in Revelation 4–5 is not a timeline. John is not shown a sequential event but is taken in the Spirit into the heavenly court to behold the throne, the scroll, and the one who is worthy to open it. This is not a rapture timestamp. It is a throne room vision—a prophetic orientation to heaven's verdicts, not a narrative chronology of earthly removal. The entire sequence is a prelude to judgment, not an escape clause. The book of Revelation itself offers abundant precedent for such thematic flashbacks and visionary overlays: the trumpet judgments are previewed before the sealing of the servants; Revelation 12 recounts the birth of Christ long after His resurrection is assumed in the timeline; the seventh trumpet is sounded before the bowls are even introduced. These are not chronological sequences but layered scenes, like panels of stained glass arranged by theme. To isolate the twenty-four elders and elevate their appearance as evidence of a Church already raptured is to confuse symbolic theater with historical documentary. John is not handed a stopwatch; he is handed a scroll and commanded to see who is worthy to break its seals.

Moreover, the identity of the twenty-four elders is not literal, but symbolic. Their number—twenty-four—is drawn directly from Old Testament priestly and judicial structures. David appointed twenty-four courses of priests for temple service, ensuring continual intercession before the Lord (1 Chronicles 24). The Jewish Sanhedrin, the governing court of Israel, likewise consisted of twenty-three elders with a high priest presiding as the twenty-fourth. This is not incidental; it is covenantal imagery. Representing the full council of God with Christ at the center of both covenants. Both Testaments speak of Jesus the Son of God, for He is the center of all Scripture. The elders, dressed in white robes and wearing golden crowns, are a picture of heavenly order, not personal autobiography. According to Thayer's Greek Lexicon, the word *presbyteros* in this context need not signify redeemed humans at all. Thayer notes that in Revelation, "the twenty-four elders are understood by many as a heavenly Sanhedrin or divine council of angels or celestial rulers, symbolic of order, judgment, and representation." In other words, they are throne room officials—not resurrected Church members. Their garb and thrones reflect their heavenly commission—not their salvific testimony.

This reading is not a modern novelty. Several ancient and scholarly sources confirm it:

- **Thayer's Greek-English Lexicon** (presbyteros, Strong's 4245):
  "In the Apocalypse, the twenty-four elders are understood by many to be either the representatives of the church, or of the heads of the Old and New Testament church, or as a heavenly council or court about the throne of God." (abridged, Thayer)
- **The International Critical Commentary (ICC), Revelation (Swete, 1906):**
  "The elders are not the representatives of the Church, but of a wider order; a celestial council or court about the throne, after the manner of the Sanhedrin." (p. 65, Swete)
- **Victorinus of Pettau, Commentary on the Apocalypse 4.4:**
  "The twenty-four elders sitting are the twelve patriarchs and the twelve apostles... who sit for the twelve tribes and the church." (ANF 7:347)

Anticipating the Pretrib Comeback: Apostolic Presence in the Vision

Some pretribulationists will counter that if the twenty-four elders are the twelve patriarchs and twelve apostles, this proves the glorified Church is present in heaven before the tribulation. They reason: "John saw the elders on thrones; the apostles are among them; therefore, the church is already raptured." But this argument does not stand up to the narrative or the symbolism of John's vision.

1. **The narrative logic:**

   John, the apostle, is himself present in the vision, observing and interacting with the elders. Nowhere in the entire account does he identify himself as one of the elders, nor does he show any recognition of familiar faces or speak to any fellow apostles as peers. When an elder questions him in Revelation 7:13, John responds as an inquirer and learner, not as a fellow council member. If the elders were literally and not symbolically the apostles—including John—it would create a logical contradiction: John would be both a participant and an observer, both present and present to himself. The vision never once hints at such self-recognition or duality.

   This is not simply an argument from silence. Rather, it is an argument from the literary stance of the text. Throughout the book, John is the recipient of revelation, the one summoned "in the Spirit" to witness what transpires before the throne. He is always on the outside of the council, never among the enthroned. He is never depicted as crowned, robed, or participating in heavenly government; his role is always that of the prophet and witness.

2. **The symbolic function:**

   As the early church fathers and major lexicons confirm, the twenty-four elders function as a symbolic, heavenly Sanhedrin—a celestial council representing the fullness of divine government and the whole people of God across both covenants. Their number is emblematic, not a literal census. Victorinus of Pettau and Oecumenius, as well as the International Critical Commentary and Thayer's Lexicon, all confirm the symbolic and representative nature of the elders.

3. **In conclusion:**

If the twenty-four elders were literal, individual apostles (including John), the vision would at least hint at such recognition or role. Instead, the elders remain a symbolic, heavenly council, and John remains the visionary, observing and receiving, never enthroned or participating. The narrative is not silent—it is clear. The elders represent not a "who," but a "what": the celestial council of God's order and redemptive purpose. This aligns with apocalyptic conventions, the language of symbol, and the literary structure of Revelation itself.

Therefore, the claim that the elders prove a pretribulational rapture for the church cannot withstand the internal logic or the symbolic grammar of John's vision.

When all the textual, historical, and theological evidence is weighed, it is clear that the twenty-four elders function as a heavenly Sanhedrin. Like the earthly Sanhedrin of Israel—an assembly of elders presided over by the high priest—these elders constitute the divine council that stands before the throne, surrounding the Lamb, rendering worship and participating in heaven's judgments. Their presence signals the order, continuity, and universality of God's redemptive plan—a plan that encompasses both covenants but does not reduce itself to a secret code for end-time escape.

The heavenly Sanhedrin motif is further underscored by their actions: holding golden bowls of incense, which are the prayers of the saints, and casting their crowns before the throne in continual worship. They are not enthroned Church members resting from tribulation, but high officials in the celestial court, bearing witness to the worthiness of the Lamb and the unfolding of God's purposes.

To insist that these elders must be the raptured Church is not only unwarranted by the text but also diminishes the sweeping vision of Revelation. The real glory of the passage is not in the Church's hidden presence, but in the visible reign of Christ, the Lamb who is worthy to open the scroll, and the multitudes redeemed from every nation, tribe, and tongue who overcome by faith.

This is the true vision set before us a heavenly council, a cosmic Sanhedrin, and the Lamb who alone is worthy.

The Elders as Observers, Not the Redeemed

Most pretribulational teachers would still assert that the twenty-four elders in Revelation represent the raptured Church, supposedly enthroned in heaven before the tribulation begins. Their main proof text is the song in Revelation 5:9–10, which, in the King James Version, reads:

"Thou hast redeemed us to God by thy blood out of every kindred, and tongue, and people, and nation; And hast made us unto our God kings and priests: and we shall reign on the earth."
(KJV, Revelation 5:9–10)

However, the earliest and most reliable Greek manuscripts including Codex Sinaiticus and Codex Alexandrinus do not say "us" or "we." They read:

"Thou hast redeemed <u>them</u> to God by thy blood... and hast made <u>them</u> kings and priests..."

This is not a trivial change. It is decisive. The elders and the four living creatures are not singing about their own redemption. They are proclaiming the Lamb's victory in redeeming others—those "from every kindred, tongue, people, and nation." Their song is not autobiographical; it is doxological. It is heaven celebrating the worthiness of Christ, not the elders recounting their personal deliverance.

Even more telling is who sings this song. It is not only the elders, but the four living creatures, the cherubim of Ezekiel's visions, who stand closest to the throne of God. These are not humans, but celestial beings who, throughout Scripture, represent the highest orders of heaven's worship and judgment. Are we to believe these angelic creatures were also raptured from the nations? That would be absurd. The song is not about a secret escape from earth; it is the entire heavenly court proclaiming the redemptive power of the Lamb for those who overcome.

This heavenly doxology shifts the focus from the elders as an exclusive group to the universal scope of Christ's work. The victory celebrated in the song is for the multitude—those who "come out of great tribulation" (Revelation 7:14), gathered from all nations and tribes. It is not a memorial of escape, but a proclamation of Christ's conquering grace for the saints who endure.

This understanding is confirmed beyond question in Revelation 7:13, where one of the elders—supposedly part of the raptured Church, according to the pretrib argument—turns and asks John:

"What are these which are arrayed in white robes? and whence came they?"
(Revelation 7:13)

If the elders are the Church, the question is incoherent. John is not among them; he is questioned by them. He does not recognize himself or any apostle as part of the council, nor does he respond as a peer or brother. His answer is as an outsider, a witness to the scene. The elder's question is priestly, even judicial, but not fraternal. He stands as a member of the heavenly court, observing the arrival of saints who have persevered through tribulation. It is worth reiterating John is not talking to himself or to any familiar earthly colleague. He is a prophetic observer, not a participant in the council.

What, then, is the true role of the elders? Revelation 5:8 gives us the answer:

"The four beasts and four and twenty elders fell down before the Lamb, having every one of them harps, and golden vials full of odours, which are the prayers of saints."

Let that image settle in. The elders along with the living creatures are far from being silent recipients of redemption. They are priestly members, holding the intercessory prayers of the saints as incense before the throne. They do not represent the saints in their own person they carry the prayers on behalf of the saints, offering them up to God as a fragrant offering.

These are not pretrib-rapture Church members reminiscing about their earthly days. They are heavenly attendants, offering the groanings of God's people who are enduring below. And yes, these are the very prayers that are handed over to the angel in Revelation

8, who then offers them on the golden altar before God. The text is explicit:

"And another angel came and stood at the altar, having a golden censer; and there was given unto him much incense, that he should offer it with the prayers of all saints upon the golden altar which was before the throne. And the smoke of the incense... ascended up before God out of the angel's hand. And the angel took the censer, and filled it with fire of the altar, and cast it into the earth..." (Revelation 8:3–5)

These are not idle prayers. They become the very catalyst for God's righteous judgments. The plagues of the tribulation are unleashed not because the Church is absent, but because the cries of the saints for justice have reached heaven and demand a response. The elders, therefore, are not commemorating escape, but mediating the justice that is soon to come.

As we've already seen and briefly touched on, this reading aligns not only with the broader testimony of Revelation but also with respected lexical and patristic sources. Thayer's Greek Lexicon observes: "In the Apocalypse, the twenty-four elders are understood by many as a heavenly Sanhedrin or council of angels or celestial rulers, symbolic of order, judgment, and representation." Early commentators and later Greek fathers echo this view, seeing the elders as the symbolic officials of God's throne a council representing the full witness of both covenants, not a secret signal of a pretribulation rapture.

The twenty-four elders are not raptured Church members, but a heavenly council and priestly assembly, joined by the cherubim of Ezekiel's visions, serving as mediators and witnesses to the drama of redemption. Their song is not a testimony of personal escape, but a celebration of the Lamb's victory for all who overcome. Their ministry is not a memorial of absence, but the catalyst for God's intervention on earth the priestly council through whom the prayers of the saints ascend, and through whom judgment is released.

The Saints' Prayers Ignite Judgment

And what happens to those prayers? Revelation 8 answers that with terrifying clarity. When the Lamb opens the seventh seal and silence fills heaven, the next vision is of the altar:

"And another angel came and stood at the altar, having a golden censer;
and there was given unto him much incense, that he should offer it with the prayers of all saints upon the golden altar...
And the smoke of the incense... ascended up before God...
And the angel took the censer, and filled it with fire of the altar, and cast it into the earth..."
(Revelation 8:3–5)

The very prayers of the saints become the fuel of divine retribution. The judgment trumpets that follow—the destruction, the fire, the hail, the plague—are triggered not by a heavenly calendar, but by a cry rising from the earth. The suffering saints below pray, and heaven responds with justice. This is the direct answer to the martyrs in Revelation 6:10 who cry:

"How long, O Lord... dost thou not judge and avenge our blood...?"

The fire cast upon the earth is not arbitrary. It is divine vengeance in answer to the prayers of the saints.

The Absurdity of the Pretribulation Argument

If the elders are the raptured Church, as pretrib teachers claim, and they are holding the prayers of saints, and those prayers trigger the plagues of the tribulation then we are forced to ask: Whose prayers are they offering? If the Church is in heaven, having escaped the tribulation, then logically these must be the prayers of tribulation saints the very people left behind. Which means the elders, supposedly representing the raptured Church, are offering up the prayers of those still suffering on earth, asking God to cast down fire, judgment, and plague. And the implication, whether pretribulationists will admit it or not, is clear: if the saints on earth are the ones praying, and the prayers cause the judgments, then the saints would be praying for their own destruction.

This is the absurdity pretrib theology cannot escape. They must, either admit that the Church is still on earth during the tribulation and crying out for justice—which undermines the pretrib-rapture entirely or claim that the prayers are somehow disconnected from the saints, which would undermine the entire priestly intercession pattern that Revelation presents. Either way, the logic breaks. The elders are not praying saints—they are angelic functionaries holding prayers. And those prayers are not about escape—they are about endurance and vindication.
The rest of the pattern confirms the point. The Church is not shown as an elite group of twenty-four enthroned elders. It is revealed in Revelation 7:

"After this I beheld, and, lo, a great multitude, which no man could number, of all nations, and kindreds, and people, and tongues, stood before the throne, and before the Lamb, clothed with white robes, and palms in their hands."
(Revelation 7:9)

And who are they?

"These are they which came out of great tribulation, and have washed their robes, and made them white in the blood of the Lamb."
(Revelation 7:14)

The true Church does not arrive in heaven through vanishing. It arrives through victory. It is not hidden in a council chamber. It is displayed in open triumph. And it is not limited to twenty-four—it is a multitude no man can number.[16]

The Misplacement of Honor

So let the irony stand. If pretribulationism is correct, then those who were "left behind" are the very ones who prayed heaven's justice into motion. They are the ones who endured, whose prayers

---

[16] *Genesis 15:5 "And he brought him forth abroad, and said, Look now toward heaven, and tell the stars, <u>if thou be able to number them</u>: and he said unto him, <u>So shall thy seed be.</u>"*

were heard, and who are raised in the first resurrection, given thrones, and made to reign with Christ. Meanwhile, the supposed pretribulation Church is reduced to a symbolic choir, holding censers and singing a borrowed song.

This is not doctrinal accuracy; it is doctrinal confusion. It represents a theological misplacement of honor. Revelation is not vague about who reigns—it is those who "loved not their lives unto the death," who "overcame by the blood of the Lamb," and who are raised to reign with Christ for a thousand years. It is their prayers, not their removal, that move heaven to act.

The vision of the twenty-four elders, far from confirming a secret rapture, showcases the justice, priesthood, and government of heaven in response to the suffering saints on earth. Their song is not a testimony of personal escape but a celebration of Christ's triumph for those who endure. The prayers they offer become the catalyst for God's righteous intervention, vindicating those who remain faithful even through tribulation.

In Conclusion

The harmony between Jesus and Paul is not fractured by artificial timelines or divided hopes. Every vision of the end points to a singular, glorious return—one resurrection, one gathering, one reign of Christ with His saints. Attempts to split the people of God or stagger His coming only blur the radiant unity of the New Testament promise. As we have seen, the story of Revelation exalts those who persevere, not those who escape. The true blessed hope is not absence from tribulation, but vindication and reward when Christ is revealed from heaven in glory.

Next Revelation:
Grace Was Always the Way: Exposing the False Gospel of Dispensationalism

In the next chapter, we will expose the root error of dispensationalism: its false gospel. Together, we will walk through Scripture and history to demonstrate that grace was never a New Testament invention. It was always the way. From Noah to

Abraham, from David to Daniel, the righteous have always lived by faith. And it is that faith—not works or ethnicity—that has always been the path to God's promise.

Chapter 12:
Grace Was Always the Way: Exposing the False Gospel of Dispensationalism

From the very first pages of Scripture, before a single commandment was carved into stone, before a priesthood was ordained, before Israel marched through the wilderness under the shadow of Sinai, one truth rang clearly from heaven to earth: God is gracious. Long before Moses, long before the Law, long before the covenant at Mount Sinai, we are told,

"But Noah found grace in the eyes of the LORD." (Genesis 6:8)

This simple sentence is more than a biographical note; it is a theological foundation. It establishes that grace is not the invention of a new covenant age. Rather, it is the eternal disposition of God toward those who believe. The flood narrative, so often viewed as a grim picture of divine judgment, is in truth an early proclamation of divine mercy. Noah was not spared because he was perfect. He was spared because he believed, and because he believed, he obeyed. He received grace, and grace carried him through the judgment that consumed the world around him. Salvation did not come before the storm, but in it, through it, by the hand of a gracious God.

This is the arc of redemption from the very beginning. It tells us that salvation is not a temporary arrangement introduced after the resurrection; it is rooted in the very character of God Himself. Grace has always been the way, not because humanity deserved it, but because God delights to show mercy. To suggest that God's redemptive posture has changed through the centuries that in some ages He required performance before mercy, and in others offers mercy without merit—is not merely theologically imprecise; it is a denial of God's immutability. The God of Noah, the God of Abraham, the God of David, and the God of the apostles is the same God. He has not changed, and His way of salvation has not changed. The flood did not alter His grace. The Law did not replace His grace. The cross revealed its fullest expression.

Dispensationalism's Distortion of Grace

The greatest threat to the beauty of this unbroken pattern of grace is not secularism or atheism; it is the theological framework that subtly redefines salvation across ages. Classical dispensationalism, as taught by figures like C. I. Scofield and John Walvoord, constructs a system that divides human history into dispensations, assigning to each a distinct way in which God governs His relationship with man. In this model, the Church Age becomes the singular home of grace, while previous and future dispensations are marked by heightened human responsibility—obedience to the Law in the past, endurance in the tribulation to come.

In the dispensational scheme, Old Testament saints were saved by "faithful obedience" to the law, while tribulation saints— those who will come to faith after the rapture—must endure and refuse the mark of the beast to attain salvation. Though these views are often cloaked in language that gives lip service to faith, the emphasis unmistakably shifts toward performance. This is no minor error; it is a fundamental reversal of the gospel's order. Scripture is clear that obedience does not produce grace; rather, grace produces obedience.

Hebrews 11 does not showcase a list of moral achievers who earned salvation through acts of strength. It reveals a lineage of believers who, precisely because they believed, acted. "By faith Noah... prepared an ark," "By faith Abraham... obeyed," "By faith Moses... forsook Egypt." Faith came first. Works followed. Always. The moment we suggest that obedience or endurance becomes the means by which salvation is unlocked, we place the burden of righteousness on the back of the sinner and nullify the sufficiency of Christ.

This misalignment is reinforced by Scofield's own commentary, which repeatedly downplays grace in earlier dispensations and reserves its full operation for the post-resurrection period. Walvoord follows the same pattern, particularly in his teachings on the tribulation, where salvation is portrayed as a strenuous combination of belief and moral fortitude. But Ephesians 2:8–9 leaves no room for such equations:

"For by grace are ye saved through faith; and that not of yourselves: it is the gift of God: Not of works, lest any man should boast."

This verse does not carry a Church Age disclaimer. It is a declaration of eternal truth. Salvation is always by grace through faith. Not by works. Not by endurance. Not by ritual. And certainly not by navigating the fine print of a man-made timeline. To teach otherwise is not merely a flawed interpretation; it is a perversion of the gospel. It is to replace the gift of God with the wage of labor and to suggest that the shed blood of Christ is not sufficient for all ages and all people.

At the heart of the problem is the dispensational misuse of the word "dispensation" itself. The Greek word is οἰκονομία (*oikonomia*), which appears in passages like Ephesians 1:10, 3:2, and Colossians 1:25. Lexically, *oikonomia* does not mean a distinct era of salvation or a shift in the way people are saved. Rather, it refers to stewardship, administration, or management of a household. According to BDAG (Bauer-Danker-Arndt-Gingrich) Lexicon:

"οἰκονομία, management of a household, direction, office, administration, arrangement, order, plan."

Thayer's Greek Lexicon states:

"οἰκονομία: the management of a household or of household affairs; specifically, the management, oversight, administration, of others' property; ... in the N.T., dispensation, stewardship, administration."

When Paul speaks of "the dispensation of the grace of God which is given me to you-ward" (Ephesians 3:2), he is not describing a new way of salvation, but the privilege of administering and proclaiming the same grace now revealed in fullness through Christ.

Early Christian writers understood οἰκονομία (*oikonomia*) in precisely this sense. Irenaeus, in *Against Heresies*, Book III, chapter 16, wrote:

"For the Lord of all gave to His apostles the power of the gospel, by whom we have known the truth ... and most copiously does he treat

of the divine οἰκονομία [oikonomia] connected with our Lord, and expound the new advent of liberty."

Here, "oikonomia" refers to God's plan and administration of redemption, not separate ways of salvation. Chrysostom, in his Homilies on Ephesians, Homily VI (on Ephesians 3), says:

> *"For this cause I Paul, the prisoner of Christ Jesus in behalf of you Gentiles... not only do we no longer loathe you, but we are even bound... for your sakes and of this exceeding grace am I partaker.*
> *Ver. 2. 'If so be that ye have heard of the οἰκονομία [dispensation] of that grace of God, which was given me to you-ward.'*
> *By 'dispensation of grace,' he means the revelation made to him... For a dispensation it was, a mighty one... For Himself said to me, 'Depart, for I will send thee far hence unto the Gentiles'... for a dispensation it was... to call one, uninfluenced from any other quarter, immediately from above... 'If so be that ye have heard,' saith he, 'of the οἰκονομία [dispensation] of that grace of God which was given me to you-ward.'"*

The "dispensation of grace" is the stewardship and unfolding of God's eternal purpose—not a fragmented gospel, but the outworking of one redemptive plan.

The tragic result is that instead of rightly dividing the word of truth, dispensationalism divides the gospel. It builds unnecessary walls between the covenants of God—walls that Scripture never erects. It paints a portrait of a God who changes not only His methods but His very attitude toward sinners depending on the era. But the God of the Bible is not like the shifting shadows of human systems. He is "the same yesterday, and today, and forever" (Hebrews 13:8). His grace does not expire. It is not seasonal. It is not bound to a dispensation. It is eternal, like the God who gives it.

Hebrews and the Law's Transformation

To understand just how deep and unbroken the thread of grace runs through the biblical narrative, we must confront the role of the law and its relationship to salvation. One of the most misapplied ideas in dispensational theology is the notion that salvation under the Mosaic covenant was somehow an exception to the rule of grace. While dispensationalists will often concede that "the law never saved," their broader framework continues to treat the Mosaic era as a system of merit-based approval, where righteousness came through external compliance. But the writer of Hebrews makes it plain that the law was not God's ultimate plan; it was a placeholder, a shadow.

"For the priesthood being changed, there is made of necessity a change also of the law." (Hebrews 7:12)

This passage does not imply that grace was introduced when the law was changed, but rather that the Levitical system—being temporary and imperfect—was always pointing beyond itself. It had to give way to a better covenant, a better priesthood, and a better mediator. Galatians 3:24 reinforces this role: the law was our schoolmaster, our guardian, to bring us unto Christ, "that we might be justified by faith." The goal was always Christ. The means was always faith. The law served grace; it never replaced it.

But dispensationalism resists this continuity. Even when it affirms that no one has ever been saved by works alone, it still insists that the framework of salvation varied from age to age. This subtle error leads to an artificial division between the old and the new covenants, as if God's disposition toward sin and mercy shifted based on historical context. Yet Scripture paints a very different picture—a picture of a God who operates by grace in every age, using different covenants to reveal the same unchanging mercy.

Nowhere is this more beautifully demonstrated than in the book of Jeremiah. In Jeremiah 3:1, God recounts a legal principle embedded in the Mosaic law:

"They say, If a man put away his wife, and she go from him, and become another man's, shall he return unto her again? shall not that land be greatly polluted?"

This statute, based on Deuteronomy 24:1–4, forbade a man from taking back a wife who had been defiled by remarriage. Yet in the very same breath, God overrides this law with grace.

"Turn, O backsliding children... for I am married unto you."
(Jeremiah 3:14)

Here we see the supremacy of grace over the technicalities of the law. God Himself acknowledges the law's restriction, then overturns it—not in defiance of justice, but in pursuit of mercy. He calls Israel, His estranged bride, back to Himself—not because the law allows it, but because His heart demands it. This is grace unbound.

The cross does not begin grace; it reveals its infinite extent. Jesus Christ did not come to alter the method of salvation, but to fulfill the redemptive promise embedded in every age. The Levitical system pointed to Him. The sacrifices foreshadowed Him. The priesthood anticipated Him. And when He came, He brought to light what had always been true: salvation is by faith in the God who justifies the ungodly.

Theological Consequences of Dispensationalism

The consequences of dispensational theology are not confined to abstract doctrinal charts or theoretical disputes among scholars. They strike at the very heart of how we understand the character of God. When a theological system teaches that God saves some people by grace and others by merit, that He withholds mercy from those born in the wrong era, or that He turns His back on sincere repentance because it happens after an arbitrarily defined line called "the rapture," it ceases to be merely flawed. It becomes dangerous.

To suggest that God is a respecter of persons—showing grace to Church Age believers while requiring tribulation saints to prove their loyalty through endurance and legalistic obedience—is to contradict the very words of Scripture. Acts 10:34 could not be clearer: "God is no respecter of persons." If He saved Abraham by faith, and if David was forgiven without works, then the idea that God would withhold grace from someone in the tribulation simply because they came to faith too late is not only unbiblical, but also unjust.

This flawed picture reaches its most disturbing form when dispensationalism portrays God as a persecutor of the repentant.

According to this system, those who come to believe in Christ during the tribulation are not embraced with compassion but are thrown into a world of divine plagues and wrath, with no promise of deliverance—only a hope of endurance. This is not the God who says, "Come unto me, all ye that labour and are heavy laden, and I will give you rest" (Matthew 11:28). This is not the Good Shepherd who leaves the ninety-nine to rescue the one.

Dual Covenant Theology

Dispensationalism subscribes to a dual covenant belief, primarily to protect its system from inconvenient verses like those found in Matthew 24, where Jesus says the elect are gathered immediately after the tribulation. By adopting this framework, dispensationalists can compartmentalize such passages, assigning them to national Israel rather than the Church. To truly strike at the heart of dispensationalism and expose how it distorts the message of grace, we must address its belief in two covenants operating simultaneously.

Dual Covenant Theology posits that Jews are saved through their own covenant with God, independent of faith in Jesus Christ. This perspective claims that modern Jews do not need to believe in Jesus for salvation, arguing that God maintains one covenant for the Church (through Christ) and another for Israel (through Abraham or Moses). The result is a system that effectively teaches two paths to salvation: one for Gentiles (through Christ), and one for Jews (through the Law or national election).

Scripture repeatedly and clearly teaches that salvation is found only in Jesus Christ, for both Jew and Gentile:

"Neither is there salvation in any other: for there is none other name under heaven given among men, whereby we must be saved."
(Acts 4:12)

"He that hath the Son hath life; and he that hath not the Son of God hath not life."
(1 John 5:12)

"Christ is the end of the law for righteousness to everyone that believeth."
(Romans 10:4)

"There is no difference between the Jew and the Greek: for the same Lord over all is rich unto all that call upon him."
(Romans 10:12)

There is one gospel for all mankind. Any theology that separates salvation into ethnic categories stands in direct opposition to this message.

Scripture is even more explicit in its warnings:

"Who is a liar but he that denieth that Jesus is the Christ? He is antichrist, that denieth the Father and the Son."
(1 John 2:22)

"And every spirit that confesseth not that Jesus Christ is come in the flesh is not of God: and this is that spirit of antichrist..."
(1 John 4:3)

"For many deceivers are entered into the world, who confess not that Jesus Christ is come in the flesh. This is a deceiver and an antichrist."
(2 John 1:7)

These verses make it clear: to reject Jesus as the Messiah is to stand in opposition to the truth, and such rejection is spiritually labeled as antichrist. It is important to clarify that "antichrist" in John's usage does not mean someone is the beast of Revelation or demon possessed. It means they are opposed to, or in place of, Christ—a theological description, not a sensational label. The New Testament never makes exceptions for religious sincerity or ethnic heritage when it comes to faith in Christ.

Paul, himself a Jew, mourned for his brethren who rejected Christ—not because they lacked a covenant, but because they were cut off from the only source of righteousness:

"For I bear them record that they have a zeal of God, but not according to knowledge... For they being ignorant of God's righteousness, and going about to establish their own righteousness, have not submitted themselves unto the righteousness of God."
(Romans 10:2–3)

Peter likewise proclaimed this truth to Jewish audiences:

"Neither is there salvation in any other..."
(Acts 4:12)

Jesus Himself told the Jewish leaders:

"If ye believe not that I am he, ye shall die in your sins."
(John 8:24)

The consistent message throughout the New Testament is that salvation is through faith in Jesus Christ alone, for both Jews and Gentiles.

To teach that Jews can be saved apart from Christ is to preach another gospel. Paul warned:

"Though we, or an angel from heaven, preach any other gospel... let him be accursed."
(Galatians 1:8)

There is no biblical warrant for an alternate path of salvation—not by birth, race, nor Law. God's covenant promises to Israel are real, but they are fulfilled in Christ. To be part of the true covenant, one must receive the Son.

In summary, the New Testament unequivocally teaches that salvation is through faith in Jesus Christ alone, for all people, regardless of ethnic background. Dual Covenant Theology, by proposing a separate path to salvation for Jews, contradicts this fundamental gospel truth. Therefore, it must be recognized as a deviation from the true gospel and addressed accordingly.

A Final Word: Dual Covenant Theology and Dispensationalism—Two Branches of the Same Root Error

It must be said plainly: the doctrines of dispensationalism and dual covenant theology may wear different clothing, but they spring from the same theological root—a denial of the consistent gospel across all time. Both divide salvation into compartments. Both imply that God's method of saving souls is determined by ethnic status or historical timing. And both, in different ways, diminish the centrality of Christ as the sole mediator between God and man.

Dispensationalism, in its classical form, introduces era-based salvation schemes—claiming that Old Testament saints were justified through legal faithfulness, that the Church is uniquely saved by grace through faith without works, and that tribulation saints must endure and refuse the mark to be saved. This creates a fragmented gospel that treats God like a time-based administrator instead of a covenant-keeping Savior.

Dual covenant theology, meanwhile, carves out an entire people group—Israel—and grants them a parallel path to God apart from the cross of Christ. It suggests that Jews, because of their national election, have an ongoing saving covenant through Abraham or Moses, and therefore need not repent or believe in Jesus to be saved. But Paul directly rebukes this idea in Romans 9:1-8. He weeps for his brethren not because they have no covenant, but because they have not submitted to the righteousness of God revealed in Christ. Their covenant was always pointing forward to Him, and without Him, they are severed branches—not heirs.

"For they stumbled at that stumblingstone; as it is written, Behold, I lay in Sion a stumblingstone and rock of offence: and whosoever believeth on him shall not be ashamed."
(Romans 9:32–33)

Jesus is not a theological option. He is the cornerstone, and the entire building of salvation collapses without Him. Whether we are speaking of Jews or Gentiles, pre-cross or post-cross, Church Age or tribulation—there is no salvation apart from the Son.

"Whosoever denieth the Son, the same hath not the Father."
(1 John 2:23)

This is the line in the sand that no theology can cross without losing the gospel. The Son is the way. The Son is the door. The Son is the life. Any doctrine—no matter how academic, how well-intentioned, or how emotionally appealing—that attempts to create a back door into God's presence apart from Jesus Christ must be rejected. Because if Jesus is not required for some, He is not Lord of all.

To say that modern Jews are saved through their own covenant, apart from faith in Jesus, is to contradict the entire testimony of the apostles, the prophets, and Christ Himself. It is to call the gospel unnecessary. It is, in Paul's words, to preach "another gospel"—and he does not hesitate to pronounce a curse upon it.

This is no small matter. It is not a disagreement over end times charts or denominational preferences. It is a matter of eternal life and death. And as shepherds of God's people, we are called to guard the flock from wolves in theological clothing, no matter how respectable their credentials or how large their platform.

Let us not be afraid to say what Scripture says: if someone denies that Jesus is the Christ, he is antichrist—not in the sense of a demonic monster, but in the theological sense John defined. He stands in opposition to the only name under heaven by which we must be saved.

Reclaiming the True Gospel in a Confused Age

In an age where even many evangelical leaders flirt with ideas of dual paths, multiple covenants, and backdoor salvations, the Church must rise again and declare what has always been true: there is one Lord, one faith, one baptism. One way. One covenant. One Gospel.

The temptation to appease cultural sensitivities or to maintain favor with the religious elite is strong. But so is the temptation to embrace systems like dispensationalism that feel tidy and logical but fracture the beauty of God's consistent character. We must resist both. We must resist any framework that suggests some people are too late, and others are too special, to need Jesus.

No, the gospel does not bend to heritage. It does not pivot for eras. It does not revise itself for national Israel or the Church. It calls every person, in every generation under heaven, to repent and believe on the Lord Jesus Christ. This gospel is not new. It is not Gentile. It is not Western. It is the everlasting covenant—the Lamb slain from the foundation of the world.

So let us preach it with boldness. Let us teach it with clarity. Let us reject the theological systems that divide what God has united. And let us call both Jew and Gentile to the same glorious hope: that whosoever shall call upon the name of the Lord shall be saved.

He is the same yesterday, today, and forever. And His grace was always the way.

Rebuttal & Answer:
"The Marriage Supper Proves a Pretrib Rapture."

The pretribulational system, while popularized in recent centuries, relies heavily on speculative sequencing and theological assumptions that are not plainly taught in Scripture. One of its most prominent pillars is the idea that the marriage supper of the Lamb must take place in heaven during a seven-year tribulation on earth. From this, it is asserted that the Church must be raptured before the tribulation begins in order to participate in this heavenly celebration. This belief is frequently supported by connecting passages such as Revelation 19:7–9 with John 14:2–3, forming an intricate timeline that—when examined closely—rests more on tradition and inference than on exegesis and clarity. The entire framework hinges on reading a preconceived system into texts that do not actually make the case. In this chapter, we will carefully deconstruct the logic of this claim, examining the relevant passages in context, identifying where the arguments rely on theological projection, and ultimately demonstrating that neither the marriage supper of the Lamb nor the judgment seat of Christ (Bema Seat) necessitate or support a pretribulational rapture. Rather, they affirm a posttribulational, public return of Christ and the vindication of His faithful bride.

The Pretrib Argument Stated

According to dispensational teaching, the marriage supper of the Lamb occurs in heaven during the same seven-year period in which God is pouring out wrath upon the earth. Pretribulationists maintain that in order for the Church—the bride of Christ—to participate in this heavenly event, she must be removed from the earth beforehand through the rapture. The logic of this position generally follows a chain of inference rather than textual demonstration. Revelation 19:7–9 is cited to argue that the marriage has already occurred in heaven, with the bride now ready and robed in righteousness, while John 14:2–3 is often brought in to suggest that Jesus has prepared a heavenly bridal chamber to which He will take the Church before returning again in power. When combined with assumptions about the judgment seat of Christ taking place in heaven prior to the Second Coming, this framework becomes a self-sustaining construct. However, the fundamental problem with this structure is not that its parts are derived from unrelated texts—which they are—but that the entire sequence is built on silence and inference, requiring the reader to insert meaning that the text itself never declares.

Exegetical Problems with the Pretrib View

The most immediate and observable flaw in the pretribulational use of Revelation 19 is the fact that the passage never actually states that the marriage supper takes place in heaven. While the vision does begin in heaven (Revelation 19:1–6), the marriage announcement itself is a declaration of the present, not a report of something already accomplished seven years prior. The phrase "is come" in verse 7 is not an announcement of completion but a signal of arrival—of readiness. And significantly, the text says nothing about the supper taking place before Christ's return. Rather, the focus is on the bride's preparation and the imminence of the union, not on a hidden feast or secret celebration. Scripture reads:

"Let us be glad and rejoice, and give honour to him: for the marriage of the Lamb is come, and his wife hath made herself ready."

(Revelation 19:7)

This statement emphasizes that the bride has now completed her preparation. She has not been passively waiting in a celestial bridal chamber but has made herself ready, a phrase that implies perseverance, cleansing, and faithful expectation. The wording here reinforces the idea that this preparation has just reached its culmination, not that it was finalized seven years earlier. The following verse continues with this forward-looking tone:

"And he saith unto me, Write, Blessed are they which are called unto the marriage supper of the Lamb."
(Revelation 19:9)

This language functions as a blessing upon those who are invited to the supper—it is an invitation, not a retrospective. The text does not depict the event itself but merely announces its arrival. There is no scene of dining, no description of setting, and certainly no indication that a seven-year feast has been in progress prior to Christ's descent. The very next image in the passage is the heavens opening to reveal Christ on a white horse, prepared for war, not emerging from a finished banquet. The supposed heavenly setting of the supper is therefore assumed without evidence, driven by the demands of a dispensational timeline rather than the text itself.

The Sequence in Revelation 19

The structure of Revelation 19 must be taken seriously, as it provides clear chronological markers that directly challenge the pretribulational interpretation. In Revelation 18, Babylon has just fallen, and in response, the voices in heaven shout hallelujahs. This praise and rejoicing continue into Revelation 19:1–6, forming a heavenly chorus of celebration over the fall of the great harlot. It is only then, in verses 7–9, that the marriage is announced. No supper has yet been shown, no celebration involving food or festivity has taken place. Instead, the marriage "is come" a phrase which again signals that the time has arrived, not that it has passed.

Immediately following this, we are told:

"And I saw heaven opened, and behold a white horse; and he that sat upon him was called Faithful and True..."
(Revelation 19:11)

This signals the moment of Christ's return—the visible, climactic Second Coming. There is no break in the narrative, no pause for a feast, no space for a seven-year wedding banquet in heaven. The progression is smooth and uninterrupted: Babylon falls, heaven rejoices, the bride is ready, Christ descends. The only supper described explicitly in the remainder of the chapter is not a seven-year marriage supper of the Lamb, but the grotesque "supper of the great God," where birds feast on the flesh of kings and mighty men:

"Come and gather yourselves together unto the supper of the great God; That ye may eat the flesh of kings, and the flesh of captains..."
(Revelation 19:17–18)

This deliberate juxtaposition between the celebratory feast of the righteous and the humiliating consumption of the wicked is not about concurrent timelines but contrasting destinies. The true marriage supper is not described as having occurred in heaven but is anticipated as part of the public vindication of Christ and His saints on earth. The absence of any actual wedding feast in heaven within the passage is not a narrative oversight—it is an interpretive correction to traditions that rely on artificial insertions.

The Biblical Pattern of Wedding Imagery

Appeals to ancient Jewish wedding customs are often used to prop up the dispensational narrative, with the claim that the groom and bride spent seven days in seclusion before a public celebration. But while such traditions may reflect elements of Hebrew culture in certain time periods, Scripture itself does not prescribe a rigid seven-day bridal chamber as the theological template for Christ's return. When we examine the biblical pattern, especially in the prophetic and apocalyptic contexts, a far simpler and more consistent order emerges: betrothal, preparation, union, and celebration—all occurring in a way that aligns with public revelation, not secret removal.

This fourfold pattern is evident throughout Scripture. In the current age, the Church is betrothed to Christ. Her role is one of active preparation, enduring tribulation, and maintaining faithfulness until the Bridegroom appears. The wedding occurs when Christ returns to claim His bride—not before. Then the celebration begins. This is not only the consistent biblical picture, but it is also reinforced by Revelation's own structure. The Church prepares herself amid suffering (Revelation 14:12), the return of Christ follows (Revelation 19:11), and the Kingdom is inaugurated with the saints reigning alongside Him (Revelation 20:4–6).

Old Testament prophecy supports this sequence. In Isaiah 25, a messianic feast is promised, but its location and timing are explicitly tied to Mount Zion and the resurrection:

"And in this mountain shall the Lord of hosts make unto all people a feast of fat things... He will swallow up death in victory; and the Lord God will wipe away tears from off all faces..."
(Isaiah 25:6, 8)

The feast is terrestrial. It follows the defeat of death and the wiping away of tears both of which occur at the time of resurrection and judgment, not seven years prior.

Likewise, Jesus' parable of the wedding feast in Matthew 22 emphasizes that the celebration follows the king's destruction of those who rejected his invitation:

"But when the king heard thereof, he was wroth: and he sent forth his armies, and destroyed those murderers, and burned up their city... Then saith he to his servants, The wedding is ready..."
(Matthew 22:7–8)

This parable places judgment first, followed by the invitation to the feast not a hidden celebration before tribulation, but a vindicating event afterward. The biblical pattern points not to secrecy, but to public redemption and restoration following trial and confrontation.

The Supper Is Celebratory, Not Escapist

It is essential to emphasize the nature of the marriage supper not merely its location or timing. Revelation 19:7 states:

"Let us be glad and rejoice, and give honour to him: for the marriage of the Lamb is come, and his wife hath made herself ready."

This is not the portrait of a bride who has been whisked away and hidden from the storms of tribulation. Rather, this is the language of victory through perseverance. The bride "hath made herself ready," which in the wider context of Revelation speaks to faithful endurance, unwavering testimony, and purification through suffering. Earlier, in Revelation 14:12, we are told:

"Here is the patience of the saints: here are they that keep the commandments of God, and the faith of Jesus."

These saints are not removed from tribulation; they are preserved through it. They overcome by the blood of the Lamb and the word of their testimony. The picture is not one of divine insulation, but one of steadfastness in the face of demonic opposition. To reinterpret the supper as an escape reward fundamentally distorts its character. The supper is a celebration of faith proven true, of love maintained under pressure, and of a bride adorned in the righteousness that was refined by fire.

Revelation does not depict the saints as bystanders watching wrath unfold on others. It shows them crying out beneath the altar:

"How long, O Lord, holy and true, dost thou not judge and avenge our blood on them that dwell on the earth?"
(Revelation 6:10)

These are not absent ones. They are participants—witnesses to judgment, co-laborers in testimony, and ultimately sharers in the glory of the returning Christ. They are called to the supper not because they were evacuated before trouble came, but because they were found faithful when it did.

Theological and Typological Errors in the Pretrib View

Beyond misreading the immediate text of Revelation 19, the pretribulational view makes a series of theological and typological missteps that distort the larger redemptive framework of Scripture. Chief among these is the failure to distinguish between the marriage and the supper. These are not synonymous. The marriage itself—symbolizing the union of Christ and His people—occurs when the Bridegroom returns. The supper is the celebration that follows. To conflate the two is to confuse covenantal language with ceremonial metaphor.

Furthermore, the pretrib view often limits the identity of the bride to the Church alone, severing the continuity of redemptive history. But Revelation 21 corrects this narrowing. The angel says to John:

"Come hither, I will shew thee the bride, the Lamb's wife… And he shewed me that great city, the holy Jerusalem, descending out of heaven from God."
(Revelation 21:9–10)

This is a corporate identity. The New Jerusalem is the final, complete expression of God's redemptive plan—a city inhabited by all the redeemed, from every age and covenant. The bride is not merely the Church raptured before the end; she is the full manifestation of God's covenant fulfilled. To isolate her to the Church alone and assign her a private banquet before the Second Coming is to diminish the glory of the Lamb's inheritance.

The Seven-Year Heavenly Feast: A Tradition of Men

The notion of a seven-year heavenly feast is not the result of scriptural exegesis but the fruit of system-driven imagination. It is an idea read into the text from assumptions about Daniel's seventieth week and the perceived need to fill the time between the rapture and the return. But this entire structure is constructed on assumptions. No passage states that the marriage supper is seven years long. No passage places it in heaven. No apostle ever teaches it. No prophet ever foresaw it.

The warning of Jesus against tradition ought to ring loudly here:

"Thus have ye made the commandment of God of none effect by your tradition. Ye hypocrites…"
(Matthew 15:6–7)

"In vain do they worship me, teaching for doctrines the commandments of men."
(Mark 7:7)

By elevating a constructed doctrine above the revealed testimony of Scripture, the dispensational system unwittingly enshrines a tradition of men. It inserts events, timelines, and meanings that the inspired writers never gave us. It reshapes eschatology not around the cross and crown of Christ, but around charts and chronological guesses. The bride of Christ deserves better than speculative pageantry. She deserves the truth—truth that calls her to prepare, endure, and reign with Him, not to escape the hour of trial through manufactured loopholes.

The True Interpretation: Consummation at the Return

Rather than envisioning a heavenly, hidden celebration stretching across the seven-year tribulation period, the proper interpretation of Revelation 19 recognizes that the marriage of the Lamb culminates with the return of Christ—not before it. The announcement that "the marriage of the Lamb is come" should be understood as a climactic moment—an arrival that coincides with Christ's descent and the inauguration of His Kingdom. The image of the heavens opening in verse 11 is not a new scene but the continuation of the one already in progress. The bride has made herself ready, the announcement has been proclaimed, and now the Bridegroom comes to consummate the union with His people through judgment, vindication, and public glory.

This return is not incidental to the marriage—it is the marriage. For it is at His appearing that He receives His own unto Himself. It is then that the righteous are gathered, resurrected, and glorified. It is then that the covenant is fulfilled in public splendor.

- 239 -

The imagery of a wedding and its supper is therefore meant to communicate joyful consummation at the very moment the King returns to establish His reign.

The idea that the bride must already be crowned and judged in order to accompany Christ in Revelation 19 is an assumption without exegetical warrant. There is no passage indicating that the bride must have already received her rewards before descending. The narrative flow of Revelation supports the opposite: she is declared ready at His coming, and she reigns with Him after the return.

"And they lived and reigned with Christ a thousand years."
(Revelation 20:4)

It is at this point, not seven years earlier, that the bride enters into her rest and reward. The feast is not a celestial retreat. It is a public enthronement. It does not take place in secret while the world burns; it unfolds as the smoke of Babylon clears and the Kingdom of God begins.

The Supper Does Not Require a Pretrib Rapture

When all the pieces are put back into place and examined within the context of Scripture, it becomes clear that the pretribulational marriage supper theory is a house built on sand. The argument collapses when tested by the structure of Revelation, the prophetic witness of Isaiah, the teaching of Jesus, and the covenantal identity of the bride in Revelation 21. The marriage supper is not described as a heavenly event prior to the return. It is not associated with escape, secrecy, or a celebratory intermission while the earth suffers. It is a vindicating celebration that follows trial, preparation, and judgment.

The rapture is not required in order for the marriage to occur. In fact, the rapture—as Paul teaches in 1 Thessalonians 4—is a gathering that takes place at the coming of the Lord, not before it. The bride is gathered at the return. The resurrection occurs at the last trumpet. The Kingdom is inaugurated when Christ descends. These events are not spread across years but are telescoped into the day of the Lord's appearing.

"Let us be glad and rejoice, and give honour to him: for the marriage of the Lamb is come, and his wife hath made herself ready."
(Revelation 19:7)

The call is not to escape but to prepare. The testimony of Revelation does not portray a bride in retreat, but a bride in readiness having endured, overcome, and been made spotless by the Lamb's blood. Her reward comes not because she was hidden, but because she was faithful.

To further fortify the argument against the pretribulational interpretation of the marriage supper of the Lamb, it is essential to examine the biblical and cultural context of wedding feasts. A survey of scriptural accounts reveals that wedding feasts often commenced prior to the consummation of the marriage, challenging the notion that the Church must be raptured and united with Christ before the celebration begins.

Biblical Precedents: Feasts Preceding Consummation

Jacob and Leah: A Feast Before Union

In Genesis 29:21–22, Jacob, having fulfilled his seven years of service, requests his wife. Laban responds by organizing a feast:

"And Laban gathered together all the men of the place, and made a feast."

The consummation occurs later that evening, leading to Jacob's realization of Laban's deception the following morning. This account illustrates that the feast was a communal event preceding the private union.

Samson's Wedding: Celebration Amidst Uncertainty

Judges 14:10–12 recounts Samson's wedding feast:

"So his father went down unto the woman: and Samson made there a feast; for so used the young men to do."

The feast, customary among young men, occurred before the marriage was fully consummated. The ensuing events, including Samson's departure, suggest that the union was not finalized during the feast.

Parable of the Wedding Feast: Invitations Before Final Judgment

In Matthew 22:2–10, Jesus describes a king preparing a marriage feast for his son. The initial guests refuse the invitation, leading the king to extend the call to others. Notably, the feast is ready before the final guest list is complete, and prior to the judgment of attendees.

Parable of the Ten Virgins: Entry into the Celebration

Matthew 25:1–10 presents the parable of the ten virgins awaiting the bridegroom. At midnight, the call announces his arrival, and those prepared enter the marriage celebration:

"And they that were ready went in with him to the marriage: and the door was shut."

The emphasis is on readiness and entry into the feast, not on a prior consummation or rapture.

Wedding at Cana: Celebration Before Consummation

John 2:1–10 recounts Jesus attending a wedding in Cana, where he performs his first miracle. The feast is underway, and there is no indication that the marriage has been consummated. This aligns with Jewish customs where the public celebration often preceded the private union .

These scriptural examples demonstrate a consistent pattern: wedding feasts commence before the consummation of the marriage. Applying this understanding to Revelation 19:7–9 suggests that the marriage supper of the Lamb does not necessitate a pretribulational rapture. Instead, it aligns with the view that the celebration occurs in conjunction with Christ's return, not prior to it.

This perspective challenges the pretribulational framework, which posits a heavenly feast during a seven-year tribulation on earth. The biblical pattern supports a posttribulational celebration, emphasizing readiness and faithfulness rather than escape from tribulation.

In conclusion, the biblical precedent of feasts preceding consummation undermines the argument for a pretribulational rapture based on the marriage supper of the Lamb. The consistent scriptural pattern supports a celebration that coincides with Christ's visible return, affirming the call for believers to remain steadfast and prepared.

FALLBACK CLAIM: The Bema Seat Must Happen Before the Second Coming

Faced with the insufficiency of the marriage supper argument, pretribulationists often retreat to a secondary claim in defense of their timeline: the Church must be raptured before the tribulation in order to appear at the judgment seat of Christ—the Bema Seat—during the seven-year interval in heaven. The assertion is that the bride must already be judged, rewarded, and glorified before returning with Christ in Revelation 19. But this fallback, like the one before it, suffers from the same fatal flaw—it is based on theological necessity, not textual declaration.

The Pretrib Pivot: The Bema Seat Must Be Pretrib

The idea that the Bema Seat occurs during a heavenly interval before the Second Coming is not found anywhere in Scripture. It is assumed because the pretrib model needs time in heaven for something to happen. The logic goes something like this: if the saints return with Christ in Revelation 19, and if they are already crowned and robed in righteousness, then they must have already been judged and rewarded. Therefore, there must be a Bema Seat judgment in heaven prior to Christ's descent, which necessitates a prior rapture.

However, none of these links are made in Scripture. There is no passage stating that the Bema Seat occurs in heaven. There is no text assigning it to a seven-year period. And there is no reason, biblically, to believe that judgment and reward cannot occur at the time of the Lord's return.

The two primary texts used to support the doctrine of the Bema Seat are clear in their message—but silent about their timing:

"But why dost thou judge thy brother? ...for we shall all stand before the judgment seat of Christ."
(Romans 14:10)

"For we must all appear before the judgment seat of Christ; that every one may receive the things done in his body..."
(2 Corinthians 5:10)

These verses affirm the reality of Christ's judgment of believers, not for condemnation, but for evaluation and reward. Yet neither verse tells us when this will occur. There is no reference to heaven. No reference to a seven-year window. No linkage to a pretribulational rapture. The idea of the Bema Seat happening during the tribulation is simply not present in the text—it is read into the text to satisfy the demands of a tradition.

As with the marriage supper, the supposed seven-year Bema Seat judgment is another case of a tradition being used to override the plain reading of Scripture. It is not an apostolic doctrine. It is not a prophetic utterance. It is a theological invention that conveniently fills a gap in the pretrib timeline. But the same warning that Jesus gave about human tradition applies again:

"Ye reject the commandment of God, that ye may keep your own tradition."
(Mark 7:9)

When doctrine is shaped not by the text, but by the assumptions we bring to the text, we are not honoring the Word of God—we are neutralizing it. The Bema Seat does not need seven years in heaven to be real. It needs only the appearing of Christ.

Scripture Places Reward and Judgment at the Return

The consistent testimony of Scripture is that reward comes when Christ returns, not before:

"For the Son of man shall come in the glory of his Father with his angels; and then he shall reward every man according to his works."
(Matthew 16:27)

"And, behold, I come quickly; and my reward is with me, to give every man according as his work shall be."
(Revelation 22:12)

"Therefore judge nothing before the time, until the Lord come…"
(1 Corinthians 4:5)

The timing of reward is anchored to the return of Christ. Scripture never places this reward seven years before His coming. On the contrary, the final trumpet in Revelation 11 is the moment when judgment and reward are announced. This is not an earlier, secret trumpet—it is the last trumpet.

The Resurrection and the Last Trumpet Collapse the Timeline

Paul's teaching on the resurrection in 1 Corinthians 15 directly contradicts the notion of a pretrib Bema Seat:

"Behold, I shew you a mystery; We shall not all sleep, but we shall all be changed... at the last trump... the dead shall be raised incorruptible."
(1 Corinthians 15:51–52)

This resurrection occurs at the last trumpet, not before. If the saints are judged and rewarded at the resurrection, and the resurrection occurs at the final trumpet, then any attempt to place the Bema Seat seven years earlier becomes impossible. The resurrection is the trigger. The appearing of Christ is the context. And the reward follows.

Revelation 11 affirms the same timeline:

"The kingdoms of this world are become the kingdoms of our Lord...
and the time of the dead, that they should be judged..."
(Revelation 11:15, 18)

There is no room here for a prior event. The Bema Seat occurs when the dead are raised, and the dead are raised when Christ returns—not seven years before.

The combined weight of Scripture decisively undermines the two primary pretribulational supports—the marriage supper and the Bema Seat. Both rely on assumptions and traditions, not on exegesis or apostolic teaching. Neither argument can stand without a system to prop it up, and once that system is removed, both collapse. Revelation does not teach a seven-year heavenly feast, nor does it teach a pretribulational judgment. These are traditions of men, constructed to fill gaps in a model that has no support in the actual text.

What Scripture does teach is a faithful Church, called to endure, purified through tribulation, and vindicated at the return of Christ. Her reward is not escape it is reign. Her supper is not secluded but it is triumphant, and it is glorious.

"Be thou faithful unto death, and I will give thee a crown of life."
(Revelation 2:10)

In this chapter, we exposed the fractured gospel of dispensationalism and reaffirmed the eternal consistency of God's grace from Noah to the cross, from Abraham's faith to the Lamb slain before the foundation of the world. Salvation was never divided by timeline or ethnicity. It was, and is, by grace through faith in Christ alone.

But if that message is so clear in Scripture, how did the early Church understand it? Did the first Christians embrace a two-track gospel? Did they expect a secret escape before tribulation? Or did they suffer and hope with the same faith we now proclaim?

Next Revelation:
What the Early Church Believed The Unified Testimony of the First Christians Against Escapism

In the next chapter, we will turn to the writings of the earliest believers those closest to the apostles themselves. We will examine their unified voice, not only on salvation, but on the Second Coming, the Antichrist, and the tribulation. What emerges is a testimony against escapism—and for a Church that stands, endures, and overcomes.

Chapter 13:
What the Early Church Believed
The Unified Testimony of the First
Christians Against Escapism

If you listen to modern pretribulationists, you'd think the Church has always believed that Jesus could return "at any moment" to whisk His people away before the world gets bad. But the voices of the earliest Christians say otherwise. The men who sat under the Apostles and their direct disciples had a very different message. They didn't teach escape they taught endurance. They didn't preach a two-stage return—they preached one appearing, one resurrection, and one kingdom, all after the Antichrist.

The early Church Fathers were unified on this: the Church would endure the great tribulation, face the Antichrist, and only afterward be vindicated at the glorious return of Christ. These weren't speculative interpretations—they were warnings born out of persecution, shaped by martyrdom, and drawn directly from the teachings of the apostles themselves. If the pretrib rapture had been part of the apostolic deposit, these men missed it entirely—and missed it consistently.

Irenaeus of Lyons (c. 130–202 AD)

Irenaeus wasn't just a church father—he was a second-generation link to the apostles. He sat under Polycarp, who walked with John. If anyone would've inherited a secret rapture doctrine, it was him. Instead, Irenaeus warned believers about being deceived by the Antichrist. He pleaded with the Church to correctly understand the number 666—not as trivia—but as a real defense against real deception.

"Such, then, being the state of the case, and this number being found in all the most approved and ancient copies [of the Apocalypse], and those men who saw John face to face bearing their testimony [to it]; while reason also leads us to conclude that the number of the name of the beast... will amount to six hundred and sixty and six... I do not

know how it is that some have erred... deducting the amount of fifty from it, so that instead of six decads they will have it that there is but one."
— *Against Heresies, Book 5, Chapter 30*

Irenaeus believed the Church would face the Antichrist—not watch him from the balcony. He didn't minimize the danger of deception. He highlighted it as a pastoral concern. His view wasn't "don't worry, you'll be gone," but "be ready, because you'll still be here."

Irenaeus also laid out a timeline of events: Antichrist comes, devastates all things, then Christ returns visibly. He also recognized the necessity of accurately identifying the Antichrist:

"But when this Antichrist shall have devastated all things in this world, he will reign for three years and six months, and sit in the temple at Jerusalem; and then the Lord will come from heaven in the clouds, in the glory of the Father, sending this man and those who follow him into the lake of fire; but bringing in for the righteous the times of the kingdom, ... and restoring to Abraham the promised inheritance..."
—*Against Heresies 5.30.4*

This reads like a commentary on Matthew 24:29–31:

"Immediately after the tribulation of those days shall the sun be darkened... and then shall appear the sign of the Son of man in heaven... And he shall send his angels with a great sound of a trumpet, and they shall gather together his elect..."

Irenaeus echoes Jesus word-for-word. The tribulation comes first, then Christ appears, then the elect are gathered. Pretribulationism reverses that sequence. Irenaeus confirms it.

Irenaeus also affirmed that the resurrection occurs after the Antichrist, not before him. That alone buries the secret rapture theory.

"For all these and other words were unquestionably spoken in reference to the resurrection of the just, which takes place after the

coming of Antichrist and the destruction of all nations under his rule... Then the Lord will come from heaven in the clouds, in the glory of the Father."
— *Against Heresies, Book 5, Chapter 35*

Compare this to 1 Thessalonians 4:16–17:

"For the Lord himself shall descend from heaven with a shout... and the dead in Christ shall rise first: Then we which are alive and remain shall be caught up together with them in the clouds, to meet the Lord in the air..."

And again with 1 Corinthians 15:52:

"In a moment, in the twinkling of an eye, at the last trump: for the trumpet shall sound, and the dead shall be raised incorruptible..."

It's the same event, same order, same imagery—clouds, trumpet, resurrection, return. Irenaeus is not interpreting the rapture as some earlier secret event. He places the resurrection at the visible return of Christ after the Antichrist's defeat. That's not pretrib—that's the exact sequence pretrib denies.

Justin Martyr (c. 100–165 AD)

Justin was another early witness who spoke plainly about what the Church should expect. He regarded the rise of Antichrist as imminent, not the sudden appearance of Christ. Justin understood that the Church would face this time of trouble head-on.

"...that it was said that he would have dominion for a time, and times, and a half a time, Daniel shows in this way... and, moreover, you are aware that this has been prophesied for the duration of the reign of Antichrist... and, moreover, you are not unaware that this has been predicted for the duration of the reign of Antichrist..."
— *Dialogue with Trypho 32*

He warns with unmistakable urgency:

"...when Antichrist shall desolate all things in this world, whoever hears or reads these words may take heed... But I and others, who are right-minded Christians on all points, are assured that there will be a resurrection of the dead, and a thousand years in Jerusalem... The time shall come, and it is even now at hand, when those who are called Christians shall dwell with their Lord for a thousand years..."
— *Dialogue with Trypho 110*

Notice carefully: Justin did not say that Christ's coming was at hand, but rather that the coming of Antichrist and the tribulation he would bring were imminent. This single detail upends the modern pretribulational framework. The earliest Christians were not expectantly waiting for Jesus to appear at any moment; they were bracing themselves for the arrival of the great deceiver—the Antichrist, "the lawless one," who would "make war with the saints."

This is the exact inverse of today's pretribulational teaching. Modern prophecy charts urge believers to look up, to expect Jesus at any instant to whisk them away. But Justin and his generation were watching the prophetic horizon for the fulfillment of Daniel's warning, knowing that the time of distress would come first.

It was the Antichrist who was "even now at hand," not deliverance from him. This isn't just a difference of timing; it's a total reversal of the Church's focus. Justin's testimony perfectly mirrors Paul's order in 2 Thessalonians 2:1–3:

"Now we beseech you, brethren, by the coming of our Lord Jesus Christ, and by our gathering together unto him... Let no man deceive you by any means: for that day shall not come, except there come a falling away first, and that man of sin be revealed..."

Paul declares that Antichrist must come first. Justin, likewise, says that Antichrist's reign was imminent. Pretribulationism, on the other hand, claims Jesus could return at any moment. One of these voices does not agree with the others.

If Justin had believed in an any-moment rapture, he would have written as much. Instead, his words call the saints to sober discernment and readiness for persecution, not a sudden escape. He called for preparation, not evacuation. He urged believers to heed the warnings, not to hope for a secret whisking away.

Justin's writings stand as a sober rebuke to escapist rhetoric. The early Church was not clinging to dreams of imminent rescue; they were holding fast to the promise of victory after tribulation— after deception, after the Beast's fury. They looked for Antichrist first, then Christ. Pretribulationism reverses the order; Justin helps us recover it.

Tertullian (c. 155–240 AD)

Tertullian was not only an apologist, he was one of the first Latin theologians to systematize doctrine and when it came to the end times, his expectations were clear: the Antichrist was coming, a literal temple would be desecrated, and the Church would be there to endure it.

Some modern interpreters try to dismiss the eschatology of 2 Thessalonians 2 by spiritualizing the "temple of God." They say it's symbolic—maybe the Church, maybe the human heart, maybe something else abstract enough to avoid having to reckon with the text. But Tertullian didn't buy that. He took Paul at his word and expected the Antichrist to commit a very literal act of blasphemy in a very real place.

"He is to sit in the temple of God, and boast himself as being God... That temple of the Jews which was destroyed... shall be rebuilt for the use of Antichrist."
— Against Marcion, Book 5, Chapter 12

That doesn't sound like metaphor. It sounds like history waiting to happen. And more importantly, it sets the stage for the Church's suffering under that future tyrant.

Tertullian, like Irenaeus and Justin before him, believed the prophetic sequence was real: a rebuilt temple, a lawless one exalted above God, a persecution that sweeps across the saints, and then the return of Christ to judge and to reign.

Tertullian didn't envision a Church removed from the scene before this tribulation unfolded. On the contrary, his very discussion presupposes a faithful body of believers still present on the earth, resisting the Antichrist's self-deification. His concern was not that the Church would be caught off guard because they missed the rapture. His concern was that the Church would be unprepared to stand against the beast.

When he wrote that the Antichrist would "boast himself as being God," he wasn't offering an abstract theological concept. He was echoing Paul's precise warning in 2 Thessalonians 2:4:

"Who opposeth and exalteth himself above all that is called God, or that is worshipped; so that he as God sitteth in the temple of God, shewing himself that he is God."

What does that mean for the saints? It means every other form of worship Jewish, Christian, and pagan is outlawed unless it bends to the Beast. That's not just a warning to Israel. That's not just for some future group called "tribulation saints." That's for the Church.

You can't worship God and survive under the Antichrist. That's the point. And that's why Tertullian, like all the early Fathers, warned believers—not to wait for a secret deliverance—but to prepare for a public confrontation.

If pretribulationalism had existed in Tertullian's day, he would have exposed it for what it is: a doctrine of avoidance. But instead, he calls the Church to boldness, vigilance, and perseverance in the face of the most terrifying idolatry the world has ever seen.

Hippolytus of Rome (c. 170–235 AD)

If Irenaeus laid the foundation, Hippolytus built the tower. A faithful student of Irenaeus and a bishop in his own right, Hippolytus carried forward the same eschatological framework he inherited: a visible return of Christ after the rise of the Antichrist, with the Church enduring tribulation until that glorious appearing. And unlike modern theories that mutate prophecy into charts and secret timelines, Hippolytus did the exact opposite—he brought prophecy down to earth and placed the Church in the thick of it.

In his Treatise on Christ and Antichrist, Hippolytus gives one of the earliest detailed expositions of end-time prophecy in Christian literature. He walks carefully through Daniel's beasts, horns, and time periods, and he connects them—not to history past, but to a future tyrant yet to come. That tyrant, he says plainly, is the Antichrist.

"As Daniel also says: 'I considered the beast... and, lo, there were ten horns upon it... and, behold, there came up among them another little horn...' ... What, then, is meant by the 'little horn,' if not Antichrist?"
— *Treatise on Christ and Antichrist 25, 63*

He doesn't reinterpret these horns as general opposition to the Church. He doesn't spiritualize the conflict. He identifies it: a specific kingdom, a specific man, and a specific war—against the saints.

"This man will come... and deceive many; and persecute the saints; and reign... until the coming of the Lord from heaven."

Notice the sequence. Antichrist appears, deceives, persecutes, reigns—then Jesus returns. Sound familiar? It's the exact timeline given in 2 Thessalonians 2:3:

"That day shall not come, except there come a falling away first, and that man of sin be revealed..."

Paul and Hippolytus are saying the same thing. The coming of the Lord isn't imminent—it's resisted. It's preceded by deception, rebellion, and the rise of the Antichrist. If pretribulationists had lived in Hippolytus' day, they wouldn't have recognized his teaching. Worse, they would have called it "missing the blessed hope."

But Hippolytus wasn't the one turning the hope upside down. Pretribulationism did that. Today, they teach that the Church should be scanning the skies for Christ's return at any moment—Hippolytus said we should be watching for the Beast.

The difference matters. One view expects deliverance before difficulty. The other expects victory through endurance. The early Church chose the latter. And they chose it with open eyes and scarred backs. They knew full well that the tribulation wasn't an abstraction—it was coming. And it was coming for them.

Revelation 13:7 affirms this sobering expectation:

"And it was given unto him to make war with the saints, and to overcome them..."

Hippolytus never denies it. He confirms it. The saints aren't raptured—they're refined. They aren't watching—they're withstanding. And they overcome not by escape, but by perseverance.

"And they overcame him by the blood of the Lamb, and by the word of their testimony; and they loved not their lives unto the death." *(Revelation 12:11)*

That's the eschatology Hippolytus believed. And that's the eschatology we recover not with fear, but with faith. Not with predictions of absence, but with the promise of presence—Christ present with His Church, even in tribulation, even in death, even in fire.

Hippolytus didn't give us charts. He gave us courage. And it's time we listened.

The Shepherd of Hermas (c. 140 AD)

While The Shepherd of Hermas is not attributed to a named Church Father, it was one of the most widely read and respected texts in the second century and was included in Codex Sinaiticus—right after Revelation. That's important, because it reflects the kind of literature early Christians were feeding on alongside the Apocalypse. And it confirms what we've seen from the Fathers: The Church didn't expect to avoid tribulation. It expected to be tested by it—and purified through it.

Hermas doesn't talk about an escape. He talks about endurance. Not evacuation, but examination.

"Happy ye who endure the great tribulation that is coming... Those, therefore, who continue steadfast, and are put through the fire, will be purified by means of it."
— *Vision Second and Vision Fourth*

That language "put through the fire" should sound familiar. It's not isolated. It's biblical. It echoes the fiery trials spoken of by Peter, the refining fires spoken of by Malachi, and the gold tested in fire in Revelation.

"Beloved, think it not strange concerning the fiery trial which is to try you, as though some strange thing happened unto you: But rejoice, inasmuch as ye are partakers of Christ's sufferings..."
(1 Peter 4:12–13)

"And I will bring the third part through the fire, and will refine them as silver is refined..."
(Zechariah 13:9)

"I counsel thee to buy of me gold tried in the fire, that thou mayest be rich..."
(Revelation 3:18)

These aren't metaphors for good times. They're road signs for the remnant. The fire is not a detour from God's plan it's part of it. The tribulation is not what the Church escapes it's where the Church is tested. And Hermas doesn't hide that. He reinforces it.

And let's be honest—if ever there was a perfect opportunity to insert a secret rapture doctrine, this was it. Visionary literature. Eschatological themes. Prophetic tone. But instead of teaching removal, The Pastor of Hermas teaches refinement. Instead of vanishing saints, we're given steadfast ones. And instead of a trapdoor theology, we get a furnace theology.

That's consistent with Revelation itself. The Church in Smyrna isn't told they'll be rescued from persecution. They're told to endure it:

"Fear none of those things which thou shalt suffer: behold, the devil shall cast some of you into prison... be thou faithful unto death, and I will give thee a crown of life."
(Revelation 2:10)

The pattern doesn't change from Jesus to John to Hermas. The Church overcomes by enduring—not by escaping. And when pretribulational theology says otherwise, it's not just departing from scripture—it's departing from the voice of the early Church.

Hermas speaks plainly: the tribulation will come. The saints will go through it. And those who remain steadfast will be purified—not removed.

That's the message the early Church lived and died by. And that's the message we must recover.

Additional Early Witnesses: Strong Precedent for Historic Premillennialism

Let's be clear: this book has focused on dismantling the secret pretribulational rapture. But that's only one side of the story. The other side is what the early Church did believe and that belief forms the root system of what we now call historic premillennialism. That's not just a label it's a framework of faith grounded in Scripture, affirmed by the earliest Christians, and diametrically opposed to both pretrib rapture doctrine and the spiritualized schemes of amillennialism and postmillennialism.

The early Church believed Christ would return after the tribulation, after the reign of the Antichrist, and before the millennium. That's the true timeline: Antichrist, return, resurrection, reign. They didn't flatten prophecy into abstraction. They expected it to unfold in real time, in real history, with real suffering and a real Savior coming to reign.

Let's walk through a few more voices in that unbroken chorus.

Lactantius (c. 250–325 AD)

Lactantius, known for his apologetics, lived during a time of great instability and persecution. And like those before him, he saw what was coming: a world descending into chaos, a tyrant rising to power, and Christ returning in judgment to set all things right.

"...he will contrive many things against the righteous, will afflict them, and put them to death... He will harass the righteous... Then

will the righteous be driven into banishment, and into concealment; and will be pursued and slain."

"...that king will not only be most wicked himself... He will sit in the temple of God, and make himself as God... And he will persecute the righteous with cruel punishments, will cause righteous blood to flow, and will attempt to destroy the law of God."

"But when the tyrant and enemy shall have devastated all things in the world, he will reign for three years and six months, and sit in the temple at Jerusalem; and then the Lord will come from heaven..."
— Divine Institutes 7.17,19,21

That's not a spiritual metaphor. That's Revelation 19 and 20 in summary form. Persecution. Antichrist. Judgment. Kingdom. The order matters and Lactantius puts it in the same sequence as Jesus, Paul, and John.

He did not teach that the Church disappears before this storm. He wrote to comfort and prepared believers for the suffering to come. His view, like those before him, left no room for a vanishing act—but made plenty of room for a victorious appearing.

Cyprian of Carthage (c. 200–258 AD)

Cyprian, Bishop of Carthage saw tribulation not as a theoretical doctrine but as a lived experience. The Church of his day was already facing affliction and Cyprian interpreted that suffering in light of the coming resurrection.

"The day of affliction has begun to hang over our heads, and the end of the world and the time of the Antichrist to draw near, so that we must all stand prepared for the battle... with the advantage of foreseeing the impending storm, that we may take shelter, and be strengthened by the protection of the Lord... let us prepare ourselves with a whole heart, and with a firm faith, for the struggle of the coming persecution; let the soldiers of Christ consider that they are being trained in the camp of this world for the crown of victory in the future warfare. Let them exhibit the discipline of a prepared mind... that they may attain to the reward of the Lord."

He didn't separate the two. He didn't offer shortcuts. He taught what Paul taught:

"If so be that we suffer with him, that we may be also glorified together."
(Romans 8:17)

Suffering precedes glory. Tribulation precedes resurrection. The cross comes before the crown. That was Cyprian's theology and its biblical theology. There is no escapist exemption here, only the promise of glorification through suffering.

Melito of Sardis (c. 170 AD)

Melito, Bishop of Sardis, was a fierce defender of the faith and one of the earliest orthodox voices to affirm both the high Christology of the Incarnation and the apocalyptic hope of Revelation. His surviving fragments are precious because they reveal just how tightly early believers linked Christ's suffering to His return in judgment—and our own participation in that pattern.

"He endured suffering in many ways: He was condemned by law, led away by witnesses, and carried by hands. He bore a crown of thorns; He was pierced by reeds; He was scourged, struck, spat upon, dishonored, and crucified. He was buried as a man, rose from the dead as God, and will come again as Judge of the living and the dead."
—Melito of Sardis, On the Passion and Coming Judgment (fragment)

There's no room in Melito's eschatology for the idea that Christ's return being divided up or delayed by a seven-year gap. His return is a reckoning. It's the final answer to injustice, persecution, and martyrdom. He endured suffering, and so will His people. But then He comes visibly, powerfully, finally to judge and reign.

Melito also affirmed the inspiration of Revelation. That matters. Because if you believe Revelation is divinely inspired and you actually take it at face value, you won't come away thinking the Church is airlifted out in chapter 4. You'll see what the early Church saw: that the saints are in the thick of the conflict—overcoming, testifying, and waiting for vindication at the visible coming of the Lamb.

And Melito wasn't a fringe figure. He was orthodox. He was respected. He stood against Gnostic distortions of the gospel and gave one of the earliest high Christological confessions in Church history.

Putting the Pieces Together: Their Timeline Is Not Ours—Unless We Return to Theirs

All of these men from Irenaeus to Melito believed the Church would go through tribulation. All of them placed the return of Christ after the rise of the Antichrist. All of them held to a visible coming, a real resurrection, and a literal kingdom that follows. And none of them taught a pretribulational rapture or a split-stage return of Jesus Christ.

That matters, because if pretribulationalism were the apostolic teaching, it would show up here. It would echo through their letters. It would be shouted from their pulpits. But what we hear instead is a unified cry: hold fast, endure, the King is coming after the trial, not before it.

Their doctrine wasn't built on fear or escapism. It was rooted in victory—through suffering, not from it. It was rooted in Christ's own pattern: cross first, then crown. And that's the pattern the Church must reclaim.

Conclusion: The Unified Testimony of the Early Church The Trumpet, Not the Trapdoor

The testimony of the early Church is not a vague echo it's a unified voice. It doesn't stutter. It doesn't hesitate. It declares plainly what our generation has buried under centuries of speculation and sentiment: that the Church will face the Antichrist, endure the great tribulation, and meet the Lord when He returns visibly, finally, and gloriously to reign.

There was no secret coming. No hidden rapture. No eschatological sleight of hand. The earliest Christians did not speak of Jesus sneaking His bride out the back door before things got rough. They spoke of Him bursting through the clouds, trumpet blasting, angels shouting, and saints rising from the grave in the twinkling of an eye. One return. One resurrection. One kingdom.

And not one of them, not one taught otherwise.

Their writings ring with urgency—not because Jesus might return "at any second," but because the Beast might. Justin Martyr didn't say Christ was at the door—he said Antichrist was. Think about that. The modern church reversed the entire timeline. Today, people watch for Jesus and ignore the Beast. But the early Church watched for the Beast and prepared for Jesus. They believed Paul's warning in 2 Thessalonians 2:1–3, that we are not to be shaken or deceived, because that day shall not come, except there come a falling away first, and that man of sin be revealed.

That's the order. Not rapture, then tribulation. But deception, tribulation, then return. The Church Fathers believed it. The Apostles taught it. And the Scriptures confirm it.

They didn't build their doctrine on speculation. They didn't need chart timelines or fill pulpits with fantasy. They stood on Scripture, they watched for the Antichrist, they resisted false gospels, and they encouraged the saints to hold fast. They knew that suffering precedes glory, and that the fire purifies the faithful. They weren't escapists. They were overcomers.

So, here's the challenge: if you trust the early Church to give you the right books, the right gospel, and the right view of Christ—why would you distrust them on the return of Christ?

The truth is, pretribulationism is a theological orphan. It has no family line in Church history. It has no inheritance from the Apostles. And it cannot sit at the table with the saints who gave their lives to defend the true hope of His return.

The early Church looked for Christ to come—not to spare them from suffering—but to vindicate their suffering. They didn't expect a rescue. They expected a resurrection. They weren't waiting for a trapdoor. They were waiting for a trumpet.

And so must we.

Rebuttal & Answer:
"Pseudo-Ephraem Said the Elect Would be Gathered After the Tribulation"

Pretribulationists often seize upon a single line from the Latin Pseudo-Ephraem as though it were a divine revelation, overlooked for centuries until finally rediscovered by dispensational apologists in the 20th century. They argue that this line offers "proof" of a pretribulational rapture in the early Church:

"For all the saints and elect of God are gathered, prior to the tribulation that is to come, and are taken to the Lord..."

At first glance, especially in English, this may sound like a rapture. But upon closer examination, both the textual integrity and historical theology collapse under scrutiny. This one line-ripped from a document falsely attributed to Ephraem, translated selectively, and torn from context-has been wielded to override not only the rest of the homily, but also the testimony of Scripture and the authentic writings of Ephraem the Syrian himself.[17]

The Fatal Omission: Pretribulationists Never Mention the Syriac Version

---

[17] The Pseudo-Ephraem text, often cited by pretribulationists as early evidence of a pretrib rapture, was translated by Dr. Cameron Rhoades at the request of Tim LaHaye and promoted by the Pre-Trib Research Center. This organization, along with affiliated scholars like Grant Jeffrey and Thomas Ice, holds a statement of faith affirming "*the personal, bodily, pretribulational, and premillennial return of our Lord Jesus Christ*." The document is not written by Ephraem of Syria and is widely dated by scholars to the 7th century or later. Its use as proof of early pretribulationism reflects confirmation bias, not historical consensus.

The greatest irony in this debate is that pretrib advocates almost never mention the Syriac version of this homily. That's because the Syriac version, more faithful to Ephraem's language and worldview, destroys their interpretation. It says:

"Pronouncing the good fortune of the deceased Who had avoided the calamity: 'Blessed are you for you were borne away (to the grave) And hence you escaped from the afflictions! But as for us, woe is us! For when we die, Vultures will serve as escort for us!' And if the days of that time were not shortened, The elect would never survive The calamities and afflictions. For Our Lord revealed (and) disclosed to us In his Gospel when He said: 'Those days will be shortened For the sake of the elect and the saints."
—Pseudo-Ephraem, Sermon on the End of the World

This line-parallel in structure to the Latin quote-doesn't describe a rapture. It describes death. A peaceful death before the tribulation. It is praising the dead, not announcing the sudden vanishing of the living.

It harmonizes with the biblical theme of death as a form of divine mercy, as in:

"And I heard a voice from heaven saying unto me, Write, Blessed are the dead which die in the Lord from henceforth: Yea, saith the Spirit, that they may rest from their labours; and their works do follow them."
(Revelation 14:13)

These texts are not pretribulational. They are pastoral, prophetic, and posttribulational.

The Authentic Ephraem Teaches Endurance, Not Escape

In writings attributed to Ephraem the tribulation is not a period from which the Church is evacuated it is a furnace through which the faithful must endure. Even the oft-misquoted fragment from Pseudo-Ephraem affirms this reality when read in context. He, like Paul, expected the apostasy and rise of the Antichrist to come before the Second Coming. He wrote:

"In those days people shall not be buried, neither Christian, nor heretic, neither Jew, nor pagan, because of fear and dread there is not one who buries them; because all people, while they are fleeing, ignore them... Then all people from everywhere shall flock together to him (Antichrist) at the city of Jerusalem, and the holy city shall be trampled on by the nations for forty-two months... But those who wander through the deserts, fleeing from the face of the serpent, bend their knees to God..., being sustained by the salvation of the Lord, and while wandering in states of desertion, they eat herbs."
—Pseudo-Ephraem, Sermon on the End of the World

There is no pretribulation rapture here. On the contrary, this teaching aligns perfectly with 2 Thessalonians 2:1–3, which declares that the day of Christ will not come "except there come a falling away first, and that man of sin be revealed." Pseudo-Ephraem joins John in Revelation and Paul in Thessalonica, bearing witness that the Church will face the deceiver, suffer persecution, and witness martyrdom. Pseudo-Ephraem also says, "all people" shall flee from him, it is inclusive language that assumes general terror in the last days but, as we have explored throughout this book, such language allows for outliers.

But perhaps the most devastating blow to the pretribulational misuse of Pseudo-Ephraem comes from what he meant by "escape." Both the Latin and Syriac versions of his writings include a blessing—not for those raptured—but for those who have already died in Christ before the affliction begins:

"Arise, O sleeping ones, arise, meet Christ, because his hour of judgment has come... the Lord shall destroy (Antichrist) by the spirit of his mouth...
—Pseudo-Ephraem, Latin Sermon on the End of the World

"Pronouncing the good fortune of the deceased Who had avoided the calamity: 'Blessed are you for you were borne away. And hence you escaped from the afflictions!"
—*Syriac Fragment*

This is not a rapture. It is a funeral. The "taking away" is death, not disappearance. The only ones counted blessed for escaping the tribulation are those who have already gone to sleep in the Lord. It is the opposite of a secret coming—it is a eulogy. Pseudo-Ephraem is saying exactly what Isaiah said

"The righteous perisheth, and no man layeth it to heart... he shall enter into peace: they shall rest in their beds, each one walking in his uprightness."
(Isaiah 57:1–2)

In both Scripture and Ephraem, death is the early gathering. It is not an act of deliverance in the sky, but a mercy granted in rest. When Pseudo-Ephraem refers to the elect being spared or taken away, he is not describing a corporate event that removes the Church from the earth; he is acknowledging the majority of the elect are gathered in death prior to the great affliction. The saints who live to see the end will face fire, but those who sleep beforehand are counted blessed. Ephraem's authentic Homilies never taught escapism. Consider the following from Homily On the Second Coming:

"What, my brethren? When the martyrs show the wounds of their sufferings and tortures, and when the noble ascetics show their asceticism and self-discipline, their patience and affliction, and their poverty, will the indolent, the sluggish, and the indifferent have anything in which to boast?[18]

This language unmistakably recalls the patience and faith of the saints in Revelation 13:10, where God's recompenses tribulation on those who trouble the Church. The hope is not escape but

---

[18] **On the Second Coming of Our Lord Jesus Christ verse 12**

preservation. The Church will be hidden, tried, refined, and ultimately vindicated.

These are the words of a shepherd warning his flock to endure suffering, trust in divine shelter, and look for the glorious appearing of Christ after the great tribulation. The Church faces the Antichrist. The Church must endure tribulation.

There is no mention of a pretribulational rescue, and certainly no invisible return of Christ to secretly collect His Church. Ephraem's witness is consistent with apostolic teaching and early Christian expectation: suffering precedes glory. Tribulation precedes rest. The grave—not the clouds—was the early Christian escape hatch. The furnace comes before the kingdom.

Reverse the Rebuke: Maybe the Dispensation Has Been Misread

It is a common tactic among pretribulational teachers to accuse posttribulationists of misinterpreting Scripture, often accompanied by the exhortation to "rightly divide the Word" and maintain dispensational distinctions. Such teachers insist passages like Matthew 24 pertain exclusively to Israel and therefore cannot refer to the Church. Yet paradoxically, the same teachers eagerly embrace isolated phrases from non-inspired texts like Pseudo-Ephraem's Latin homily—written centuries after the apostles and wrongly attributed to an author who never wrote in Latin—as unquestionable evidence of the Church's pretribulational rescue.

Consider the irony inherent in their logic: Matthew 24, directly spoken by Christ—the very Head of the Church—explicitly places the gathering of the elect after the tribulation. Yet dispensational teachers claim the elect cannot represent the Church. Conversely, a brief and ambiguous line from a late, pseudonymous medieval sermon is seized upon to declare with absolute certainty that the elect gathered before tribulation must indeed be the Church. If dispensational distinctions forbid applying Christ's explicit teaching about the elect in Matthew 24 to the Church, how is it consistent to apply the far vaguer use of the term "elect" in Pseudo-Ephraem's Latin homily to that same Church?

The dispensational principle is being selectively employed, exposing not careful exegesis, but a desperate attempt to preserve a cherished doctrinal tradition. This selective method reveals the contradiction inherent in pretribulational hermeneutics: Scripture itself can be casually set aside, yet isolated fragments from medieval sources can be dogmatically elevated.

What This Really Is: Elevating Tradition Above Christ

In truth, the pretribulational interpretation of Pseudo-Ephraem collapses once the broader context and details are acknowledged. To sustain their reading, advocates must systematically ignore: Ephraem's authentic works, which teach plainly that believers must endure persecution; the explicit meaning of the Syriac homily, which clearly identifies death—not rapture—as the blessed escape; the overall context of both Syriac and Latin versions, which describe martyrdom and suffering for living saints during the tribulation period.

Most importantly, pretribulationalists must disregard the explicit teaching of Christ Himself, who declared without ambiguity:

"Immediately after the tribulation of those days... He shall send His angels... and they shall gather together His elect." (Matthew 24:29–31)

To reject Christ's clear chronological description of the gathering of the elect in favor of an obscure, disputed passage from a pseudonymous, medieval homily is to elevate human tradition above divine revelation. It is to invert the very principle they claim to uphold the authority of Scripture.

Conclusion: Death Before Tribulation Is a Mercy, Not a Rapture

The unified testimony of Ephraem's authentic Syriac writings, the explicit language of the Syriac version of the Pseudo-Ephraem sermon, and the consistent Scriptural witness all point decisively to one conclusion: the saints who are "received" or "taken away" before the tribulation are received through the merciful means of death, not through a pretrib rapture.

To extract a doctrine of bodily rapture from an isolated Latin phrase, divorced from its Syriac context, the author's authentic theology, and the clear statements of Christ Himself, is neither sound exegesis nor faithful interpretation. Rather, it reveals theological desperation, a determined effort to find evidence where none exists, and to supplant the unambiguous teaching of Jesus with the ambiguity of human tradition.

The truth remains clear and unassailable: Christ gathers His elect after the tribulation. Those who are spared the tribulation's horrors before that day are indeed blessed—but their blessing is found in peaceful death, rest from labor, and reception into the Lord's presence—not in secret escape or hidden rapture. The Word of God, spoken clearly by Christ Himself, must always prevail over speculative interpretations of any medieval sermon, however convenient its wording might seem.

Let us then return to the old path the path walked by the apostles, preached by the early Church, and preserved by the faithful under fire. From Ignatius to Irenaeus, from Tertullian to Ephraem, the testimony is clear: the Church must endure tribulation, but she shall be vindicated at the visible return of Christ. This is not a modern theory, but the ancient faith. We are not waiting for escape—we are waiting for glory. As Jeremiah declared:

"Thus saith the Lord, Stand ye in the ways, and see, and ask for the old paths, where is the good way, and walk therein, and ye shall find rest for your souls"
(Jeremiah 6:16).

Let us walk in that good way, even if it leads through the fire, for beyond the fire is the kingdom.

Next Revelation:
Preparing the Church for Tribulation Calling the Saints to Endure, Not Escape

The book of Revelation does not call the saints to escape—it calls them to overcome. The Lamb leads His people through the storm, not around it, and the promise is reserved for those who endure to the end. The next chapter will explore that call to perseverance, for Scripture declares:

"In all these things we are more than conquerors through him that loved us" (Romans 8:37).

The path may be narrow, but the victory is certain—for those who follow the Lamb wherever He goes.

Chapter 14:
Preparing the Church for Tribulation
Calling the Saints to Endure, Not Escape

From the very beginning, Jesus never sugar-coated what it meant to follow Him. He did not offer a comfortable journey but a costly calling—one marked by daily self-denial, patient endurance, and unwavering faithfulness. Yet in recent generations, a comforting but unbiblical teaching has taken root: the idea that believers will escape the tribulation through a secret evacuation before Christ visibly returns. This modern myth has lulled many into spiritual passivity. But Christ never promised evacuation. He promised endurance. He never invited us to bypass suffering but called us to walk the narrow road—one that leads through the valley of testing, not around it. The call has not changed. The cross still waits for every disciple.

Indeed, Jesus explicitly called us to deny ourselves, take up our cross daily, and follow Him. This is a daily walk in the footsteps of the One who literally carried the cross for our sins. The weight of that cross was heavy, crushingly heavy. We read how Jesus collapsed under its burden, physically spent from beatings, bleeding, and exhaustion He endured willingly for our sake. Yet, in those final moments of anguish, Simon of Cyrene was told to step in and help Him bear that cross up to Golgotha's hill. Even Christ, in His humanity, received help bearing that awful burden. So, when our burdens seem too heavy and the trials of life too overwhelming, we find comfort in knowing Jesus Himself strengthens us. He shares our burden and helps us carry the cross so that we may endure faithfully to the very end. In this same spirit of assurance, He promises, "My yoke is easy, and my burden is light" (Matthew 11:30).

No dispensational framework, no matter how elaborate or attractive, can override this fundamental call to follow Christ through hardship and perseverance. Any doctrine failing to affirm, "Hereunto are you called to suffer as Christ suffered," should immediately be treated with suspicion. The apostle Paul, echoing the words of his Master, wrote plainly:

"For to me to live is Christ, and to die is gain"

(Philippians 1:21).

Far too often believers have been crippled by a spirit of fear rather than emboldened by a call to courage and endurance. This has resulted in the glorious hope of vindication, promised in Christ's triumphant return, being quietly replaced by doctrines of stealthy and secret retreat. What motivation do we have to embrace such a diminished expectation—one devoid of the glory vividly portrayed in Scripture? The answer is clear: fear. It is fear of plagues, fear of persecution, fear of wrath—fear of hardship itself. Yet we have not been called to cowardice but courage, to boldness rather than retreat. The calling upon our lives is not to secretly vanish but to steadfastly proclaim the glory and power of Christ's second coming.

Let us therefore choose courage over cowardice, strength over fear, and biblical truth over comforting myths. Let us embrace the cross-bearing, self-denying, perseverance-oriented Christianity modeled by our Savior Himself. The path may be difficult, but it leads to glory. For Christ did not promise an easy escape—He promised a sure victory.

Jesus' Call to Stay Ready: Lessons from His Parables

When Jesus told stories, He wasn't entertaining—He was equipping. His parables were not given to create imaginative distractions but to train the hearts and minds of His disciples for perseverance. Each story was a summons to vigilance, endurance, and fruitfulness under pressure. Think about the parable of the faithful and wise servant (Matthew 24:45–51). The servant is not praised for escaping danger or foreseeing a hidden departure; he is honored because, in the face of apparent delay, he remained loyal to his duty. His reward was not based on how quickly he left, but how steadfastly he stayed. The unfaithful servant, by contrast, saw the delay as an opportunity to let down his guard—to become abusive, indulgent, and careless. His downfall came not because he missed the exit but because he failed the test of enduring responsibility during the Master's apparent absence.

Or consider the ten virgins (Matthew 25:1–13). This parable is often remembered for its imagery, but its message is deeply sobering. All ten were waiting. All ten expected the Bridegroom to come. But only five had prepared with enough oil to endure the delay. The others assumed the wait would be short. They neglected to carry what was necessary for the long night. The lesson is not that the bridegroom came unexpectedly, but that some failed to endure with readiness. Jesus does not commend the swift, but the steady— the ones who anticipate delay and maintain their spiritual reserves until the door is opened.

And then there is the parable of the talents (Matthew 25:14–30). Here, the master departs and leaves his servants with varying responsibilities. The ones who put their talents to work—who labored, multiplied, invested, and endured the long stretch of absence—are rewarded when the master returns. But the one who feared hardship and took the posture of passive preservation is condemned. He hid his gift. He waited, but he did not work. He anticipated the master's return but did nothing in the meantime. His problem was not disbelief in the return, but failure to act in light of it. He represents all who claim to wait for Christ yet live as if hiding from hardship justifies unfaithfulness.

In all three parables, Christ is preparing His Church for faithfulness. He does not speak of servants disappearing early, virgins raptured before the cry, or stewards rewarded for hiding out. He presents a consistent picture: the faithful endure. They labor in the delay, keep watch through the night, and stay ready regardless of how long the wait becomes. There is only the call to vigilance, endurance, and spiritual stewardship until the King returns. These stories are not puzzles to decode—they are warnings to take up the cross and endure until the end.

Revelation 3:10: The Promise to Those Who Endure

Jesus makes an incredible promise in Revelation 3:10:

"Because thou hast kept the word of my patience, I also will keep thee from the hour of temptation, which shall come upon all the world, to try them that dwell upon the earth."

Many have read this as a ticket out of tribulation but look carefully. This promise is to those who've demonstrated patience— those who've already endured. It speaks of protection through trial, not removal from it. Just as Noah was preserved through the flood and Israel through Egypt's plagues, God's protection doesn't always mean evacuation—it often means empowerment to endure.

This aligns perfectly with Jesus' prayer in John 17. Knowing full well the trials His followers would face, Jesus prayed explicitly:

"I pray not that thou shouldest take them out of the world, but that thou shouldest keep them from the evil." (John 17:15)

Think about that! Jesus didn't ask for evacuation. He prayed for divine protection right where we are. He asked the Father to strengthen and shield us through trouble, not to remove us from it. If escape were His intent, wouldn't He have prayed differently? Clearly, Jesus wanted us firmly planted, protected, and productive—even in tribulation.

Yet, the pretrib teaching contradicts this. It removes from the scene the very believers commended for perseverance, eliminating any need for endurance at all. This contradiction undermines Christ's call to faithfully stand strong.

Practical Encouragement: Watch, Pray, Endure

Jesus didn't leave us guessing about what to do. He plainly instructed in Mark 13:37:

"What I say unto you I say unto all, Watch."

Watching isn't passive sky-gazing; it's about spiritual alertness, vigilance, and constant readiness. It serves as a vital antidote to complacency, equipping us to recognize spiritual dangers and remain steadfast amid challenges.

In Luke 21:36, Jesus further clarifies:

"Watch ye therefore, and pray always, that ye may be accounted worthy to escape all these things that shall come to pass."

Yet, as we've discussed previously, the "escape" mentioned here is not a reference to evading persecution or everyday trials—it specifically denotes deliverance from the divine wrath to come.

Believers are explicitly appointed to endure trials and hardships (Acts 14:22), but they are never destined to suffer God's wrath (1 Thessalonians 5:9). Thus, our prayerful vigilance is not aimed at finding an easy exit from troubles, but rather at receiving divine strength and grace to remain faithful through them.

Historically, the Church has always faced trials and tribulations, just as Christ explicitly warned: "In the world ye shall have tribulation" (John 16:33). From the first-century persecutions of Rome, through the severe trials faced by early believers like Polycarp and Ignatius, down to the faithful martyrs of every age, God's people have consistently borne witness through endurance. Jesus never promised exemption from difficulty; He promised His presence and ultimate triumph amid difficulty. Trials are not aberrations in the Christian life; they are normative. Each generation of believers has faced unique tests, and the Church's legacy is not one of escaping hardship but overcoming it by faith.

Jesus reinforced this message clearly:

"He that shall endure unto the end, the same shall be saved" (Matthew 24:13).

This enduring salvation is assured for those who remain faithful, not those who speculate sensationally or wait passively for escape. Endurance requires spiritual depth, patience, and resilience. Christ's teaching calls for a faith that is active, steadfast, and immovable, a faith rooted deeply enough to withstand even the harshest storms. The Church has never thrived by retreating; it has flourished through perseverance, courage, and unwavering loyalty to the One who conquered sin and death.

Martyrdom: Honored Testimony, Not Tragic Defeat

The idea of martyrdom unsettles many Christians in the modern era. Yet, from a biblical perspective, martyrdom is not a defeat but the highest form of victory. The book of Revelation offers a sobering but hopeful perspective:

"They overcame him by the blood of the Lamb, and by the word of their testimony; and they loved not their lives unto the death"

(Revelation 12:11).

Here, triumph is not defined by preservation of one's own life, but by a steadfast witness that values Christ above all, even to the point of death. The testimony of the martyrs stands as a profound affirmation of Christ's supreme worth; their faithfulness exposes the poverty of a faith preoccupied with safety or escape.

Peter reinforces this calling with unmistakable clarity:

"For even hereunto were ye called: because Christ also suffered for us, leaving us an example, that ye should follow his steps"
(1 Peter 2:21)

The life of discipleship, as Peter and the other apostles understood, is patterned after the suffering and endurance of Christ Himself. The earliest generations of believers did not shrink back when faced with opposition; they viewed suffering as an opportunity to draw nearer to their Lord. Ignatius of Antioch, who faced execution in Rome, wrote with striking serenity, "Let me be food for wild beasts... I am God's wheat, ground by beasts to become pure bread for Christ." The apostles themselves rejoiced that they were counted worthy to suffer for the name of Jesus (Acts 5:41). Their hope was never anchored in deliverance from suffering, but in the assurance of God's presence through it.

Jesus spoke to this reality with characteristic directness:

"If any man will come after me, let him deny himself, and take up his cross daily, and follow me"
(Luke 9:23).

To follow Christ is to embrace this daily call not a one-time sacrifice, but a continual pattern of self-denial and faithfulness, whatever the cost. And in this calling, Christ offers His own assurance, "My sheep hear my voice, and I know them, and they follow me. And I give unto them eternal life; and they shall never perish, neither shall any man pluck them out of my hand" (John 10:27–28). The believer's security is not found in avoiding difficulty, but in trusting the Good Shepherd who leads us through every trial and promises life that endures beyond the grave.

The path of suffering has always been the Church's calling and privilege. To follow Christ is to walk where He walked, to endure what He endured, and to rest in the promise that nothing can separate us from His love or from the hope of resurrection. True security is not found in escape, but in unwavering allegiance to the One who overcame the world.

Don't Fear God's Judgments—They're Not Meant for You

Many believers today find themselves living under a persistent shadow of fear, largely because they misunderstand the message of Revelation's plagues. As we have explored earlier in this book, the trumpets, bowls, and seals described in Revelation do not signify indiscriminate calamity for God's people but represent God's measured response against those who persecute the saints. These judgments are not directed at the faithful, but at those who oppress and afflict them. Paul expresses this principle with clarity, teaching that tribulation is appointed not for God's children, but for those who trouble the Church, "Seeing it is a righteous thing with God to recompense tribulation to them that trouble you; and to you who are troubled rest with us, when the Lord Jesus shall be revealed from heaven with his mighty angels" (2 Thessalonians 1:6–7).

The book of Revelation reinforces this divine reversal. The martyrs, whose blood has been shed by the world's violence, cry out beneath the altar, "How long, O Lord, holy and true, dost thou not judge and avenge our blood on them that dwell on the earth?" (Revelation 6:10). God's answer is not to remove His saints from the world, but to bring forth justice on their behalf. Revelation 8:4–5 portrays the prayers of the saints rising up before God, and in response, judgment is cast upon the earth. The plagues that follow are not random disasters, but God's deliberate intervention to defend and vindicate His people.

Despite this clear biblical testimony, pretribulational doctrine often teaches believers to fear the very judgments that are, in reality, God's answer to the Church's prayers for justice. This mindset not only breeds anxiety but also distorts the character of God's redemptive plan. It is as if Israel, upon hearing of the plagues sent against Egypt, had trembled in fear rather than recognizing those judgments as their deliverance. In the same way, it is neither logical nor scriptural for the Church to dread the righteous acts of God that are designed to liberate the faithful and hold oppressors to account.

The apostle Paul counseled Timothy, and by extension all believers, not to be governed by fear, "For God hath not given us the spirit of fear; but of power, and of love, and of a sound mind" (2 Timothy 1:7). The message for the Church is clear: we are called to reject fear-based teaching and to recognize the judgments of Revelation as expressions of God's faithfulness to His promises. These plagues are not threats to God's people, but the means by which He answers the cries for justice that have ascended from His saints throughout the ages.

Revelation itself echoes this exhortation:

"Rejoice over her, thou heaven, and ye holy apostles and prophets; for God hath avenged you on her"
(Revelation 18:20)

Far from inciting dread, God's righteous judgments are grounds for hope, celebration, and confidence in the ultimate victory of Christ and His Church.

Spiritual Preparation Over Political Confidence

Today, it's tempting for the Church to put a lot of hope in political victories and cultural influence. And while believers certainly have a role in standing up for biblical values, we must be careful never to confuse earthly political power with genuine spiritual strength. Political engagement is valuable and its often part of how we live out our convictions, but it should never replace the core disciplines of the faith. Our primary allegiance isn't to any earthly party or politician, but to Christ's eternal kingdom.

We must remember that, according to biblical prophecy, earthly governments will ultimately succumb to deception and opposition to Christ. Scripture shows us clearly that, in the last days, global politics will be dominated by the Antichrist's political-religious system until Jesus returns. So, while it's natural—and even important—to care deeply about our society's direction, we can't put our final hope there. The early Church changed the world not because they had political power (they had none), but because their lives overflowed with holiness, compassion, boldness, and deep trust in God, even amidst persecution.

Genuine preparation for tribulation starts with spiritual practices like repentance, discipleship, prayer, and nurturing strong communities of faith. Politics can be an expression of our beliefs, but it can never substitute for a vibrant, enduring relationship with Christ. When persecution comes—and Scripture assures us it will—only those rooted deeply in spiritual maturity and unwavering trust in God's sovereignty will stand strong.

The Final Call: Overcome Through Christ

Revelation 12:11 and 3:21 declare the victory that belongs to the people of God:

"They overcame him by the blood of the Lamb, and by the word of their testimony... To him that overcometh will I grant to sit with me in my throne."

Christ is returning not for a bride that has retreated or vanished, but for one that stands firm in the midst of trial. He offers true gold refined in fire (Revelation 3:18), not the allure of a cheap escape. His call remains unchanged, "Be thou faithful unto death, and I will give thee a crown of life" (Revelation 2:10). The Church is invited not to fear the flames, but to shine brightly within them, overcoming through Jesus Christ, our hope and our strength.

Some may respond sincerely, "I still believe in the pretrib rapture because it gives me hope. I just don't want to be here for all that." This is perhaps the most honest objection, for it rests not on exegesis, but on emotion—a very human longing to be spared the darkest hour. Who would not desire relief in the face of suffering? Yet true, biblical hope has never been rooted in escape. It is built on the character of God—His justice, His faithfulness, and His unbreakable promise to be present with us, even in the deepest valleys.

If our concept of hope requires that we be removed from tribulation, then what do we say to generations of believers who have faced fire, prison, and sword? Did God love them less, or fail to keep His promise? The testimony of Scripture and history says otherwise. Jesus never promised to remove us from every trial, but to be present in the midst of them. His word was never, "Fear not, for you will escape trouble," but rather:

"Fear thou not; for I am with thee: be not dismayed; for I am thy God: I will strengthen thee; yea, I will help thee; yea, I will uphold thee with the right hand of my righteousness."
(Isaiah 41:10)

The kind of hope that is built on avoiding trouble is not true hope at all; it is denial shaped by fear. Denial cannot sustain faith when the world is shaking. True biblical hope is what empowered martyrs to sing while the flames climbed higher, what steadied the apostles when prisons and wild beasts awaited, what carried saints through the cruelties and the darkness of totalitarian regimes. This is the hope Jesus offers—unshakable, enduring, able to stand because it knows who stands with us.

Remember the story of Shadrach, Meshach, and Abednego. Their faith did not spare them from the furnace. On the contrary, they were thrown into a fire heated seven times hotter than before. The miracle was not that God delivered them from the flames, but that He met them in the fire. The astonished king saw not three, but four men walking unharmed, "and the form of the fourth is like the Son of God" (Daniel 3:25). Their deliverance was not found in avoiding the trial, but in the presence of God within it. This is biblical hope. This is the kind of God we serve: not one who always spares us from the fire, but one who joins us in it and leads us through to victory.

Let us, then, anchor our hope in the One who overcomes, who is with us always, and who has promised that the crown of life awaits those who are faithful unto the end.

The Last Rebuttal:
"But I Feel Like…"—When Emotion Becomes Theology

As this conversation draws to a close, perhaps the most persistent objection is not one of exegesis, tradition, or even logic, but of feeling. Many believers—sometimes quietly, sometimes with urgency—confess, "I just feel like God wouldn't let us go through that. I feel like the rapture is our blessed hope. I feel like I couldn't endure if things became that dark." These are deeply human responses. The longing to avoid pain, to be spared tribulation, and to find comfort in the idea of escape is not new. In fact, it is as old as humanity itself.

It is important to say plainly: our feelings matter to God. He is not indifferent to our anxieties or our hopes. The Lord who wept at the tomb of Lazarus and sweat drops of blood in Gethsemane knows the weight of human emotion. But He also knows how easily fear and longing can shape our expectations—even in the realm of doctrine.

This is the essence of emotional theology: This "Emotional theology" is not simply having feelings about God or the future; it is allowing those feelings—especially our fears, longings, and instinct for self-preservation—to become the architects of what we believe, sometimes in direct contradiction to what Scripture actually teaches. When doctrine is built on emotion rather than revelation, it becomes untethered from the truth that alone can sustain us when the testing comes. The heart may be sincere, but sincerity is not the measure of sound doctrine.

This is where emotional theology quietly supplants biblical faith. We want assurance, and so we imagine a doctrine that promises safety rather than suffering. We are comforted by the thought of absence from tribulation, and so we begin to interpret Scripture in ways that insulate us from discomfort. The danger is subtle but profound: when feeling becomes the architect of belief, truth is reduced to the measure of our preferences.

Yet, as we have seen throughout Scripture and the testimony of the early Church, God has never promised to spare His people from tribulation—only to walk with them through it. Our hope is not found in the promise of an early exit, but in the presence of Christ who sustains, vindicates, and redeems His people in every circumstance. Biblical hope is not the denial of difficulty, but the assurance that God's faithfulness is greater than every storm.

No one modeled this reality more vividly than Christ Himself. In Gethsemane, the Son of God faced dread, agony, and a foreknowledge of suffering so intense that His sweat became as drops of blood. Jesus prayed, "Father, if it be possible, let this cup pass from me; nevertheless not my will, but thine, be done." The cross was not a hypothetical possibility for Him; it was the appointed path. The One who was beloved of the Father endured not only death, but the full weight of human pain, betrayal, and injustice. Out of love, He submitted Himself to suffering, "for the joy that was set before him" (Hebrews 12:2).

Jesus also taught with uncompromising clarity:

"A servant is not above his master, nor a messenger above the one who sent him"
(Matthew 10:24)

If God did not spare His own Son, but delivered Him up for us all, how can we imagine ourselves exempt from the suffering that Christ endured? We are not better than He is. The way of the Master is the way of the disciple. Jesus Himself warned, "If they have persecuted me, they will also persecute you" (John 15:20).

The history of the apostles stands as a solemn testimony to this pattern. Of the twelve, all but one were killed in brutal ways for their witness to Christ—and even the one who was spared martyrdom, John—the most beloved apostle—suffered exile and endured many hardships for the sake of the gospel. Their lives were not marked by escape, but by enduring faith. Their hope was not found in a promise of being kept from trouble, but in the certainty that God would vindicate them, that their labor and suffering would not be in vain.

There is a deeper wisdom at work in God's dealings with His people, a wisdom that transcends our natural desire for ease or comfort. As the Lord declared through Isaiah, "For my thoughts are not your thoughts, neither are your ways my ways, saith the Lord. For as the heavens are higher than the earth, so are my ways higher than your ways, and my thoughts than your thoughts" (Isaiah 55:8–9). We are invited to trust a God whose perspective is infinitely greater than our own, even—and especially—when we do not fully understand His reasons for allowing suffering.

Also consider God's response to Job. Job was a righteous man who suffered profoundly, and yet God never explained the reasons for his trials in terms that satisfied human curiosity or emotion. Instead, the Lord drew Job's attention to His sovereignty, His wisdom, and the vastness of His works. "Where wast thou when I laid the foundations of the earth? declare, if thou hast understanding" (Job 38:4). Job's comfort ultimately did not come from answers, but from an encounter with the God who is present in suffering and whose purposes reach beyond what human minds can grasp.

To anchor faith in feeling is to build on sand. The storms will come—history guarantees it, and prophecy confirms it. What endures is not the theology that soothes our anxieties, but the truth that equips us to stand firm. We are not called to follow our hearts wherever they lead, but to follow Christ who has already gone before us, bearing the cross, despising the shame, and securing for us a hope that will not disappoint.

There is a tenderness and a warning here. God is not the author of confusion or fear, but He does call us to trust Him in the face of both. Hope is not the assurance of escape, but the confidence of presence—His presence with us in every fire and storm. The faith that endures is anchored in the character of God, not in the comfort of our feelings. Only then can we say, with Job, "Though he slay me, yet will I trust in him" (Job 13:15), and with Paul, "We are troubled on every side, yet not distressed... cast down, but not destroyed" (2 Corinthians 4:8–9).

Let us build our faith not on what we feel, but on who God is—trusting that His ways are higher, His wisdom is perfect, and His promises are sure. God will, in the end, vindicate His people, wipe away every tear, and make all things new. The pain of the present is not the end of the story. Our hope is not in avoidance of tribulation, but in the unfailing presence and ultimate justice of the One who conquered death itself.

"Who shall separate us from the love of Christ? shall tribulation, or distress, or persecution, or famine, or nakedness, or peril, or sword? As it is written, For thy sake we are killed all the day long; we are accounted as sheep for the slaughter. Nay, in all these things we are more than conquerors through him that loved us. For I am persuaded, that neither death, nor life, nor angels, nor principalities, nor powers, nor things present, nor things to come, Nor height, nor

depth, nor any other creature, shall be able to separate us from the love of God, which is in Christ Jesus our Lord."
(Romans 8:35–39)

EPILOGUE
Sounding the Alarm

We are not appointed to wrath, yet neither are we appointed to retreat. The wrath of God is not intended for the faithful, but for the rebellious, the unrepentant, and the Beast-worshipers who have shed the blood of the saints. Yet somehow, amid the confusion of modern eschatology, this wrath has been misassigned—portrayed as something the Church must frantically escape rather than endure under the preserving hand of her Lord.

The result has been a false comfort and a tranquilized watchfulness. The Bride, instead of diligently trimming her lamp and staying awake in anticipation of the Bridegroom, has been lulled into dreaming of an early departure. Yet Jesus did not call His Church to nap peacefully before the wedding feast; He called her to remain vigilant and alert, watching steadfastly through the night.

True biblical hope is not fragile, nor does it demand an escape route to survive. Rather, it thrives in tribulation precisely because it is rooted in the unwavering promise of divine vindication. Just as Israel stood firm at the Red Sea, witnessing the salvation of God while the armies of Egypt drowned, so too will the faithful Church be preserved—not by absence from trouble, but by the powerful presence of God within it.

When Christ returns in glory, the tables will dramatically turn. The world will tremble, the skies will split apart, and those who have been maligned, martyred, and mocked will rise triumphantly to meet their King. That day is not to be feared but longed for. It is the day of recompense, the hour when God will openly display those who truly belong to Him. This, then, is the real promise—not evacuation before the storm, but enduring rest after the refining fire. This promised rest is worth every difficult step of the tribulation that precedes it.

Let this, therefore, serve as the final call: stand firm. Reject the soft gospel of escape that seeks comfort at the expense of truth. Do not mistake physical safety or ease for spiritual faithfulness. The true Church will overcome—not by vanishing from adversity, but by persevering through it. The blood of martyrs throughout history continues to cry out—not for mere relief, but for justice. And be assured: justice is coming.

Prepare your heart. Strengthen your hands. Be counted among the wise virgins who kept their lamps burning bright through the prolonged darkness. Christ is coming, bringing with Him a kingdom that cannot be shaken.

"Strive to enter in at the strait gate: for many, I say unto you, will seek to enter in, and shall not be able."
(Luke 13:24)

And as you faithfully await that glorious day, may the ancient blessing first spoken by Aaron rest gently upon you, bringing peace, comfort, and strength for every trial ahead:

"The Lord bless thee, and keep thee:
The Lord make his face shine upon thee, and be gracious unto thee:
The Lord lift up his countenance upon thee, and give thee peace."
(Numbers 6:24–26)

With this divine promise of God's favor and presence, go forward with courage and confidence, knowing He who has begun a good work in you will be faithful to complete it.

About the Author

Joshua Dobbs is an independent minister based in Kentucky and the voice behind the Truth in Christ channels on YouTube, Rumble, and TikTok. Known for his clear exegesis and in-depth lexical studies, Joshua specializes in biblical eschatology and the defense of historic Christian doctrine. His teaching is rooted in Apostolic Christian originalism—a return to the faith, order, and doctrine of the early Church as revealed through Scripture and upheld by the apostles.

Joshua's work blends accessible teaching with theological depth, helping believers navigate modern confusion with biblical clarity. His content challenges popular end-times assumptions with rigorous study and conviction, calling the Church back to the unshakable hope found in Christ's return.

Truth in Christ – Joshua Dobbs's main YouTube channel:

https://www.youtube.com/c/truthinchrist

Truth in Christ (@truthinchrist85) – the official TikTok account:

https://www.tiktok.com/@truthinchrist85